Lighting: In
and Ex

Lighting: Interior and Exterior

Robert Bean

PhD CEng MIEE CPhys MInstP FCIBSE FSLL FRSA

ELSEVIER

AMSTERDAM • BOSTON • HEIDELBERG • LONDON • NEW YORK •OXFORD
PARIS • SAN DIEGO • SAN FRANCISCO • SINGAPORE • SYDNEY • TOKYO

Architectural Press is an imprint of Elsevier

Architectural
Press

Architectural Press
An imprint of Elsevier
Linacre House, Jordan Hill, Oxford OX2 8DP
200 Wheeler Road, Burlington, MA 01803

British Library Cataloguing in Publication Data
A catalogue record for this book is available from the British Library

Library of Congress Cataloguing in Publication Data
A catalogue record for this book is available from the Library of
Congress

ISBN 0 7506 5552 6

For information on all Architectural Press publications
visit our website at www.architecturalpress.com

Typeset by Genesis Typesetting Ltd, Rochester, Kent
Printed and bound in Great Britain

Contents

Preface   vii

Illustration acknowledgements   viii

Introduction   1

Part One   Lighting concepts and resources   3

1   Living in the luminous field   5
2   The importance of daylight   13
3   How much light is needed?   17
4   How lighting levels are set   25
5   Ensuring visual comfort   29
6   The importance of illuminance variation and
    the role played by shadows   37
7   Colour in lighting   45
8   The lit appearance of the room and the occupants   57
9   Calculations and measurements in lighting design   65
10 'Lumen' methods   97
11 The significance of mounting height in an
    interior lighting installation   109
12 Daylight calculations   115
13 Energy management   123
14 Electric lighting: light sources and luminaires
    (including emergency lighting)   129

Part Two   Interior lighting   163

15 Lighting for offices   165
16 Industrial lighting   185
17 Lighting for educational buildings and sports halls   193
18 Lighting for shops and stores   201
19 Lighting for public buildings and atria   207
20 Domestic lighting   221

Part Three   Exterior lighting   **227**

21   Displaying a building after dark   229
22   Outdoor sports lighting   245
23   Motorway and high speed road lighting   257
24   Lighting for urban, amenity and residential areas   275

Appendices
Appendix 1   Typical lamp data   *283*
Appendix 2   Typical maintenance factor data   *284*
Appendix 3   Illuminance, illuminance ratios, cavity
*   reflectance, glare: examples and observations*   *287*

Glossary   *301*

Bibliography   *307*

Index   *309*

Preface

Lighting is a fascinating subject, which has physical, psychophysical and aesthetic aspects.

It is no longer considered to be merely the province of the electrical engineer who arranges its installation or of those who manufacture lamps and luminaires. Over the past two decades there has been an increasing emphasis on architects, designers and building professionals having a more in-depth understanding of lighting and lighting matters within the context of the built environment and for lighting engineers to take greater interest in the wider aspects of design than merely that of engineering. This book endeavours to provide a text that furthers such understanding and interest.

I am indebted to those who have assisted with various aspects of the book and particularly wish to thank Ron Simons, Peter Thorns, Peter Raynham, Peter Tregenza, Dave Bridgers, Jonathan David, Bob Bell, Hugh King and Peter Stone. I am also especially grateful to my wife, Jacquie, for her many hours of work in word processing the manuscript and for her assistance with the diagrams and illustrations.

Robert Bean

Illustration acknowledgements

The following Figures are reproduced by kind permission of Thorn Lighting: 2.1, 8.2, 8.3, 8.4, 8.5, 8.7, 14.26, 14.28, 14.29, 14.30a, 15.2, 15.3, 15.4, 15.5, 15.11, 16.1a, 16.1b, 16.1c, 17.1, 17.4, 18.1, 18.2, 18.3, 19.1, 19.2, 19.3, 19.5, 19.6, 19.7, 20.1, 20.2, 20.3, 21.1, 21.2, 22.1, 22.2, 24.1, 24.2 as are all the front and back cover images.

The permission of CIBSE and the Society of Light and Lighting to reproduce the following is gratefully acknowledged: Figure 17.3 is from LG5 (1991) and Figures 7.1(a), (b) and (c) are from LG9 (1997) Figs A2.1, A2.2(a) and (b) respectively. Figures 14.10 (a) and (b) and 14.14 are from the 1994 Code for Interior Lighting, pp. 97, 98 and 99 respectively.

Figures 23.7, 23.8 and 23.9 from BS 5489 Figs 1, 3 and 12a respectively, and extracts from BS 5489 Part 2 Table 1, Part 3 Table 1, and Part 10 Table 1 are reproduced with the permission of the British Standards Institution under licence number 2003SK/095. BSI publications can be obtained from BSI Customer Services, 389 Chiswick High Road, London W4 4AL (Tel +44 (0) 20 8996 9001; email cservices@bsi-globval.com).

Figure 15.1(b) is reproduced courtesy of Bob Bell and Figure 23.6 is courtesy of Siemens Lighting and Bob Bell. Figures 18.4 and 19.8 are reproduced courtesy of Siemens Lighting. Figure 15.1(a) is reproduced courtesy of Peter Boyce and the Electricity Council. Figures 14.2 and 14.16 are reproduced courtesy of LIF. Figures 14.7, 14.8 and 14.15 are reproduced courtesy of Osram Ltd. Table 17.1 is reproduced courtesy of Pfee.

Every effort has been made by the author and publishers to trace and acknowledge copyright holders. If any has been inadvertently overlooked the publishers will be pleased to make the appropriate arrangement at the earliest opportunity.

Introduction

This book is intended for people who need to get to the heart of the subject as quickly as possible. Therefore, to suit this aim, it adopts a different style to that often found in textbooks. Nevertheless, the intention is to be rigorous in imparting the necessary information and ideas.

For the benefit of those for whom this is the first serious contact with the subject, Part One deals with lighting concepts and resources. These chapters also act as a review for those who have some knowledge of the subject.

Parts Two and Three deal with applications, while the Appendices supply additional examples and other relevant information. It is intended that this approach will allow the reader to quickly achieve an understanding of the relationship between the various topics and their relative importance. This should enable more detailed later studies to be undertaken with confidence and an appreciation of the need for those studies.

One objective of this book is to meet the needs of those studying lighting topics as part of a wider course on the built environment. It will also meet the requirements of those who are studying with the intention of pursuing a career in lighting design.

It is the intention to use the reader's time economically whilst providing a first class introduction to the 'lighting' aspects of lighting engineering. The questions, answers and solutions at the end of the chapters are part of this process.

The first chapter emphasizes the importance of the fact that lighting is provided in a building for the benefit of the people who inhabit or pass through that building. It is the needs, performance and characteristics of the people who occupy the building that should be the primary concern of the lighting designer. Although energy efficiency and conservation are important considerations, they should never be allowed to seriously impede the visual performance, visual comfort or visual satisfaction of those occupying the building since, in the final analysis, it is that use that merits the building's existence.

The lighting of a building can perform a number of functions, but those functions all relate to the usefulness of the lighting to the people for whom the building was constructed and the lighting must be such that it promotes, rather than diminishes, their well-being.

Lighting also plays its part in allowing movement between buildings, in displaying buildings after dark and in supporting outdoor activities. Therefore, Part Three attends to these equally important matters.

Lighting concepts and resources

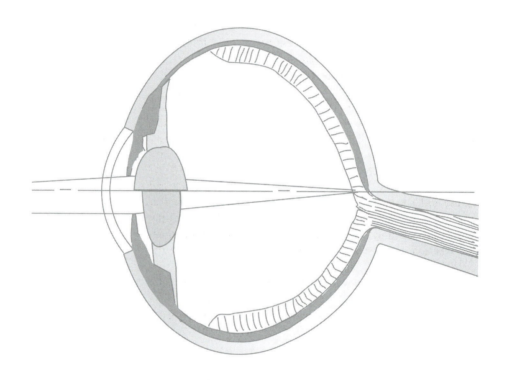

Living in the luminous field

We are in intimate contact with the luminous field through our eyes, except when we are asleep, just as we are in intimate contact with the atmosphere through our lungs. All the time we are absorbing electromagnetic energy, which we call light, and we are evaluating, consciously or subconsciously, the messages it dictates to us about the world around us.

The data we receive in this way is continually compared with previously received information to help us with this evaluation. For example, you are sitting in a room which has a wall that is brown in colour. The sun is streaming through the window and its light falls on one end of the wall. The other end of the wall is in dark shadow. Thinking about the appearance of the wall, you realize that what you see is that the end of the wall in dark shadow appears dark brown; the middle section of the wall appears light brown and the end of the wall where the sunlight falls is a pale, almost luminous brown. However, you know that the wall is painted only one colour, a particular shade of brown. You appreciate that the impression of different colours is caused by the way in which the light falls upon the wall. Such an interpretation depends upon the brain evaluating the whole scene in a routine way.

A similar thing happens when you look at a white ceiling in a daylit room. You may see various shades of grey, as well as white, but you know that the ceiling is actually painted white and not grey. It would be possible to deceive the eye/brain combination with a carefully created visual scene, but in most contexts the brain makes the correct deduction.

Appreciation of this ability of the brain to use previously absorbed information to evaluate the meaning of a visual scene is obviously important in understanding how people react to the lighting they encounter. It emphasizes the point that often their feelings and opinions are related to evaluations of which they are not fully aware.

In every developed human being there is a vast store of reference data that the senses use to evaluate the present.

Much of that data is shared human experience and awareness of the past. Since sight is one of the primary senses, much of that reference data is stored in visual images with associated emotional reactions. Basic to this is the experience of warm and sunny days and also of cold and dark nights, while there are others linked to private memories. Each person has a vast store of memories, many of which only emerge as emotions when particular situations are encountered. Since people vary in this way, some like certain things that others dislike. Therefore, it is not possible to arrive at a common consensus about such subjective things as art, decoration and sometimes lighting.

A 'natural' designer is someone who has absorbed the experiences of living in the luminous field in such a way that they find it easy to create luminous fields themselves that are appropriate for the building or space to be lit and their creativity is rather like that of Beethoven who, when asked where his musical creativity came from, said simply 'It comes unbidden'.

However, most designers need the conscious observation of the luminous field as it presents itself day by day, together with the effort of analysis, so that ideas can come to them when bidden in order that good lighting designs are achieved. Observation of the luminous field is the key to being able to create good lighting schemes, and in lighting, as with other areas of design, there is often a tension between the past and the present.

In some spaces and situations it is sequence that is important, for instance, when moving from space to space, such as passing through a museum, department store or supermarket. While in some types of building it is the need to locate a particular service or to find the means of escape in an emergency. In other spaces, such as a waiting area, it is a feeling of relaxation rather than stimulation that is required.

The first stage in any design is simplification – finding one word or sentence to describe the aim of the space that the lighting is to assist. This could be inspiration, stimulation, relaxation, progression, interest, awareness, performance, satisfaction, etc. The strength of the lighting attributes to be provided will also depend upon the time spent in a space. For instance, a theatrical type of display that has some very bright lights may be ideal for short stay stimulation, but disastrous for permanent occupation. Design means exploring the full purpose of the lighting and carefully *crafting* the solution. Start by simplifying, but end by avoiding over-simplification.

Some designers would claim to have no need of calculation, measurement or the like but, in the final analysis, no design can be translated into reality without the fruits of measurement and evaluation. It is this interaction of art and science that has always been the key that has made the world function and made it worth living in.

Our response to the luminous field is also affected by other factors, such as our physical state. For example, if we have a headache then our tolerance of the amount of light we can cope with is usually reduced and we reach for dark glasses. In terms of emotional state, bright sunshine stimulates us with feelings of well-being, whilst a heavily overcast sky can lower our spirits and, in more extreme cases, can result in Seasonal Affective Disorder (SAD). Electric lighting can exhibit similar contrasts and so have similar effects.

Another whole area relating to visual perception is the physical behaviour of the eye itself. An example of this is that it has been found that the eye is moving all the time, as part of its 'scanning' procedure. Boundaries which represent rapid or sudden change are brought to our notice so that the information implied by this change can be evaluated.

The eye itself is a most remarkable visual device worthy of a brief study.

Figure 1.1 shows a cross-section of an eye. Light entering the eye is focused on the light-sensitive layer at the back of the eye (called the retina), where it produces an inverted image. The outer surface of the eye has a curved surface which provides about 70% of the refraction required for focusing. The lens in the eye provides the fine adjustment and does this by changing its shape from flattened to rounded.

The sensitivity of the retina is not uniform, but rather depends upon which region the light falls on and upon the lighting level. The retina is a light-sensitive nervous layer, which contains two types of light sensor:

Figure 1.1

The eye showing near and distance vision

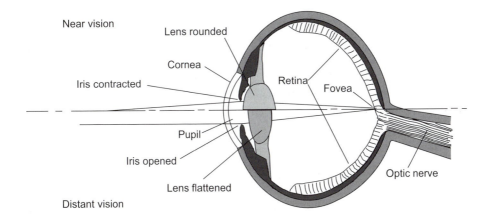

Near vision · Lens rounded · Cornea · Iris contracted · Retina · Fovea · Pupil · Iris opened · Lens flattened · Distant vision · Optic nerve

- **cones**, which operate at high lighting levels (photopic conditions), and
- **rods**, which operate at low lighting levels (scotopic conditions).

There are about 7 million cones and about 100 million rods (so called because of their shape) in the eye. Together, these communicate with the brain via the optic nerve.

The cones are mainly concentrated on the optical axis of the eye to give sharp daytime vision, whereas the rods are spread over the rest of the retina. As the distance from the optical axis (a region called the fovea) increases, so fewer and fewer cones are found and, therefore, rods predominate. Rods are much more sensitive to light than cones, but because many more of them share the same nerve fibres they give a far less detailed image. This is why details are not very clearly seen under low lighting levels, such as moonlight. In addition, the rods do not give the sensation of colour.

The iris is an aperture that automatically adjusts in diameter according to the light level and state of adaptation. At high light levels the reduced size of the aperture (pupil) gives a sharper focus by reducing spherical aberration of the lens and also gives a greater depth of visual field. This also reduces chromatic aberration.

Our colour vision is produced entirely by the cones. This visual process is mainly photochemical and cones are found with three different types of photochemicals which have three different, but overlapping, wavebands. These cover the whole visual spectrum and produce three responses that make up the colour information evaluated by the brain. Some indication of the existence of this colour vision system is found in the after-images seen when a strongly coloured light is viewed and then followed by exposure to white light. The fatiguing of the colour receptors that responded to the strongly coloured light leaves a coloured image in the field of vision which is the complementary colour that remains after the strong colour is subtracted from white light.

The retina has a very large range of operation, as is obvious from the fact that it must operate over a range of from, say, Middle Eastern sunlight to starlight. However, it can only operate over part of this range at any one time. The process of changing its range is called adaptation. Adaptation from dark to light is relatively rapid, since it mainly consists of contraction of the iris and bleaching of the photochemicals in the rods. Adaptation from light to dark is a much more lengthy process, since it consists not only of dilatation of the iris but also of the regeneration of the photochemicals in the rods. These effects have been experienced by most people, when, for example, leaving or entering a cinema.

Let us return now to the effect of lighting installations on individual impressions. It has been suggested that the effects of lighting can represent a language. For example, if you want people to look at something in particular you light it brightly; for when someone walks into a room their attention is usually drawn first to the brightest object in that room. This is called phototropic attraction – from which a moth suffers to a self-destructive degree. In the case of a brightly lit object the message conveyed by the lighting is simply 'Look here!'. However, if a lamp or lighting fitting (luminaire) is much too bright, so that it physically hurts the eye or makes it impossible to see past the light, then the message conveyed by the light is, in effect, 'Go away' or, at least, 'Look away'. Considerations such as these are very important in detailed lighting design and they will play a significant part in analysing lighting requirements for particular situations.

J.A. Lynes has suggested a very useful approach to lighting design based on the idea of lighting as a language. Just as a verbal language differentiates active from passive, subject from object, so lighting design also distinguishes the light source from the lit surface. So, in this approach 'active' elements such as lamps, luminaires and daylight are considered to differ fundamentally from 'passive' elements such as illuminated objects. The purpose of the lighting then becomes to reveal or modify certain perceived attributes of the passive element, such as colour, texture, modelling or sheen. In this approach the art of lighting is to apply effectively suitable adjectives to a given noun.

Question 1.1 Choose a word or write a sentence that describes for you an aspect of the following situations to which the lighting can contribute:

QUESTION

(a) a primary school classroom
(b) a senior school classroom
(c) a lecture theatre
(d) a hospital waiting room
(e) a hospital ward
(f) a dental surgery

Answer 1.1 The following are an appropriate set of answers:

(a) a bright and cheerful atmosphere
(b) a focused and stimulating atmosphere
(c) a formal focused atmosphere
(d) a comfortable and relaxing atmosphere
(e) a pleasant and restful atmosphere
(f) a sense of calm efficiency

ANSWER

The importance of daylight

The presence of windows to allow daylight to enter a space and to allow the occupants to look out is a major factor in the satisfaction or otherwise of those who use that space (Figure 2.1). Everyone gifted with sight can attest to this fact. However, sometimes it is necessary to exclude daylight for operational purposes, and sometimes the space is located within a building where daylighting cannot be provided.

The shape, size and location of windows is really beyond the province of the ordinary lighting designer. This is because windows have such an important effect, not just on the interior lighting but also on the view of the outside world and the outside appearance of the building. Additionally, they have a major effect on the energy efficiency of the building.

The first input into the design process is quite rightly that of the architect, who has overall control of the building's design and layout. Although people prefer a well-daylit room there must also be provision for electric lighting, since daylighting is not always available or may be inadequate. However, once the windows of a building have been designed and installed, it is seldom possible to do anything to their performance other than to change the glazing or provide blinds to control the daylighting and the heating effect or heat loss.

Therefore, detailed window design and calculations are beyond this book, but some indications of the sort of calculations that can be made and the thinking behind them is worthwhile and is given in Chapter 12.

The daylight available in a room varies with the time of day and the time of year and because of this it is usual to express the daylight performance of the windows of a room by the daylight factor that they provide within the room. This daylight factor can be for a point in the room or an average for all the surfaces in a room or, commonly, for the horizontal working plane similar to that used for electric lighting calculations. The daylight factor relates the lighting level within the room to that existing outside the building from an unobstructed sky (see Chapter 12).

There are two distinct situations for which lighting design is required. One is for a new building and the other for an existing building. Some lighting designers are fortunate in being able to specialize in lighting for new buildings where, in consultation with the architect, they can influence the daylighting design as well as the electric lighting. However, the majority of lighting design is required for existing buildings and, although

Figure 2.1

A window to look through is usually an important aspect of an interior

the integration of the electric lighting with daylighting is equally important, the main design feature to be formulated is that of the electric lighting. For this reason much of this book attends to manipulating the electric lighting to ensure suitable visual conditions in buildings, both when daylight is available and when it is not.

QUESTION

Question 2.1 What is the most important thing that daylighting adds to a room? Place the following aspects of daylighting in what you consider to be the order of importance:

(a) saves lighting energy
(b) gives a pleasant appearance to people within the space
(c) gives light of a good colour
(d) gives the opportunity to focus on a distant scene
(e) affords variability of the light
(f) gives a sense of contact with the outside world

ANSWER

Answer 2.1 The following is an appropriate (but not exclusive) answer:

(f), (d), (b), (c), (a), (e)

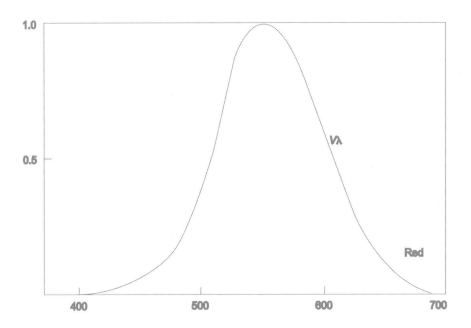

How much light is needed?

Chapter Three

In the early days of electric lighting the main requirement was to have sufficient light by which to work, and so the most important consideration was the amount of light to be provided on the workbench or desk. Later, the problem of over-bright lamps and luminaires was also taken into account.

In recent years attention has been paid to providing adequate lighting on walls and vertical surfaces and to ensuring a satisfactory appearance of both the room and the people occupying it. In recent times the need to avoid reflections in display screens has become a factor in lighting design.

Many different visual tasks have to be performed by workers in commerce, industry, etc. Although the amount of light required for a particular task may vary from individual to individual, depending upon their visual capacity, for example age or eyesight, it is possible to determine a lighting level that will meet the requirements of most of the people.

In general, the more difficult the visual task the higher the level of lighting required. As the lighting level is raised the smaller the detail that can be seen. Similarly, the poorer the contrast between the task or object and its background the greater the amount of light needed. Speed of vision also improves with an increased lighting level.

The law of diminishing returns

Lighting levels are measured in **lux** (see later in this chapter). It has been found that although increasing lighting levels improves visual performance, after a certain level of performance has been reached further increases in the lighting level bring relatively little improvement (Figure 3.1).

In this respect sight obeys similar laws to the other senses, such as hearing. With respect to vision, some relate it to a power-type law and others to a logarithmic scale with regard to the stimulus required to produce a particular level of sensation.

Figure 3.1
*Typical visual
performance curve*

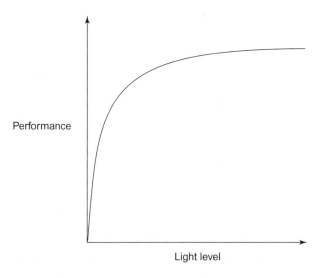

Performance

Light level

We might conclude from this that very high levels of illuminance are never justified. However, this is not true. Some tasks are so important that very high levels of illuminance are provided to give the necessary accuracy of vision. The work of a surgeon at the operating table would be an example. Lighting levels up to one hundred times those recommended for a general office are often provided over small areas of an operating table.

Therefore, it is important to have a schedule of recommended lighting levels for different types of work or situations. Such a set of schedules is provided by the *CIBSE Lighting Code*. (CIBSE stands for Chartered Institution of Building Services Engineers and the CIBSE inherited this type of Code from the Illuminating Engineering Society with which it merged in 1978, and now within CIBSE there exists a Society of Light and Lighting.)

The means of indicating what is required

The first requirement is for those who need the lighting to communicate with those who can provide it. The owner, employer or manager would ask an architect, consultant, contractor or manufacturer of lighting equipment to submit proposals. In turn, they would produce a technical specification for the suggested lighting.

Lighting, like any commodity, needs some means of indicating its quantity. If we buy an ordinary filament lamp, often called a light bulb, we buy it in terms of wattage, e.g. 60W, 100W, etc. We know that our 100W lamp will give more light than a 60W lamp of the same type. However, when it comes to a technical specification for, say, a large office, then such a simple approach is inadequate.

Offices are often lit with tubular fluorescent lamps. A typical white 100W tubular fluorescent lamp gives almost seven times as much light as a 100W domestic type of filament lamp. Therefore, watts are an inadequate measure of the amount of light provided.

Differences in light output for a given wattage of lamp can be caused by several factors. The main reason for a fluorescent lamp being far more efficient than a filament lamp lies in the fact that the atomic process for producing light is more efficient in the fluorescent lamp than in the filament lamp (see Chapter 14). Another reason is that when the electrical power in watts is converted into light the amount of light produced depends upon its wavelength (that is to say, colour). This is because the eye is more sensitive to some colours than to others, for example, under daytime or photopic conditions the eye is far more sensitive to the yellow/green wavelengths than it is to the red or blue wavelengths. The relative magnitude of the difference is indicated in the curve shown in Figure 3.2.

To determine the output of a lamp the fundamental method is to measure the power emitted in watts over a series of narrow wavebands covering the whole spectrum of the lamp and to multiply each value by the relative response of the eye (called the spectral luminous efficiency, $V\lambda$). These values are then added together and multiplied by a constant (**683**) used to relate all light output measurements to an internationally agreed base. This quantity of light, which depends upon wavelength as well as electromagnetic power, is expressed in **lumens**.

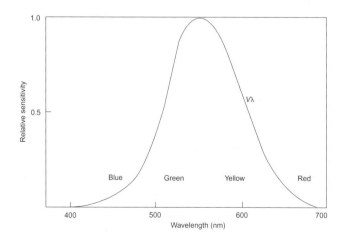

Figure 3.2

The eye is more sensitive to yellow/green wavelengths than to red or blue wavelengths

An example of this calculation is shown below in a simplified form. In particular, the wavelength intervals are 25 nm, whereas the usual interval is 1 nm.

Example 3.1 A 100W tungsten filament general service lamp has a power distribution as shown in Table 3.1. Calculate the lamp output in lumens.

Table 3.1

Wavelength (λnm)	Power radiated W per wavelength interval	Spectral luminous efficiency (Vλ)	$683 \times W \times V\lambda$ Light output per wavelength interval (lumens)
400	0.062	4×10^{-4}	0.017
425	0.096	7.26×10^{-3}	0.476
450	0.133	3.8×10^{-2}	3.452
475	0.176	0.1226	14.74
500	0.234	0.3230	51.62
525	0.298	0.7932	161.44
550	0.365	1.0002	249.34
575	0.433	0.9154	270.72
600	0.505	0.6310	217.64
625	0.575	0.3210	126.06
650	0.644	0.1070	47.06
675	0.712	0.0232	11.28
700	0.790	4×10^{-3}	2.21
	Total 5.023 watts		Total 1156.10 lumens

From such a process it is found that a 100 watt general service filament lamp typically produces 1200 lumens, a 2400 mm 100W tubular fluorescent lamp about 8000 lumens and a 100W high pressure sodium lamp about 10000 lumens (see Chapter 14). Dividing the lumen output by the wattage gives a useful indication of the relative efficiencies with which light is produced. The results for the lamps mentioned above are: filament lamp 12 lm/W; fluorescent tube 80 lm/W; high pressure sodium lamp 100 lm/W.

These are not ratios of like quantities, therefore they are not termed efficiencies, but since they do indicate the 'efficiency' with which light is produced from the electrical power supplied to the lamp, the term **efficacy** is used.

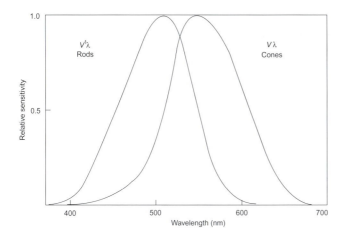

Figure 3.3
The two spectral luminous efficiency functions

In the above calculation the $V\lambda$ data was used in the formula to convert watts into lumens. This $V\lambda$ function related to cone vision or photopic vision and not rod or scotopic vision. There is another spectral luminous efficiency function $V'\lambda$ which relates to rod vision, but this is not used in calculating the light output of light sources in lumens. The two spectral luminous efficiency functions are shown together in Figure 3.3.

During adaptation from a very high level to a very low level of lighting the sensitivity curve of the eye moves from the photopic curve towards the scotopic curve and in doing so passes through the mesopic region of adaptation. In this condition both rods and cones are operative.

Road lighting often operates under lighting levels where some mesopic conditions are encountered.

A simple but inadequate specification

The simplest form of lighting specification might require 100 000 lumens to be fed into the room via the lamps and luminaires. The problem with such a simple specification is that it does not ensure that the light is received where it is needed most. So, although the outcome of the lighting designer's calculations may be to conclude that 100 000 lumens are required in that room, it is not the starting point. The starting point is to specify the required density of light (light flux) required at various points in the room. This density of the light flux is specified in terms of lumens per square metre and given the name **lux**. This is a measure of the illuminance received by the surface or point in space. For example, the CIBSE Code calls for 500 lux at desk height in a generally lit office.

QUESTION

Question 3.1 A light source has a uniform distribution of power throughout the visible spectrum. If the total radiated power is 20 W, calculate the output of the source in lumens.

ANSWER

Answer 3.1 The power per wavelength interval is 20/13

Then $683 \times 20/13 \ \Sigma V_\lambda$ = output in lumens

$683 \times 20/13 \times 4.286 = 4504$ lumens

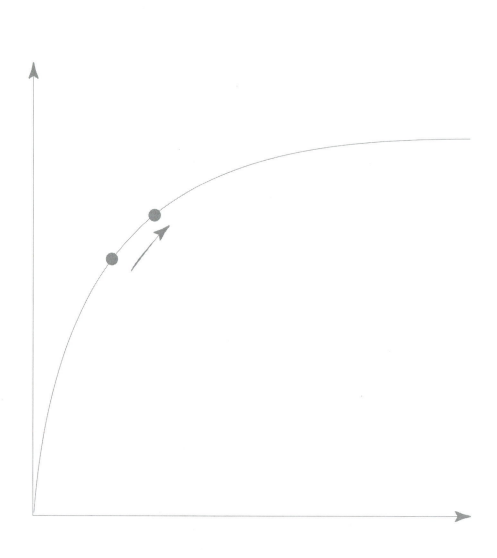

How lighting
levels are set

The lighting levels referred to here are those for performing tasks or moving safely through an interior. Many experiments have been carried out to try to find a simple way of setting lighting levels for different tasks. None of these has been entirely successful. This is partly because of differences between individuals and experiments, but also because laboratory results, in this field, do not transfer easily to the workplace.

Over the years as the value of worker productivity has risen relative to the cost of the lighting, recommended lighting levels have increased. In the 1950s the level recommended by the IES Code for general office lighting was 20 lumens per square foot, or 220 lux. Today the CIBSE Code recommends 500 lux.

This raises the question 'If the lighting level can be varied by more than one hundred percent in this way, why is it necessary to be able to specify levels or calculate them accurately?'. The answer is twofold. First, when lighting is being purchased the buyer needs to know that they have received what they requested and paid for. They also need to be able to compare one quotation with another and know that the difference in price is because one system is cheaper than another, whilst providing the same amount of light.

The other and equally important factor is that lighting levels are incorporated in standards or schedules which, when complied with, are known to be satisfactory. When the recommended lighting level is increased the result is to move the operating point of the installation up the performance curve. The amount of the change depends upon which part of the curve the two points lie on (Figure 4.1). The operating point chosen depends upon economic factors, such as the cost of labour versus the cost of the lighting. The health and comfort of the workers are also important factors in selecting lighting levels.

Figure 4.1

The change in visual performance depends on which part of the curve the two points lie on

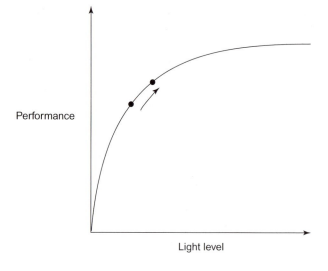

When a lighting code is being revised, a committee set up by the appropriate institution goes through the process of evaluation. This committee usually includes academics who have contact with the appropriate vision research, practising engineers and architects who have been applying the existing code, as well as others who are expert in presenting recommendations in the clearest and most useful way.

One source of discussion would be the consideration of the lighting codes and recommendations in use in other countries. Any significant differences would be noted and an attempt made to understand why it is so and then to form an opinion as to the importance of this difference in considering the revision.

Those working in the field as lighting designers might carry out opinion surveys to see if the levels already in use seem to have been found generally satisfactory. The academics and researchers would seek to show the extent to which formulae based on experiment could be used to calculate appropriate lighting levels. Calculations would be carried out and the results compared with currently recommended values. Frequently the outcome of these calculations are values that differ greatly from current practice. Even when they give values similar to those used in practice, the necessary calculations of task size etc. to apply the formula are often not considered practical; in the sense that they would not be carried out by the majority of designers who want a table of recommended values rather than a complex formula. In the CIBSE Lighting Code there are over

100 recommendations by name of task or workplace. In Europe, and hence the UK, lighting codes are being harmonized and so committees have a European membership.

The need for any lighting code to make clear the significance of its recommended values is of considerable importance. For example, the CIBSE Code gives recommended values that are intended to be standard maintained illuminance values at the task. This is a minimum value at which maintenance procedures are carried out to make sure that the level does not fall any lower (clean the lamps and luminaires, etc).

Lighting levels can be set with reference to different criteria, such as those given below:

1 The levels required to meet appropriate health and safety regulations.
2 The levels required to produce a given standard of task performance.
3 The levels required for the workers to be satisfied with the lighting.

In general, given the opportunity to set the lighting level, many workers choose higher levels than are strictly necessary for the performance of the task. However, in recent years, this tendency has been modified by the need to operate visual display screens with the ensuing contrast problems.

There is, of course, far more to lighting a building interior than choosing an appropriate lighting level for tasks to be performed. Lighting also has an important role in revealing the form of an interior, especially in buildings of high architectural merit. Additionally, buildings of relatively little architectural merit can be made more visually pleasant by carefully designed lighting. This issue receives further consideration in Chapters 6 and 8.

Question 4.1 Since there is not a precisely correct level of lighting for a particular task, but only a specified or recommended level, what are the advantages and disadvantages of this situation?

QUESTION

ANSWER

Answer 4.1 An advantage is that minor differences in achieving the specified lighting level are unlikely to cause any practical problems.

A significant disadvantage is that, sometimes, specified lighting levels are taken so seriously that there is a possibility of legal action if those levels are not achieved precisely. One consequence of this can be a tendency to overlight in order to ensure that such a situation is avoided.

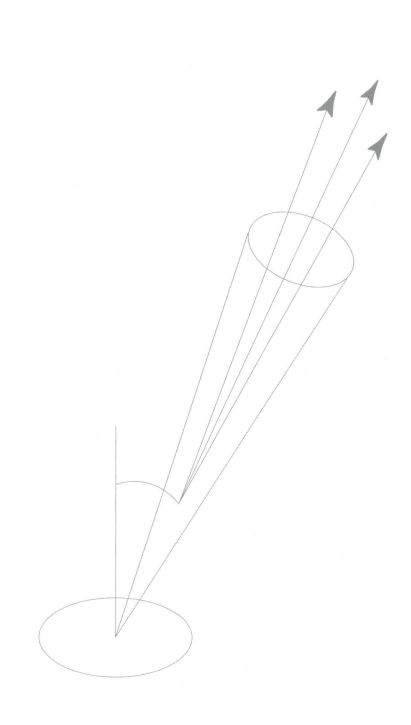

Ensuring visual comfort

Visual comfort is usually dealt with by seeking to eliminate any causes of visual *dis*comfort. It is a common experience that lights that are too bright relative to their surroundings can cause discomfort. This discomfort can range from the just noticeable to the intolerable.

This visual discomfort is called **discomfort glare**. The causes of visual discomfort may be due to natural lighting, such as light from windows or artificial lighting such as interior lighting fittings (called luminaires). In considering this problem it is useful to have a means of measuring and specifying the 'brightness' of a lamp or luminaire or a surface such as a wall.

The non-linear relationship, mentioned earlier (Chapter 3), between the physical light density and our perception of its effect, means that the term 'brightness' is normally restricted to the visual response to the physical stimulus. The physical stimulus that produces the effect is called the **luminance** of the light source or surface.

In practice, the luminance of a surface often changes with the direction of view. This means that any definition of luminance has to take into account direction as well as magnitude. A simple illustration of the change of luminance with direction of view would be a magazine with shiny paper where the ease or difficulty of reading depends upon the angle of it relative to the source of light. In some positions the luminance produced by reflection of the light source creates a bright image which makes reading the print very difficult indeed. It is for this reason that the definition of luminance has to be more complex than might at first be thought necessary.

The luminance of a surface may be due to reflection from a surface and this reflectance may be large or small and is indicated by a value less than one; for example, 0.6. This means that 60% of the incident light is reflected. This could indicate the total amount reflected by a surface in all directions or it could relate to a specific direction, such as in a mirror-type reflection. The luminance could be due to transmission through glass or some other medium and the amount of light transmitted would be indicated in a similar way by its transmittance; for example 0.4 or 40% of the light passing through the medium. Transmittance can also relate to specific directions (see Daylight Coefficients, Chapter 12).

Luminance

Any small element of a surface, whether it is the surface of a light source or a surface reflecting or transmitting light, can be considered as a small light source in its own right. Such a light source element is shown in Figure 5.1(a) and (b).

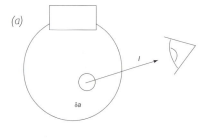

Figure 5.1

(a) A light source; (b) a reflecting surface. Each can be considered as a light source when considering luminance

The amount of light travelling from the element in a particular direction can be measured in terms of its **luminous intensity** (*I*), which is the solid angular density of the light flux; the smaller the **solid angle** (ω) the more specific is the direction.

The luminous intensity is the ratio of the light flux in the solid angle to the size of the solid angle (see Figure 5.2a).

$$\frac{F\,(\text{lumens})}{\omega\,(\text{steradians})} = I \text{ candelas}$$

It is given the symbol *I* and is measured in **candelas (cd)**. The size of a solid angle is defined in terms of the area (*a*) cut out by the solid angle at the surface of a sphere and the radius of the sphere (Figure 5.2b). The solid angle $\omega = \dfrac{a}{r^2}$ steradians. The definition is independent of the size of the sphere. For example, the solid angle subtended by the whole surface of a sphere is given by:

$$\omega = \frac{4\,\pi\,r^2}{r^2} = 4\,\pi \text{ steradians}$$

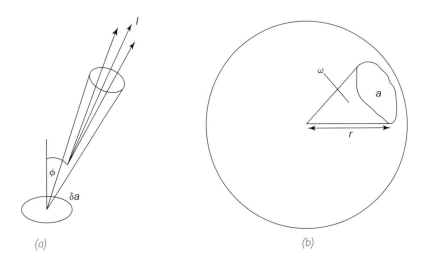

(a)   (b)

The luminance of an element of a surface is defined in terms of the luminous intensity it produces divided by the area apparently producing the intensity. Therefore, if the element is viewed at an angle ϕ then it is the projected area of the surface in that direction that is included in the formula.

At an angle ϕ to the normal of the element of surface area the luminance

$$L = \frac{I}{\delta a \cos \phi} \ \text{cd/m}^2$$

See Figure 5.3.

This definition of luminance gives us a means of measuring the physical 'brightness' of an element of a surface or of the

Figure 5.2

(a) Luminous intensity is the solid angular density of the light flux; (b) the definition of solid angle, $\omega = a/r^2$

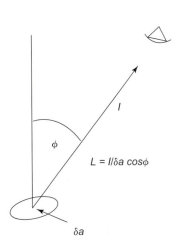

$$L = I/\delta a \ \cos\phi$$

Figure 5.3

Luminance equals intensity per unit projected area

whole surface, but the sensation of brightness experienced in a practical situation depends upon more than just the physical 'brightness'.

It is a common experience that a car headlight gives a much greater sensation of brightness when seen in the dark at night than when seen during daylight. This is because the sensation depends not just upon the luminance of the light source, but also upon the luminance of the background against which it is seen and the state of adaptation of the eye.

Visual comfort

Visual comfort depends, to a large extent, on eliminating or reducing the following three things:

1 Discomfort glare.
2 Disability glare.
3 Flicker.

Discomfort glare

A great deal of work has been carried out over many years to establish the main physical factors relating to discomfort glare. Various formulae have been proposed to enable levels of discomfort glare to be calculated for interior lighting schemes from the luminaire photometric data, room size and reflectances, luminaire mounting height and lamp output data. These calculations can be made *before* the lighting is installed, enabling the probable level of discomfort glare to be predicted. This enables limiting values of permissible discomfort glare to be recommended. If the calculations show that the glare from the installation should be below the recommended limiting value then it is assumed that the installation can go ahead without any concern about discomfort glare.

The CIE has developed a formula for a Unified Glare Rating (UGR) for interior lighting that has now been adopted by the CIBSE in the UK. The formula is

$$\text{Unified Glare Rating (UGR)} = 8\log \frac{0.25}{L_b} \sum \frac{L_s^2 \omega}{P^2}$$

where $L_s \, (cd/m^{-2})$ = luminance of the light source towards the observer

L_b = background luminance cd/m^{-2}

ω = solid angle (steradians) subtended at the eye by the source

P = a position index which increases as the light source considered moves away from the line of sight.

The constants 8 and 0.25 are introduced to provide a convenient range of values.

Values of UGR can be calculated by hand, but it is more usual to use manufacturers' tables or computer programs for this purpose. Limiting values of UGR are published for a wide range of situations and the CIBSE Lighting Code lists over 100 different situations with limiting values of UGR where appropriate. An example of a UGR calculation is given at the end of this chapter and in Chapter 15.

Disability glare

Disability glare occurs when the high brightness or size of light source is such that it affects adaptation and gives higher level of light scattering within the eye, so that the contrast of features within the visual scene is so reduced that vision is impaired. Seeking to see in these conditions can cause eye strain and fatigue.

Direct disability glare from most interior lighting installations is usually controlled if discomfort glare is eliminated. However, indirect disability glare can occur when images of light sources are reflected from a task. A particular case of this is reflection in a visual display screen. Large area sources that give no discomfort glare can often cause disability glare.

Disability glare is important in road lighting and is controlled by specifying limiting values of Threshold Increment (*TI*) (see Chapter 23).

Flicker

When operated on an alternating current supply the light output of a lamp varies with the changing current. On a 50 HZ supply this gives a 100 HZ flicker. Most people are unaffected by the flicker caused by this light output modulation. This modulation is least with incandescent lamps and greatest with discharge lamps, such as low pressure sodium lamps. Under fluorescent lighting it has been found that about 10% of people experience headaches that are thought to be due to subliminal effects of flicker.

A further effect of light modulation is the apparent slowing of moving machinery (stroboscopic effect), which, in certain circumstances, could be very dangerous. These problems can be overcome by the use of high frequency operation lamps (see Chapter 14) and also, in the case of stroboscopic effects, by operating the lamps on different phases of a three phase supply.

QUESTIONS

Question 5.1 A circular patch of a surface has a luminance of 500 cd/m^2 when viewed at an angle of 45°. If the patch has a diameter of 0.1 m, what is the luminous intensity of that patch in the direction of view?

Question 5.2 If the position index for a light source viewed directly in the line of sight is $P = 1.0$, calculate the UGR value for a spherical source in this position at a distance of 3 m seen against a background luminance of 20 cd/m². The sphere is 0.25 in diameter and has an intensity of 100 cd in all directions.

ANSWERS

Answer 5.1

The intensity is equal to the luminance multiplied by the projected area in the direction of view, in this case

$$I = LA \cos \phi$$

$$= 500\pi \left(\frac{0.1}{2}\right)^2 \cos 45°$$

$$= 2.88 \text{ cd}$$

Answer 5.2

$$UGR = 8 \log \frac{0.25}{L_b} \sum \frac{L_s^2 \omega}{P^2}$$

$$L_b = 20 \text{ cd/m}^2$$

$$L_s = \frac{100}{\pi \left(\frac{0.25}{2}\right)^2} = 2037 \text{ cd/m}^2$$

$$\omega = \frac{A}{r^2} = \frac{\pi \left(\frac{0.25}{2}\right)^2}{3^2} = 0.005 \text{ steradians}$$

$$P = 1.0$$

There is only one light source so,

$$UGR = 8 \log \frac{0.25}{20} \left(\frac{(2037)^2 \times 0.005}{(1.0)^2} \right)$$

$$= 19.3$$

The importance of illuminance variation and the role played by shadows

Chapter Six

Visual constancy

The illuminance received on an object or a surface depends upon the size of the light source, its light output and distribution, the distance of the object or surface from the light source and the orientation of the object surfaces with respect to the direction of light.

Illuminance variation due to distance or orientation is a major component in revealing the form of a room or the shape of an object. Consider a simple example (see Figure 6.1). In the room shown the illuminance received from the daylight entering the window on an overcast day onto the floor will gradually reduce as the point considered moves away from the window.

End wall

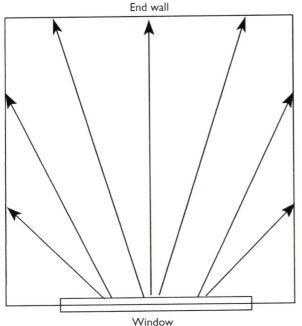

Side wall

Window

Figure 6.1

Variation of illuminance with distance and orientation in a side-lit room

This is also true of the side walls and the ceiling. However, the illuminance on the wall facing the window will be significantly higher than that on points on the side walls, floor or ceiling at the same distance because the angle of incidence of the light is closer to the normal.

This view of the way in which illuminance is distributed in a daylit room when looking into the room of this type from the direction of the window is a common experience and so we would always expect the illuminance distribution to vary in this way. If, in fact, the end wall looks darker than the adjacent wall surfaces, we would attribute this to the end wall having a darker or lower reflectance finish than the adjacent wall surfaces.

This evaluation, where the brain separates the action of the light falling on the surface and the effect of surface orientation from its surface finish, is called visual constancy and it is this routine evaluation capability that enables us to make sense of what we see. When the situation is manipulated so that this visual constancy is broken down, then illusions occur. Sometimes these illusions can be for a purpose and are welcomed, such as in a theatrical display, but in everyday situations they are to be avoided.

Visual constancy is broken down when the illuminance variation gives confusing or misleading patches of brightness or shadows which cannot be directly referenced to the light sources creating the effect.

Object form   The form of an object is revealed in context when the variation of illuminance across its surface is that which would be expected in a commonly experienced lighting situation. A curved object such as a terracotta flower pot which has a matt finish reveals its shape by the change in illuminance as its surface gradually turns away from the source of light (Figure 6.2). This type of illuminance variation is often called shading. Visual constancy makes us conclude that the form of the flower pot is revealed in this way because the source of light is on the left – even though it is not in the picture.

Highlights   The illuminance received by a surface or an object can have many components: light received from a window, light received from a lighting fitting (luminaire), light reflected from other surfaces.

When the surface receiving the illuminance is matt and scatters the light received in all directions these components

Figure 6.2
*The form of the flower
pot revealed by light
from the left*

are integrated and their distinctness is lost, but when the
surface has a specular or mirror-like component of reflection,
some of this distinctness is retained. The most obvious
example of this is a mirror, where the images of all those things
reflecting light onto the mirror are to be seen in the reflections.

Many objects and surfaces have two reflected components: a matt one due to the base material and a specular one
due to a transparent coating. Sometimes a clear image is super-
imposed upon the object – for example, a tiny reflected image

Figure 6.3

A distorted image appears on the object as a highlight

of a window, or if the image is distorted out of recognition – and then a highlight appears on the surface; that is, a bright patch standing out from the general brightness of the object or surface (Figure 6.3).

The visual scene

Any visual scene produces an illuminance variation at the observer's eye caused by the light source and each object or surface reflecting light towards the eye. When operating correctly, the optical system of the eye preserves the distinction between the individual components of the illuminance. This illuminance variation falling upon the retina provides visual information interpreted by the brain. However, the interpretation given to this illuminance variation also depends on the state of adaptation of the eye. This adaptation is related to the *average* value of the illuminance at the eye.

In terms of our visual experience nature has provided us with a set of data which is stored away in our earliest days and referred to as we seek to evaluate any subsequent visual scene. It is from this stored data that the emotional messages created by a lighting situation are selected. The experience stored from enjoying a pleasant summer day is labelled in our visual memory and our pleasure at encountering visual conditions that suggest such a day is magnified. A similar experience with negative memories associated with dark or dismal visual conditions also occurs. There is almost certainly a geographical aspect to these experiences, where the blazing heat of a desert situation is seen as something to eschew, rather than view it as a pleasant sunny day.

The role of shadows

Shadows play a very significant part in our perception of the visual environment and our ability to perform tasks. A shadow is a particular case of illuminance variation. It is generally thought of as the existence of an extreme difference in illuminance between two adjacent areas of a visual scene, caused by a sharp difference in surface orientation or an obstruction in front of the receiving surface.

An important example of the use of shadows in revealing a possible hazard is stair lighting. It is usually recommended that there is a flow of light from the top to the bottom of the stairs. This arrangement keeps the risers in shadow, whilst illuminating the treads. This helps to indicate clearly the form of the steps. It also makes it less likely that a bright light will be placed to shine up the steps and distract someone who is descending the stairs.

Returning to the example given at the beginning of the chapter of the effect of daylight from the window of a side-lit room, if a wall finish is textured, to reveal that texture under daylight the finish should be used on the side walls at right angles to the flow of light. The texture is then revealed by its shadowing effect as the light flows across the wall. Similarly, if a wall finish has a sheen that is to be emphasized then that finish is best placed on the wall at the end of the room directly opposite the window, where the bright reflection from the window reveals the sheen.

In some situations, such as floodlighting of historic buildings, the shadows created can be as important as the illumination in displaying the form of the building after dark. This is also true in other display situations.

However, unwanted shadows can distort our perception of a space or make a visual task more difficult. A light in the wrong position can make it very difficult to perform a task such as writing if it casts a shadow of the writer's head or hand across the task.

The foregoing has important implications for the use of the different types of light source and associated luminaires; a spot light, for example, gives a different message to that from a diffusing fluorescent luminaire.

QUESTIONS   **Question 6.1**   What would be missing from our visual experience if none of the objects or surfaces ever had a specular component?

Question 6.2

If you were in an interior environment where the lighting was *completely* shadowless, what would enable you to recognize objects and surfaces?

ANSWERS

Answer 6.1
The stimulation and interest that comes from reflected images. Reflected glare from specular surfaces. An absence of mirrors!

Answer 6.2
Differences in colour, self luminance, or reflectance.

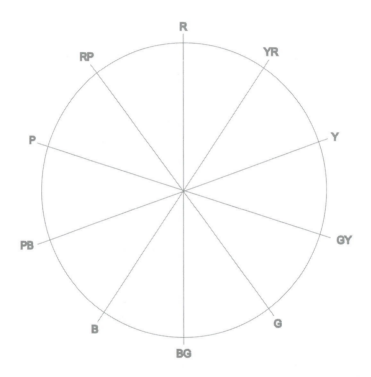

Colour in lighting

Colour makes an immense contribution to our appreciation and response to the visual scene and to the performance of many visual tasks. A black and white photograph of a flower garden is devoid of much of the information that a colour photograph contains and is quite unlikely to evoke the same interest or feelings of pleasure.

The intrinsic colour of an object is determined by the wavelengths of light that it reflects (or transmits) and the relative strength with which it reflects (or transmits) the various wavelengths. The rendering of this intrinsic colour by the light source depends upon the wavelengths of the light that the light source emits and the relative strength of emission of the various wavelengths (see Figure 7.1).

The colour sensation experienced by the observer also depends upon the observer's colour vision and the influence of other colours in the field of view which affect the observer's colour adaptation. Exposure to large areas of bright colour tends to fatigue the colour receptors, so that when viewing a subsequent scene of different colour after-images are seen. If the subsequently viewed surface is the complementary colour then these after-images may be masked.

In terms of lighting, there are two distinct aspects of colour that relate to the light sources:

1 The colour that the light sources themselves exhibit.
2 The colour that the light emitted by the light source makes other surfaces and objects exhibit.

In Chapter 1 reference was made to the three different types of colour response provided by the cone receptors that are responsible for photopic vision. Colour television pictures are created by energizing the red, green and blue phosphors of the television tube and this is only possible because of the three-colour response system of the eye. However, because

Figure 7.1

(a) The spectrum from 200 to 1000 nm; (b) spectral distribution of a white fluorescent lamp; (c) spectral distribution of an incandescent lamp

(a)

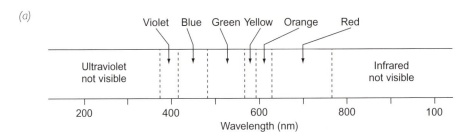

(b)

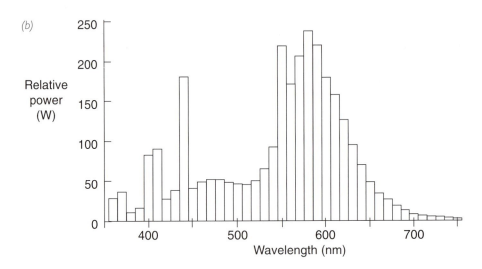

(c)

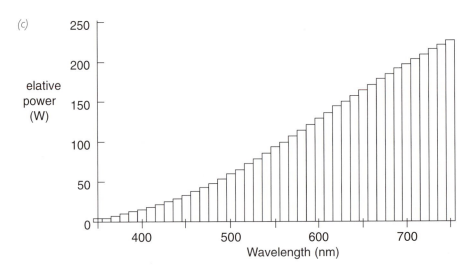

the three response systems have wavebands that overlap, it is possible for two colours to appear to be the same even when their spectral distribution is actually different. Two light sources can appear to be the same in that they exhibit a similar colour appearance, but when used to illuminate coloured objects they produce different effects.

This means that two pieces of information are required before you can be sure about the usefulness of a particular lamp for a specific task:

1   Specification of the colour it itself exhibits.
2   Indication of its colour rendering properties.

Specification of colour appearance

The three-colour response characteristics of the eye mean that a colour matching system can be established where any colour can be matched using red (R), green (G) and blue (B) primary radiations.

Consider the colour equation given below:

$$1.0(C) \equiv r(R) + g(G) + b(B)$$

This states that one unit of the colour to be matched can be matched by r proportion of (R), g proportion of (G) and b proportion of (B) such that

$$r + g + b = 1.0$$

r, g and b are the chromaticity co-ordinates of the colour (C).

It is only necessary to specify two of the three to identify the colour because r, g, b add up to unity. Unfortunately, sometimes, particularly when matching the pure spectral colours, it was found necessary to use the equation in a form such as,

$$1.0 = g + b - r$$

In order to avoid this idea of negative values of colour the CIE developed a system whereby the co-ordinate axes lay completely outside the locus of real colours and so all colours could be specified in positive values.

In this system the primaries are specified as X, Y and Z and the chromaticity co-ordinates as x, y and z and x + y + z = 1.0 for all colours. A diagram can therefore be plotted in terms of x and y (Figure 7.2).

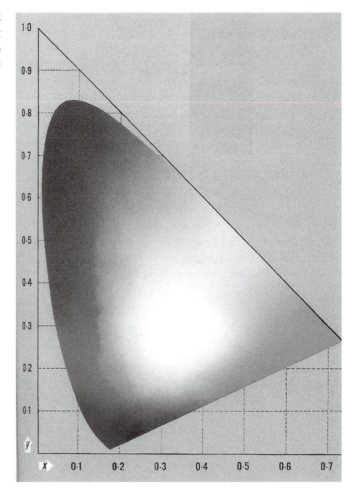

This is the basic method of specifying the colour appearance of a light source. However, for convenience, an approximate method, which is widely used, has been developed for indicating the colour of a light source and this is described below. This is based on the idea of correlated colour temperature.

If the voltage on a filament lamp is increased steadily from a low value up to its full operating voltage it will begin to glow red and then pass through a series of increasingly whiter colours as its temperature increases. If the voltage is then continually increased beyond its operating value it will emit whiter and whiter light until the filament reaches a temperature at which it is destroyed. This would be an example of how different white colours could be associated with different temperatures.

It is possible to envisage a perfect radiating body that emits more of each wavelength of radiation at a given temperature than any practical heated body. The formula relating the amount of radiation at each wavelength to the temperature for this body is well known and is called the full radiator formula.

$$M^{th} = \frac{C_1}{\lambda_5} \left(e^{(C_2/\lambda T)} - 1\right)^{-1} 10^{-9} \ (\text{W m}^{-2} \ \text{nm}^{-1})$$

where C_1 and C_2 are constants and M^{th} = watts emitted from unit area per unit wavelength interval.

The formula contains only two variables: wavelength, λ, and the absolute temperature, T. If the temperature is specified then the amount of radiation for each wavelength interval can be calculated and from this wavelength distribution the x and y co-ordinates of the full radiator can be calculated and plotted on the CIE chromaticity diagram. Figure 7.3 shows the CIE diagram with the locus of points for the full radiator.

Figure 7.3
The CIE diagram with the locus of points for the full radiator

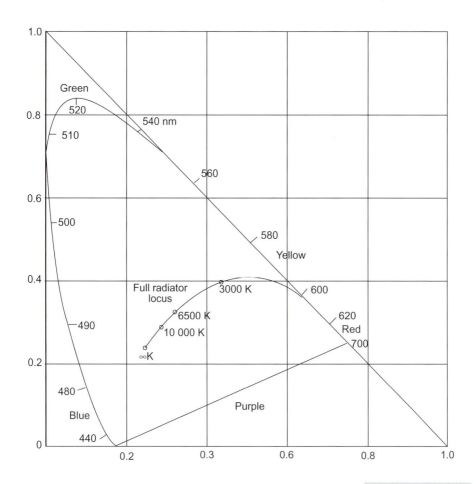

If the x and y co-ordinates are calculated for a particular lamp, say a fluorescent tube, and plotted on the diagram its correlated colour temperature can be found.

A typical value of correlated colour temperature might be 4000 K. This means that the *colour* of the tube is close to that which the full radiator would have at 4000 K. This is entirely a specification of colour and not temperature, since the outside wall of the fluorescent lamp could be at about 40°C. It is interesting to note that the *higher* the colour temperature the cooler the lamp looks.

Subtractive colour mixture

The colour appearance of a light source can be altered by using a colour filter, which could simply be a coloured coating on the lamp or a filter added to a projector. Such colour change is caused by removing wavelengths from the spectral distribution of the light source. A similar process is involved in mixing paints, where the different pigments are selective in their reflectance and absorb the other wavelengths. Such a process is often called 'subtractive' colour mixture. The additive system of colour mixture is complete when the result is white. The subtractive system of colour mixture is complete when the colour achieved is the absence of all the wavelengths, i.e. black.

Colour rendering

The colour an object or surface exhibits depends upon the wavelengths of the radiation it reflects, but if it is illuminated by a light source that provides none of those wavelengths then it will appear black. This is the extreme case, but it serves to emphasize the importance of the colour rendering properties of the light source.

The precise colour rendering properties of a light source are indicated by its spectral distribution curve, but for everyday practice an approximate method of indicating colour rendering performance is used. This is the CIE general colour rendering index. The index indicates the accuracy with which a set of specially selected sample colours are reproduced by the lamp under test relative to the same samples under a specially chosen reference light source. In general, a set of eight colour samples are used. The index is based, in effect, on plotting the chromaticity co-ordinates for each of the samples onto a modified version of the CIE diagram for each of the light sources. If the points are in agreement then the general colour rendering index for the test lamp is 100. The greater the average of the differences between the two points for each sample the lower the index value and the poorer the colour rendering properties of the source under test are rated.

Like all approximate methods this is satisfactory for most everyday situations, but where colour rendering is of vital importance a more accurate method must be used. Table 7.1 gives correlated colour temperature classes and colour rendering groups used in the CIBSE Code for Interior Lighting (SLL)

Table 7.1 Correlated colour temperature classes and colour rendering groups used in the Code for Interior Lighting

Correlated colour temperature (CCT)	CCT class
Below 3300 K	Warm
3300 K to 5300 K	Intermediate*
Above 5300 K	Cold

Colour rendering groups	CIE general colour rendering index (R_a)	Typical application
1A	$R_a \geq 90$	Wherever accurate colour matching is required
1B	$90 \geq R_a \geq 80$	Wherever accurate colour judgements are necessary or good colour rendering is required for reasons of appearance
2	$80 \leq R_a \leq 60$	Wherever moderate colour rendering is required
3	$60 \leq Ra \leq 40$	Wherever colour rendering is of little significance but marked distortion of colour is unacceptable
4	$40 \leq R_a \leq 20$	Wherever colour rendering is of no importance at all

*This class covers a large range of correlated colour temperatures. Experience in the United Kingdom suggests that light sources with correlated colour temperatures approaching the 5300 K end of the range will usually be consdered to have a 'cool' colour appearance.
Source: Society of Light and Lighting (1994) Code for Interior Lighting, Table 1.1, p. 23. Reproduced with permission.

Colour sample systems

Often the lighting designer has little control over the colour of the room surfaces, but where this is possible then an appreciation of a colour sample system, such as the Munsell System, is useful. This is a long-standing logical means of ordering colour samples. The samples are ordered in terms of three attributes: hue, value and chroma.

Hue

Hue is defined as the attribute of visual sensation that gives rise to colour names, such as red, green and blue. The ten basic hues are blue, blue green, green, green yellow, yellow, yellow red, red, red purple, purple and purple blue. The hues are referred to by their initials: B, BG, G, GY, Y, YR, R, RP, P and PB.

Value

Value indicates increasing lightness on a scale from 0 to 10, 0 being black and 10 being white; greys having values from 1 to 9. This attribute is extended to non-achromatic colours.

Chroma

Chroma represents numerically the increasing intensity or vividness of the colour.

Figures 7.4 and 7.5 show the hue circle and the Munsell arrangement of samples.

Figure 7.4

The basic Munsell hues

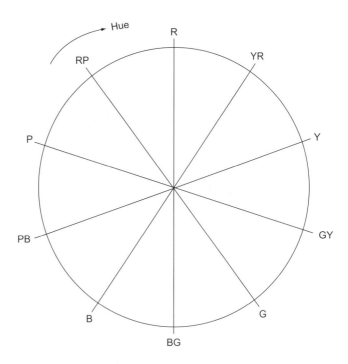

In the Munsell notation there are 10 steps between each main hue, with the main hue numbered 5. So, for example, 5Y5/8 is the main yellow hue with a value of 5 and a chroma of 8.

The Munsell system of displaying samples – hue, value and chroma – produces an uneven layout on the pages of a colour

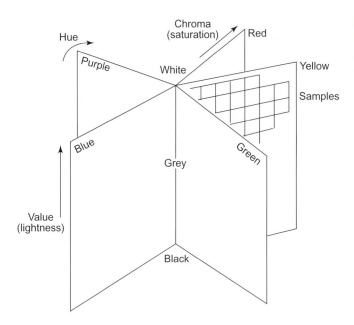

Figure 7.5

*Hue, value and chroma
in the Munsell
arrangement*

'atlas'. This is because high chroma (vivid) yellows have a high value, whereas high chroma reds and blues have low value. This gives rise to the idea that the value that is desired and the intensity of colour (chroma) should be chosen before finally selecting the hue. This is because if the hue is chosen first it may be found that it cannot provide the required value or chroma.

(Note: value does not directly equate to reflectance (%) but an approximate relationship is $R = V(V - 1)$.)

It is also worth remembering that strongly coloured surfaces can affect other surfaces by reflecting strongly coloured light onto them. However, the eye adapts to predominant colours and this reduces the effects of interreflection. Nowhere is personal observation and experience more valuable than in seeking to understand the interplay of colour with our visual mechanism.

The distinctness of different colours existing on the same flat plane, e.g. walls and doors, can be enhanced by using linear white elements such as door frames and skirting boards to delineate them. This is because white elements appear white under large variations of the light level and composition that is incident on them. White surfaces within a room, even relatively small ones, serve as a visual reference for evaluating the other colours in the space.

QUESTIONS

Question 7.1   Of the colour temperatures marked on the diagram in Figure 7.3 to which one do the coordinates $x = 0.3133$ and $y = 0.3235$ relate? What is the z value?

Question 7.2   A lamp emits radiation that has a colour which has chromaticity co-ordinates of $x = 0.57$, $y = 0.43$. Why would it be inappropriate to indicate its colour by a correlated colour temperature?

Question 7.3   Go into a room lit by incandescent lamps as dusk begins to fall. Switch on the electric light. Note how the appearance of the room changes. Apart from the lighting level, what is the most dramatic change?

ANSWERS

Answer 7.1
6500 K
$z = 1 - 0.3133 - 0.3235 = 0.3632$

Answer 7.2   The colour is almost monochromatic and lies well clear of the full radiator locus.

Answer 7.3   The colour.

The lit appearance of the room and the occupants

The human body is so constructed that our natural direction of view is parallel to the horizontal plane. This means that vertical surfaces play an important role in our visual scene. In interiors the brightness of the walls has a strong bearing on our impression of the brightness of the space. Light-coloured, well-lit walls make a room seem larger, while dark, poorly lit walls make it seem smaller. A bright ceiling gives the sense of greater height. However, in a working environment all the good impressions are negated if the task area is poorly lit, so that task performance is difficult.

Daylighting from side windows provides both bright vertical surfaces and also dark surfaces on the window walls. This visual experience is a natural one, which is often found acceptable, since it gives a sense of orientation to the space and a feeling of normality. Associated with this is the fact that daylighting also gives wide variations of illuminance during the day and the year, especially in the UK, which again gives a feeling of the passing of time and of normality. Therefore, the size and position of the windows plays a very large part in creating an appropriate visual impression.

It goes without saying that, wherever possible, daylighting should be the major component of the lighting during daylight hours. The vertical component of daylighting and the spectral distribution of the light is such that the appearance of people's faces is also found very acceptable. Where side windows are confined to one wall the problem of disability glare is usually present. This can affect visual tasks and when a person has their back to the window their features become very difficult to discern. Often a very bright window can also cause discomfort glare (Figure 8.1).

Once the window apertures and the glazing have been fixed then shades and blinds have a role to play in reducing glare. Associated with this there is often the need for supplementary electric lighting to provide satisfactory working

Figure 8.1

Disability glare makes features difficult to discern

conditions within the space. When darkness falls the need for electric lighting is self-evident. Electric lighting invariably produces a quite different effect to that of natural daylight. However, those who use it expect this to be so and there is little point in trying to make electric lighting simulate daylighting. Electric lighting has the great advantage of controllability and, therefore, predictability, which are important assets.

The after dark appearance of a room can be most powerfully affected by the form of electric lighting installed. In general the lighting should seek to follow the reflectance hierarchy in the room and only go against it when dramatic effect is required. It is clearly wasteful to strongly illuminate a surface to counteract low reflectances. However, there is some value

Figure 8.2

Consider the message that the orientation and arrangement of luminaires conveys

in seeking to provide a visual structure to a room lit by electric lighting. In the simplest case, coherent lines of light will emphasize the rectangular shape of an office, corridor or walkway. Thought should be given to the message that the orientation and arrangement of the luminaires conveys (Figure 8.2).

A major factor in determining the appearance of a room and its occupants is whether the lighting is direct or indirect or a combination of the two.

Direct lighting is the most efficient in terms of energy use. It also allows for a wide range of shadow formations depending upon the type and number of luminaires. Unless the room surfaces are of very low reflectance, even a direct lighting system produces an indirect component due to interreflection. This can vary from very weak to quite strong, depending on reflectance values. As an example, in some supermarkets the light-coloured floors and cabinets reflect a significant amount of light onto the ceiling, even though the general lighting louvred luminaires have no upward component (Figure 8.3).

Figure 8.3

In this supermarket the ceiling receives reflected illuminance from a light-coloured floor

Indirect lighting onto the ceiling is less efficient in providing light on the working plane or into the room envelope below. However, it can be very effective in giving a softer, more luxurious aspect to the space. It can be rather bland if used on its own, but when used in conjunction with spotlights it can be effective, where energy efficiency is not a prime concern. Many fluorescent luminaires are now designed to give a significant upward component as well as direct lighting. This can be a happy combination in terms of the appearance of the room and its occupants, providing a bright environment with a good indirect component to give balance to the lighting on vertical and horizontal surfaces.

Figure 8.4

An indirectly lit white ceiling with dark coloured walls

With indirect systems some very interesting effects can be achieved. For example, Figure 8.4 illustrates the impression that can be obtained by lighting a white ceiling from coves, where the walls above the coves are painted a dark colour.

Indirect lighting in the form of compact fluorescent wall lights can improve otherwise uninteresting wall areas, but it must not be used in an indiscriminate way, which contradicts the intended function of the space.

Direct luminaires can produce scalloped effects when sited close to the wall and these can either add interest or confuse the architectural message of the space (Figure 8.5).

An example of such confusion is where spotlights are placed in a church on a wall that is pierced with gothic arches. If the light is placed directly above the point of the arch the scallop effect could emphasize the shape of the arch, but if the light is placed off-centre it competes with it (Figure 8.6).

The scalloped effects caused by the luminaires are more noticeable at a distance, probably because they are focused closer to the optical centre of the eye.

There are many and varied effects of this type that can occur either by design or accident, but through observation, once the designer is aware of the possibilities, care can be taken to adopt useful techniques whilst avoiding the pitfalls.

Figure 8.5

The wall scallops from the recessed spotlights make an interesting border to the bar area in this restaurant

Figure 8.6
The off-centre light scallop competes with the arch

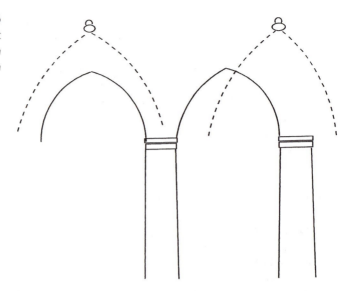

Figure 8.7
The appearance of people depends on the ratio of vertical to horizontal illuminance

Although the boundaries of the room are important aspects of the visual environment, the space within the room envelope is equally important, since it is in this space that people move and work. The appearance of people and objects within a room depends to a large extent upon the ratio of vertical to horizontal illuminance within the space (Figure 8.7).

The uniformity or otherwise of this ratio of illuminances has a large bearing on the variation of appearances throughout the space. Additionally, the ratio of maximum vertical illuminance to the average vertical illuminance at a point gives an indication of the variation of modelling of features in the horizontal direction. These simple illuminance ratios can be used to evaluate the variation of appearance that can be expected throughout a space.

Another approach to evaluating the strength and direction of modelling within a space is to use the vector scalar ratio. The vector illuminance is the maximum difference in illuminance occurring at the point considered and the scalar illuminance is the average of the illuminance from all the directions at that point. If the vector illuminance is zero then all the illuminances at the point are balanced by equal illuminances in the opposite direction. Under this condition the vector scalar illuminance ratio would be zero and the modelling would be expected to be negligible.

A weakness of this approach is that there *could* be a considerable difference of appearance with orientation, even though the vector was zero, because pairs of balancing illuminances could be quite different from each other. However, in practice, the vector scalar approach has been found satisfactory in most situations.

See Chapter 9 for the calculation of mean vertical illuminance and scalar illuminance.

Question 8.1

An early attempt at producing a modelling ratio was to suggest that the ratio of downward to upward illuminance in a generally lit interior could serve this purpose. How useful do you think this would be in practice?

QUESTION

Answer 8.1

This ratio would suggest that modelling in a space is solely a function of the reflectance of the working plane or floor. This is fairly true in a large indirectly lit space, or where there is a luminous ceiling, but it does not allow for the light distribution produced by individual luminaires. Variation in vertical illuminance is an important feature of many lighting installations.

ANSWER

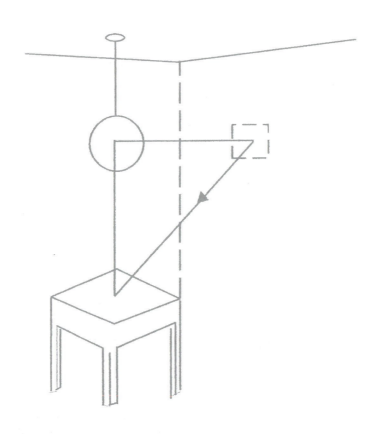

Calculations and measurements in lighting design

Lighting was first provided long before there were adequate calculational techniques, and so if the designer was experienced much design could be done with little calculation. This is certainly so in theatre lighting. However, calculations have their place. For the inexperienced they provide a means of producing an acceptable lighting scheme. For the experienced designer they provide a valuable check that is always worth making. When a totally new situation is encountered they are a means of proceeding with confidence. When a very large scheme is undertaken they enable judgements to be made between possible alternatives, where an error of 30% would represent a lot of wasted energy and money.

Lighting level schedules and lighting calculations should be viewed in the following way:

1 They can enable the beginner to produce a satisfactory lighting scheme.
2 When experience is added to these they enable the designer to produce a very good lighting scheme.
3 When to that experience is also added the special quality of flair they enable an exceptional lighting scheme to be produced.

Luminous intensity

In Chapter 5, when considering the brightness of a light source or surface, the concept of luminous intensity was introduced. The concept depends upon each light source or element of a light source being treated as a point source. The point source idea works in practice because most large light sources can be divided up into areas small enough to be considered to be point sources for calculational purposes. The great value of the concept of luminous intensity is that it can be measured for a lamp or luminaire and plotted or tabulated and used for flux and illuminance calculations. However, the idea is based on something that is non-existent, for a true point source would not emit any light since it would have no area from which to emit the light!

In fact, the assumption of a point source has to be carefully handled, since it can lead to all sorts of impossible answers. However, as long as it is accepted that a point source of light is simply a small source relative to the distance at which the measurements are being made or at which the calculations apply, then accuracies of the order of 1% can be achieved.

The inverse-square law

A small light source placed at the centre of an enclosing sphere illuminates an area A on the inside of the sphere at a distance r equal to the radius of the sphere (Figure 9.1). This area is equal to the solid angle multiplied by the radius squared ωr^2, since ω is defined as $\omega = \dfrac{A}{r^2}$ (see Chapter 5).

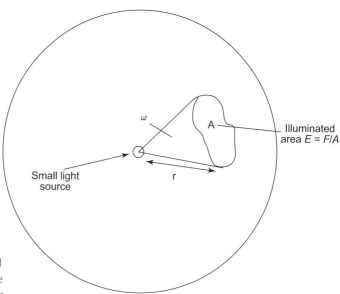

Figure 9.1

A small light source illuminating the inner surface of a sphere

The illuminance produced (E) is given by F/A. So,

$$E = \frac{F}{A}$$

$$= \frac{F}{\omega r^2}$$

where F/ω is the luminous intensity (I) of the light source in the direction of A, giving

$$E = \frac{I}{r^2}$$

If we now reduce the size of area A until it can be considered to be a point element (P) on a plane surface the inverse-square law can be written as $E = \dfrac{I}{D^2}$ lux, where D is the distance between the light source and the illuminated point.

$I = ED^2$ is a fundamental relationship for a point source of light in any direction in which light is emitted. The intensity I is a property of the light source in a particular direction and E is the effect that this intensity has at distance D from the source. If we know the intensity I in a particular direction then we can calculate the illuminance that the source produces at any distance from the source. We also have a means of measuring I since if we measure E at a fixed distance D

$$I = ED^2 \text{ cd}$$

This relationship is the basis of many lamp and luminaire photometers.

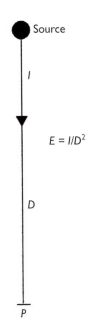

Figure 9.2

When the illuminated area is reduced to a point element $E = \dfrac{I}{D^2}$

Figures 9.3 (*a*) and (*b*) show a very simple intensity distribution photometer.

In this photometer a lamp or luminaire is supported from a wall or separate structure and a pivoted arm rotates a photo-cell at a fixed distance from the source. The movement of the arm is measured on an angle scale. The light source can also be rotated in the horizontal plane to enable measurements to be taken in different vertical planes; again measured against another angle scale. The room and the structure are painted black to eliminate reflections.

These photometers can sometimes be very large, both to accommodate large luminaires, but also to ensure that the light path is sufficiently long to be able to apply the $I = ED^2$ relationship. It can be shown mathematically, and proved experimentally, that a large light source such as a 1.5 m fluorescent luminaire obeys the inverse-square law to better than 1%, provided that the distance of measurement from the centre of the light source to the photocell is at least 5 times the major dimension of the source. In this case $1.5 \times 5 = 7.5$ m. Such photometers often employ mirrors to fold the light path and so reduce the size of the room required to house the photometer.

Intensity distribution photometry

Figure 9.3

(a) Side view of a simple intensity distribution photometer; (b) front view of the same photometer

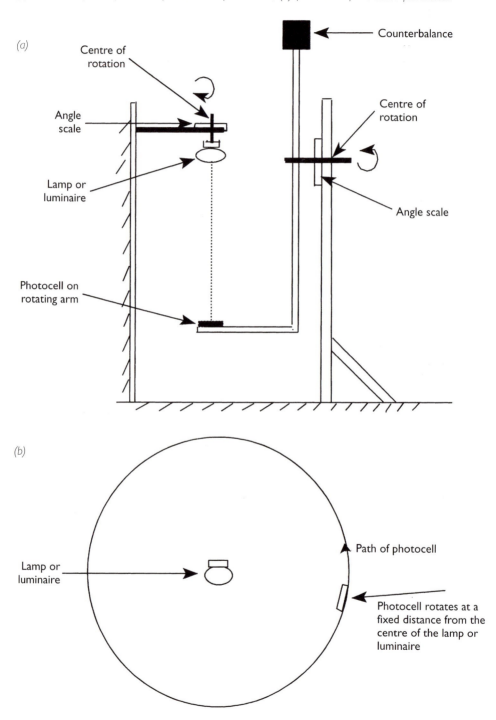

These photometer measurements are used to produce intensity data in the form of I tables or polar curves. Figure 9.4 gives part of a typical I table. The angular co-ordinates relate to directions around the source and are related to a co-ordinate system. Figure 9.5 shows a commonly used system, the C,γ system. The sphere and co-ordinate lines look like those on a world globe, but in the C,γ system γ = 0° is at the 'south pole' and not at the 'equator'.

γ (deg) mid zone	C (deg) mid zone angles				
	5	15	25	35	45
5	220	190	120	80	50
15	240	200	140	90	70
25	260	220	190	120	90
35	280	250	200	150	100
45	300	270	200	180	150

Figure 9.4
Part of an I table

I tables are fed into computers where they are used to provide luminaire intensity data for lighting programs and for the production of technical data sheets and diagrams.

A commonly used diagram is the polar curve. These curves give the intensity data for individual C planes. Figure 9.6(a) shows a typical polar curve that might be obtained from a diffusing globe luminaire (Fig 9.6b).

On a polar curve the distance, to scale, from the origin to the curve gives the luminous intensity in that direction. The globe luminaire is given in this example because its intensity distribution would be effectively the same in *all* C planes. If the polar curve is rotated about the 0–180° axis a polar solid,

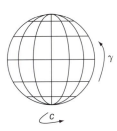

Figure 9.5
The C,γ co-ordinate system

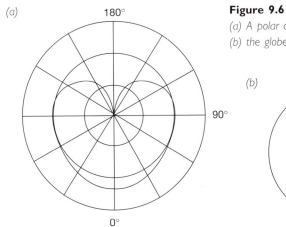

(a)

180°

90°

0°

Figure 9.6
(a) *A polar curve from a diffusing globe luminaire;*
(b) *the globe luminaire*

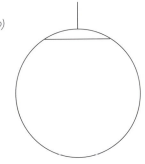

(b)

which would be apple shape, would be swept out and the polar curve would be a cross-section of this solid. This rotation could not be done for a linear fluorescent luminaire because the polar curves in different C planes are not all the same shape.

A different form of photometer is generally used for measurements on floodlights. This is because the photometric distance for accurate measurement is arrived at in a different way. When an optical system, such as a parabolic mirror, is involved it is not simply the size of the luminaire that is critical, but the size of the image produced in the mirror.

If the photocell is placed too close to the mirror the image in the mirror will not fill the whole area of the mirror. However, until the image fills the whole of the mirror the inverse-square law cannot be assumed to apply. This is because at different distances the image will have a different size and so have a different intensity. The component of total intensity produced by the lamp directly would, of course, obey the inverse-square law from close to the lamp. The reflected image will only stop increasing in size with increased distance from the projector when its fills the whole area of the reflector. For a photocell placed on the axis, this is when the ray reflected from the outside edge of the reflector crosses the axis, as shown in Figure 9.7. Beyond this point the relationship $I = ED^2$ = constant (for a given direction) applies.

Figure 9.7

The determination of the distance at which the inverse-square law would apply for a parabolic floodlight

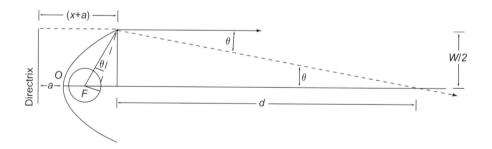

For floodlights this requires a photometric distance of about 30 m. This cannot be achieved with the ordinary type of photometer where the photocell or mirror is rotated about the floodlight. Instead the floodlight is mounted at one end of a black tunnel with a fixed photocell facing along the tunnel towards the floodlight (Figure 9.8).

The floodlight sits in a stirrup, which can be rotated in a horizontal direction and it can also be tilted in the vertical direction. Therefore, to correctly represent this arrangement

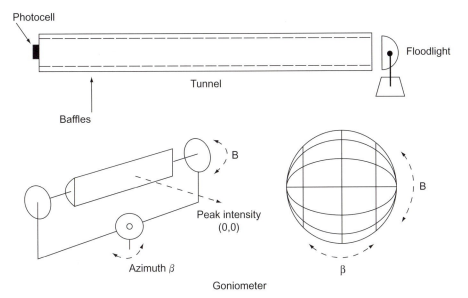

the polar axis of the co-ordinate system must be rotated through 90°. This gives the B,β system, where the B angles give the planes of measurement and β the angular measurement on the B plane. A similar system is sometimes labelled as $V, H,$ where V corresponds to B and H corresponds to β. B,β and C,γ are related and either can be translated into the other. Details of this and other co-ordinate transformations will be found in Chapter 1 of *Lighting Engineering: Applied Calculations* (Simons and Bean, 2001).

Figure 9.8
Photometry of a floodlight using the B,β co-ordinate system

Practical lighting calculations require more than the inverse-square law relationship. Consider Figure 9.9, where a luminaire is shown lighting a table.

The general point source illuminance formula

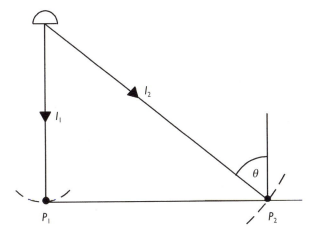

Figure 9.9
The inverse-square law alone is inadequate for illuminance calculation

To calculate the illuminance at point P_1 we can assume that an enclosing sphere through which the light flux would pass is at that point coincident with the table; that is, the table is tangential to the sphere. In this case $E = I_1/D^2$ will give the answer we seek. However, in the case of P_2 further down the table the larger enclosing sphere passes through the point, but the table is not tangential to it.

Consider Figure 9.10. Here a narrow pencil of light arriving at point P_2 is effectively parallel.

Figure 9.10

The cosine law

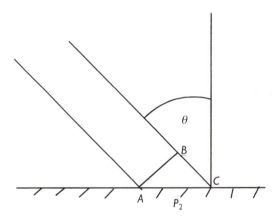

When compared with a similar light pencil at point P_1, because of its angle of incidence this pencil is spread over a wider area. The increase in area is proportional to $\dfrac{1}{\cos\theta}$, since one side of the cross-section of the pencil intercepted is now the hypotenuse of a right angle triangle; that is, AC instead of AB. This increase in area results in a lower illuminance than that predicted by the inverse-square law alone. To compensate for this effect of the angle of incidence the illuminance formula is modified to incorporate the cosine law as well as the inverse-square law. The general point source formula is then

$$E = \frac{I\cos\theta}{D^2}$$

where θ is the angle between the direction of the intensity and the normal to the illuminated point.

Example 9.1   In Figure 9.9 calculate the illuminances at points P_1 and P_2, given that the source is 1.5 m directly above P_1 and the distance from P_1 to P_2 is 1 m. The intensity towards P_1 is 100 cd and that towards P_2, 120 cd.

Answer:

(1) E at P_1

$$E = \frac{I_1 \cos \theta}{D_1^2}$$

$$= \frac{100 \times 1.0}{(1.5)^2} \quad \text{Since } \theta = 0°$$

$$= 44 \text{ lux}$$

(2) E at P_2

$$E = \frac{I_1 \cos \theta}{d_2^2}$$

$$\theta = \tan^{-1}\left(\frac{1}{1.5}\right) = 33.7°$$

$$\cos \theta = 0.83$$

$$D_2^2 = (1.5^2 + 1^2) = 3.25$$

$$E = \frac{120 \times 0.83}{3.25}$$

$$= 30.6 \text{ lux}$$

Other forms of the point source illuminance formula

Before linear fluorescent luminaires were introduced most general lighting luminaires were symmetrical about the vertical axis and the intensity distribution could be conveyed by a single polar curve. In this circumstance the traditional form of the illuminance formula was used because for the horizontal plane the angle of incidence θ was also the angle that the intensity could be read from the polar curve.

A modified form of the formula was often used for the horizontal plane produced by substituting for D in terms of the mounting height of the luminaires, H (Figure 9.11).

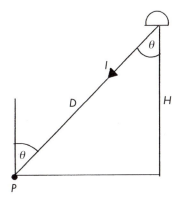

Figure 9.11
The $\cos^3\theta$ form of the general point source formula

From Figure 9.11,

$$D = \frac{H}{\cos\theta}$$

So,

$$E = \frac{I\cos^3\theta}{H^2}$$

The advantage here was that H is constant and θ gave both $\cos^3\theta$ and the angle at which the intensity was read from the polar curve.

With the advent of asymmetric luminaires, for general interior use, θ no longer gave the angle for reading the intensity from a single polar curve. Once this advantage has gone another version of the formula has some advantages.

The point source formula based upon D^3

Consider Figure 9.12(a). Here the illuminated plane is sloping.

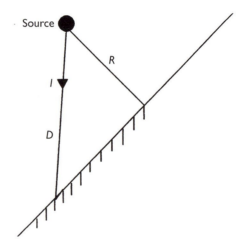

Source

R

I

D

Figure 9.12a

$$E = \frac{I\cos\theta}{D^2}, \quad \cos\theta = \frac{R}{D}$$

So,

$$E = \frac{IR}{D^3}$$

where R is the shortest distance between the source and the plane containing the illuminated point P.

Consider Figure 9.12(b). Here the illuminated point lies on a vertical surface such as a wall, where R is the shortest distance of the light source from the wall.

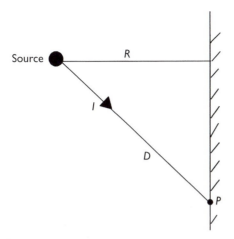

Figure 9.12b

Consider Figure 9.12(c). Here the illuminated point lies on the horizontal plane and $R = H$, the mounting height of the luminaire.

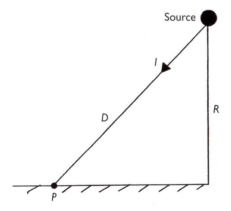

Figure 9.12c

(1) Calculate the illuminance at a point on a church tower clock which is 8 m above the ground.

Example 9.2

The floodlight is sited directly beneath the clock and 4 m from the base of the tower. It is aimed so that its peak intensity of 10 733 cd is directed at the clock (Figure 9.13).

$$E = \frac{IR}{D^3}$$

$$D^3 = (4^2 + 8^2)^{1.5}$$

$$= 715$$

Figure 9.13
*Calculation of
illuminance of a clock
on a church tower from
two floodlight positions
using the D^3 form of
the general point source
formula*

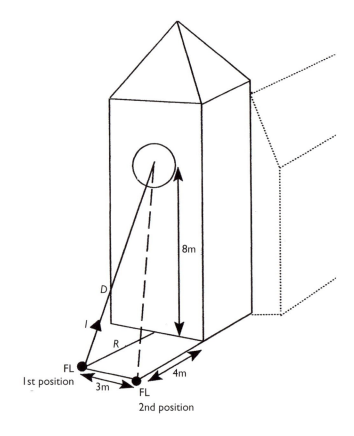

So,

$$E = \frac{10\,773 \times 4}{715}$$

$$= 60 \text{ lux}$$

(2) Now repeat the calculation assuming that the floodlight must be displaced by 3 m parallel to the front of the tower to be opposite the right hand side of the tower, as shown.

$$E = IR/D^3$$

$$D^3 = (4^2 + 8^2 + 3^2)^{1.5} = 840$$

$$R = 4, \text{ as before}$$

So,

$$E = \frac{10773 \times 4}{840}$$

$$= 51 \text{ lux}$$

In this form the point source illuminance formula can still be applied to the horizontal plane, as before, without difficulty and it is easier to apply to other cases such as exterior flood-lighting or indoor wall washers and spot lights.

Mean vertical illuminance (cylindrical illuminance)

In Chapter 8 it was mentioned that the appearance of people and objects within a room is greatly influenced by the ratio of vertical to horizontal illuminance. Direct mean vertical illumi-nance at a point is usually called cylindrical illuminance. This is to avoid a clumsy expression when mean values over an area are specified; that is, 'mean cylindrical illuminance' instead of 'the mean value of mean vertical illuminance'.

For a point source the mean vertical illuminance can be calculated by considering the average illuminance on an infini-tesimal vertical cylinder at the point of interest (Figure 9.14a).

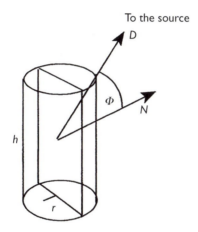

To the source

Figure 9.14

(a) Mean vertical illuminance as the average illuminance on an infinitesimal vertical cylinder

The vertical illuminance at the cylinder will vary across the surface of the cylinder as the surface of the cylinder turns away from the direction of the source. However, a simple way of calculating the average value of the illuminance on the cylin-der is to consider the flux received by a rectangular cross-section across the diameter of the cylinder normal to the plane containing the intensity directed towards the cylinder as shown. Any flux received by the rectangle through the top of the cylinder is compensated by flux received at the bottom of the cylinder not being received by the rectangle.

The vertical illuminance on the rectangle is given by

$$E_v = \frac{I \sin\theta}{D^2}$$

since ϕ, the actual angle of incidence measured from the normal, equals $(90° - \theta)$ and $\cos(90° - \theta) = \sin\theta$ *(Figure 9.14b)*.

It is worth noting that cylindrical illuminance is commonly associated with the horizontal illuminance as a ratio. That is the reason why in this case the cylindrical illuminance angle of incidence ϕ is expressed in terms of the horizontal plane illuminance angle of incidence θ and the shortest distance, denoted by N. In this case R would refer to the horizontal plane illuminance calculation, which in Figure 9.14(b) corresponds to H.

The flux received by the rectangle is $E_v \times 2rh$. This is also the flux received by the cylinder, so the average illuminance of the cylinder vertical surface is

$$E_{cyl} = \frac{E_v \times 2rh}{2\pi rh}$$

where r is the radius of the cylinder and h is the height of the cylinder

$$= \frac{E_v}{\pi}$$

$$E_{cyl} = \frac{I\sin\theta}{\pi D^2}$$

Figure 9.14
(b) The cylindrical illuminance at a point from a small light source

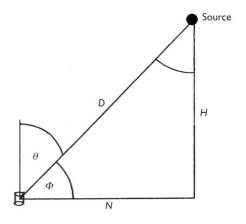

Referring to Figure 9.14(b),

$$\sin\theta = \frac{N}{D}$$

So,

$$E_{cyl} = \frac{IN}{\pi D^3}$$

Calculate the value of cylindrical illuminance for the point P in Figure 9.14 (b) given that $I = 700$ cd, $H = 2$, $N = 2$. Also calculate the ratio of cylindrical to horizontal illuminance at the same point.

Example 9.3

$$E_{cyl} = \frac{IN}{\pi D^3}$$

$$= \frac{700 \times 2}{\pi (2^2 + 2^2)^{1.5}}$$

$$= 19.7 \text{ lux}$$

$$E_{cyl} = \frac{I \sin\theta}{\pi D^2} \text{ and } E_h = \frac{I \cos\theta}{D^2}$$

So, $\dfrac{E_{cyl}}{E_h} = \dfrac{\tan\theta}{\pi}$

$\theta = 45°$, $\tan 45° = 1.0$

So, $\dfrac{E_{cyl}}{E_h} = \dfrac{1}{\pi} = 0.318$

The above example is based on direct illuminances at a point and does not take into account interreflections. In practice it is the ratio of the average value of cylindrical illuminance to the average value of horizontal illuminance that is of interest for a general lighting scheme (see Chapter 8). A graph of this ratio for typical luminaire types and room sizes is given in Figure 10.3 of Chapter 10.

Here again the term scalar illuminance provides a simpler expression. Consider Figure 9.15.

Mean spherical illuminance (scalar illuminance)

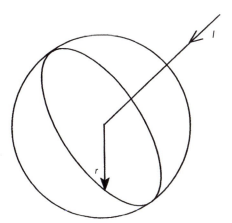

Figure 9.15

Scalar illuminance as the average illuminance on an infinitesimal sphere

The approach is similar to that for cylindrical illuminance, but since orientation is not a feature the derivation is simpler. The illuminance on a circular cross-section of the infinitesimal sphere is given by

$$E = \frac{I}{D^2} \text{ since } \theta = 0°$$

the flux received by the circular cross-section is

$$E \times \pi r^2 \text{ where } r \text{ is the radius of the sphere.}$$

This is also the flux received by the sphere, so the average illuminance on the sphere surface is

$$E_s = \frac{E \times \pi r^2}{4\pi r^2}$$

$$= \frac{I}{4D^2}$$

Example 9.4 Repeating Example 9.3 but for scalar illuminance:

$$E_s = \frac{I}{4D^2}$$

$$= \frac{700}{4(2^2 + 2^2)}$$

$$= 21.9 \text{ lux}$$

The ratio of scalar to horizontal illuminance is given by

$$\frac{E_s}{E_h} = \frac{I}{4D^2} / \frac{I\cos\theta}{D^2}$$

$$= \frac{I}{4\cos\theta}$$

$$\theta = 45° \cos\theta = 0.707$$

$$\frac{E_s}{E_h} = \frac{I}{4 \times 0.707}$$

$$= 0.354$$

Luminance measurement

At the beginning of this chapter it was pointed out that even though the inverse-square law was developed by assuming a point source of light, all real light sources must have area if they are to emit light. Therefore, we can re-write the illuminance equation for a point source as

$E_p = L\omega\cos\theta$ where $\dfrac{\delta a\cos\phi}{D^2} = \omega$ (see Figure 5.3)

L = luminance in cd/m^2

where, $L\delta a\cos\phi = I$

and $L = \dfrac{E_p}{\omega\cos\theta}$

The form of the formula suggests a simple way to measure the luminance of a surface or a light source such as an overcast sky. A simple black tube is used to define the solid angle (Figure 9.16).

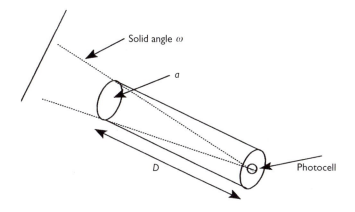

Solid angle ω

a

D

Photocell

Figure 9.16

Measurement of luminance – a black tube used to define the solid angle

Any part of a light source viewed by the aperture a, and filling the aperture, which produces the same value of illuminance at the opposite end of the tube as another source, must have the same value of luminance as the other source. Therefore, this is a simple way of comparing luminances.

In general, luminance meters work on the principle of an aperture illuminating a photocell in this way, although often lens and mirror systems are used to image the area being measured. In the simple instrument shown cos θ = 1. So,

$L = \dfrac{E_p}{\omega}$ and ω is defined by the tube as $\dfrac{a}{D^2}$.

Obviously, L could be calculated from the measured E_p and the known value of ω, but it is more usual to calibrate the instrument against a source of known luminance.

Earlier in this chapter the use of the point source illuminance formula was illustrated by calculating the illuminance from a

Direct and reflected light

floodlight on a church clock. This example was chosen because it only involved direct light from the luminaire. However, in interior lighting calculations almost always involve not just direct light from the luminaires (or windows), but also reflected light from the room surfaces.

Two approaches are commonly used to deal with the complex requirements of estimating the direct and inter-reflected illuminances in a lighting installation. One is to use the lumen method utilization factor based on pre-calculated data (see Chapter 10 and Appendix 3) to obtain average illumi-nance values. The other is to use the computer's capacity to perform a vast number of relatively simple calculations. Some computer lighting programs simply divide a space and the luminaires up into small elements and apply the point source formula to each, treating room surface elements as secondary light sources. The reflected light is added cumulatively through repeated reflectance calculations until the change in value falls below a certain level, say 5%. Part of a very simple interior lighting calculation is given below to illustrate the steps involved.

Figure 9.17

Calculation of direct and reflected illuminance

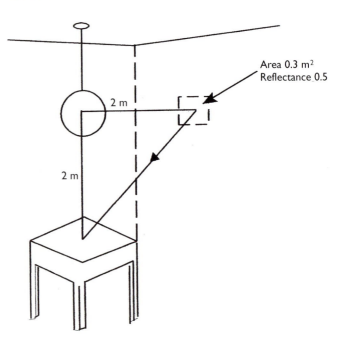

Consider Figure 9.17. In this example an opal spherical luminaire directly lights a table and light is also reflected from the other room surfaces to add to the direct illuminance on the table. The reflected light will produce continuous interreflections until all the light has been absorbed by the room surfaces or transmitted out of the room via any window. Our example will calculate:

1 the direct illuminance from the luminaire
2 the light initially reflected from one small patch of the wall surface to the same point on the table.

To calculate the direct illuminance from the luminaire it is necessary to know the luminous intensity of the luminaire in the direction to which the calculation relates. This is usually provided by the manufacturer. We will assume that the lamp flux creates a uniformly bright sphere, having the same value of luminous intensity in all directions, in order to obtain an estimate of the luminous intensity.

We assume a lamp output of 5000 lumens and a light output ratio of the luminaire of 0.8. This gives an output of 5000×0.8 lumens. The luminous intensity has the same value in all directions, so we can divide the total luminous flux by the total solid angle of the sphere.

$$I = \frac{4000}{4\pi} = 318 \text{ cd}$$

(Note: we have not been told the size of the sphere so we cannot calculate its luminance.)

The luminaire is directly above the table and so the direct illuminance is given by

$$E_D = \frac{I}{D^2} = \frac{318}{4} = 79.5 \text{ lux}$$

Additionally, since the sphere is directly opposite the patch of wall we have chosen, the illuminance at its centre will have the same value as that on the table, namely 79.5 lux.

We must calculate the intensity of the reflected light in the direction of the table, in order to calculate the illuminance on the table reflected from our patch on the wall. The flux received by the patch is equal to the illuminance multiplied by the area. So,

$$F = E \times A$$

$$= 79.5 \times 0.3$$

$$= 23.9 \text{ lumens}$$

In order to move to the next stage in the calculation and determine the luminous intensity of the patch in the direction of the

table, we have to know the reflection characteristics of the
wall; not just the amount of flux reflected but how it is distributed in terms of intensity, so we need to know the polar curve
of the reflected intensity. The most commonly used wall finish
is a matt finish and so this is often assumed for this type of
calculation. The advantage of this assumption is that we
immediately know the shape of the polar curve. It is a sphere
tangential to the reflecting surface and this is established as
follows. A perfectly matt or uniformly diffuse surface reflecting
light has the same luminance at any angle of view (see Figure
9.18).

Figure 9.18

*Polar curve of reflected
light from a uniformly
diffuse surface*

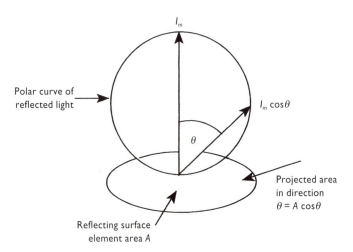

At any angle $L = \dfrac{I_\theta}{A\cos\theta}$ since a flat plane of area A viewed
an angle θ to the normal has a projected area equal to $A\cos\theta$.
So, for L to be constant at all angles of view I_θ must equal
$I_m\cos\theta$, where I_m is the intensity normal to area A; that is

$$L = \frac{I_m\cos\theta}{A\cos\theta} \text{ or } L = \frac{I_m}{A} = \text{constant}$$

The polar distribution of the reflected light is given by $I_\theta =
I_m\cos\theta$. We still need to establish the value of I_m in relation to
the reflected flux. This can be established for a uniform diffuser
in a very simple way. Consider Figure 9.19.

If a uniformly diffusing element of area δa is considered to
be part of a sphere, then the illuminance of the inside of the
sphere from the element δa is given by

$$\delta E = \frac{I_m\cos^2\theta}{D^2} = \frac{I_m\cos^2\theta}{(2r\cos\theta)^2} = \frac{I_m}{4r^2}$$

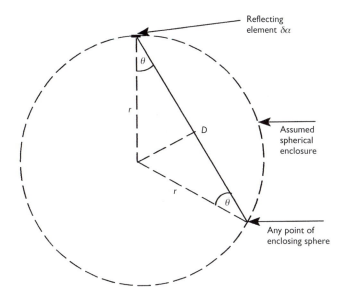

Figure 9.19

Calculation of the relationship between the flux emitted and the maximum intensity for a uniform diffuser

that is, it is constant over the interior area of the sphere. The flux on the inside of the sphere is

$$F = 4\pi r^2 \times \frac{I_m}{4r^2}$$

$$= \pi I_m$$

$$\text{So, } I_m = \frac{F}{\pi}$$

In our problem the flux received by the patch of wall is 23.9 lumens. The value of reflected flux is the incident flux multiplied by the reflectance, which is 0.5 or 50%. So,

$$I_m = \frac{23.9 \times 0.5}{\pi}$$

$$= 3.8 \text{ cd}$$

From Figure 9.18, both the angle for the intensity towards the table from the wall patch and the angle of incidence at the table is 45°, so the illuminance produced by this one reflection is given by

$$E_r = \frac{3.8 \times \cos 45° \times \cos 45°}{(2^2 + 2^2)}$$

$$= 0.238 \text{ lux}$$

This may seem a negligible value, but in a square room with the luminaire at the centre there would be four identical patches and, considering only the wall area below the luminaire, the area we have dealt with is only one sixty-fourth of the total reflecting area. Additionally, we have only considered one reflection. Interreflection from walls, ceiling and working plane commonly doubles the illuminance in such a small room with this type of intensity distribution from the luminaire.

We will calculate the luminance of the sphere and of the wall patch for the first reflection to complete this illustration. As mentioned earlier, we need the size of the sphere to calculate its luminance. We will assume it to be 0.5 m in diameter. The luminance is given by the luminous intensity in a given direction divided by the apparent, or projected, area in that direction; in this case, the area of a circle.

From page 83, the luminous intensity is the same in all directions, namely 318 cd, and now we have the sphere diameter we can calculate the projected area: $A = \pi d^2/4$. So,

$$L = \frac{I}{A} = \frac{318}{\pi \frac{(0.5)^2}{4}}$$

$$= 1619.6 \text{ cd/m}^2$$

The wall luminance produced by one reflection is given by

$$L = \frac{I}{A} = \frac{3.8}{0.3} = 12.7 \text{ cd/m}^2$$

By interreflection this value is likely to be doubled.

Uniform diffusion and the integrating sphere

In the previous section the concept of a uniform diffuser was introduced and it was shown that its intensity distribution could be characterized by $I_\theta = I_m\cos\theta$, where θ is the angle between the direction of interest and the normal to the element of surface considered. It was also shown that, for a spherical enclosure, light emitted or reflected uniformly diffusely from an element of its interior surface has an illuminance on other parts of that interior surface given by $E = \frac{I_m}{4r^2}$.

The spherical enclosure combined with the uniformly diffused nature of the emitted or reflected light means that the angle of emission or incidence is *missing* from the illuminance equation. This means that any element δa on the inside of the sphere produces the same value of illuminance at all points on the interior surface of the sphere. It also means that, regardless of the initial distribution of the direct flux from a light source within the sphere, the reflected flux will be uniformly distributed over the interior surface of the sphere. The assumption of uniform diffusion allows interreflection calculations to be performed in a relatively simple way. A practical example of such a calculation is that for the integrating sphere used for relative flux measurements in photometric laboratories.

If the sphere is coated with a matt paint of reflectance ρ, it is possible to obtain, by simple calculation, an estimate of this reflected illuminance when a light source is suspended within the sphere (see Figure 9.20).

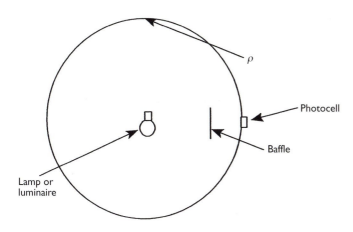

Figure 9.20
The integrating sphere

If we use the principle of the conservation of energy we can set up an energy balance equation for an integrating sphere, as follows. All the light emitted by the lamp is eventually absorbed by the sphere, but at any moment the total flux F received on the inside of the sphere equals the direct flux emitted by the lamp F_D plus the reflected flux F_R. So,

$$F = F_D + F_R$$

$$= F_D + \rho F$$

$$\text{giving } F = \frac{F_D}{1 - \rho}$$

The reflected flux:

$$F_R = F - F_D$$

$$= \frac{F_D}{1 - \rho} - F_D$$

$$= \frac{F_D \rho}{1 - \rho}$$

Dividing both sides by the area of the sphere gives the reflected illuminance E_R in terms of the direct illuminance E_D and the sphere reflectance.

$$E_R = \frac{E_D \rho}{1 - \rho}$$

This type of calculation is similar to that sometimes used to calculate the effect of interreflections in rooms to produce utilization factors. However, the complexity of the calculation increases rapidly as the number of equations required increases. This method is used to obtain the cavity reflectance formula developed in Appendix 3 and used in Chapter 15.

The practical integrating sphere

Figure 9.20 shows the arrangement in a practical integrating sphere. The reflected illuminance is measured at a convenient point in the side of the sphere. A baffle is fixed within the space between the light source and the photocell to ensure that only reflected illuminance is measured.

Integrating spheres are often large to accommodate fluorescent luminaires. A common use is for the measurement of the light output ratio (*LOR*) of a luminaire by measuring the lamp output and then the luminaire output with the lamp installed,

LOR = luminaire output/lamp output.

In practical integrators an auxiliary lamp, which is baffled to produce only reflected illumination within the sphere, is often provided. Readings are taken with the unlit light source on its own and then with the luminaire to determine the relative amount of the interreflected light each absorbs, so that a correction can be made for the difference in size of the lamp and the luminaire.

Other shapes of integrator are sometimes used for convenience, e.g. rectangular enclosures. These only give accurate results when both the light source and the luminaire are similar in shape; for example, linear.

Fundamental measurement and calculation of luminous flux

Although integrators are used for comparison of luminous flux output, the fundamental way of calculating luminous flux from a light source is to calculate it from intensity measurements using zone factors. For completeness zone factors are derived below.

Consider Figure 9.21. The flux emitted through the elemental strip of the sphere = Illuminance × Area of strip

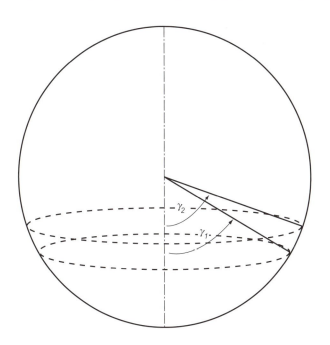

Figure 9.21
The calculation of zone factors

$$F = \frac{I_\gamma}{r^2} \times 2\pi r \sin\gamma \times r \, d\gamma$$

$$= I_\gamma \times 2\pi \sin\gamma d\gamma$$

If $I\gamma$ is the mid-zone intensity (assumed to be the average intensity) over a zone between γ_1 and γ_2, then

$$F_{\gamma_1 \gamma_2} = I_\gamma \times 2\pi \int_{\gamma_1}^{\gamma_2} \sin\gamma d\gamma$$

$$= I_\gamma \times 2\pi[-\cos\gamma]_{\gamma_1}^{\gamma_2}$$

$$= I_\gamma \times 2\pi[\cos\gamma_1 - \cos\gamma_2]$$

$2\pi[\cos\gamma_1 - \cos\gamma_2]$ is called the zone factor and is, in fact, the solid angle subtended by the zone at the centre of the sphere.

In general, for flux calculations

Flux emitted = Luminous intensity
× Solid angle through which it acts

The above treatment assumes that an average polar curve has been obtained for the azimuth direction. Zone factors for 10° zones are given in Table 9.1. As a simple example, we will calculate the flux output from a uniformly diffuse planar source

Table 9.1　Zone factors

Zone limits (degrees)	Zone limits (degrees)	Zone factors
0–10	170–180	0.095
10–20	160–170	0.283
20–30	150–160	0.463
30–40	140–150	0.628
40–50	130–140	0.774
50–60	120–130	0.894
60–70	110–120	0.993
70–80	100–110	1.058
80–90	90–100	1.091

Table 9.2　Flux calculation for a uniform diffuser using zone factors

	I_θ	ZF	Lumens
0–10	$I_m \cos\ 5° = 0.996\ I_m$	0.095	$I_m\ 0.095$
10–20	$I_m \cos 15° = 0.966\ I_m$	0.283	$I_m\ 0.273$
20–30	$I_m \cos 25° = 0.906\ I_m$	0.463	$I_m\ 0.419$
30–40	$I_m \cos 35° = 0.819\ I_m$	0.628	$I_m\ 0.514$
40–50	$I_m \cos 45° = 0.707\ I_m$	0.774	$I_m\ 0.547$
50–60	$I_m \cos 55° = 0.574\ I_m$	0.894	$I_m\ 0.513$
60–70	$I_m \cos 65° = 0.423\ I_m$	0.993	$I_m\ 0.420$
70–80	$I_m \cos 75° = 0.259\ I_m$	1.058	$I_m\ 0.274$
80–90	$I_m \cos 85° = 0.087\ I_m$	1.091	$\underline{I_m\ 0.095}$
			$I_m\ 3.150$

of maximum intensity I_m (Table 9.2). The mid-zone intensity is required for each zone.

　　The exact value which was calculated on page 85 was πI_m or $3.142I_m$. The zonal value is 0.2% high. This difference was caused by using finite zone sizes necessary for dealing with practical distributions.

Computer programs　Understandably, computer programs for lighting design have become a basic calculational tool for most lighting consultants. In addition to the average illuminance values provided by utilization factor calculations (see Chapter 10), they offer arrays of point by point calculations. The facility is often provided to allow for the mixture of luminaires in an installation, so that unusual or customized arrangements can be considered in detail.

Visualization programs also bring another dimension to examining possible design solutions. One drawback has been the time and cost taken to feed the information concerning the space to be lit into the computer and the selection and placing of the luminaires. However, there is continuous development in this area and it can be expected that this will become easier and quicker.

An issue has been the accuracy of the different programs available. Various calculational methods are embedded in these programs, such as cyclic inverse-square law calculation, some types of ray tracing and radiosity. It is easy in this field, as in others, to assume that a computer calculation has greater accuracy simply because it is generated by a computer. However, computer generated information is as good as the input data allows it to be and as good as the computer algorithm used. Compared with manual computation, it is probably true to say that computers can help make 'better' mistakes, and then repeat them again and again. This is mainly because any mistakes are not so easily noticed, unless the user of the program has the experience to recognize that the results do not make sense. However, the value of the flexibility that computer programs afford and the simple way in which changes can be made and evaluated far outstrip the limitations. Nevertheless, the question of accuracy is an important one.

A simple way of checking the consistency of a computer program is to use it to calculate the illuminances on the ceiling, walls and floor. Multiplying these illuminances by the areas of these surfaces gives the values of incident flux on each of them. The flux that is not reflected must be absorbed and so, in each case $(1 - \rho)$, where ρ is the reflectance, gives the proportion of the flux absorbed. For example, if the ceiling reflects 70% of the incident flux 30% must be absorbed. Multiplying the incident flux on each surface by $(1 - \rho)$ for that surface gives the amount of absorbed flux. Adding the values of this absorbed flux for ceiling, walls and floor gives the total flux absorbed. This should equal the total flux supplied into the room by the luminaires. For a general lighting system, this would be the total lamp flux multiplied by the light output ratio of the luminaires. Any significant discrepancy between these two values should cast doubt on the accuracy of the program because it does not adequately account for the flux supplied by the installation.

Programs that rely on dividing all the surfaces and luminaires into elements small enough for the inverse-square law to apply are usually iterative. The cycle of calculation is repeated again and again to allow for interreflection and the result of the present calculation is compared to the previous calculation. This is continued until the change in values falls below a pre-set percentage of, say, 5%.

The CIBSE has a report TM28 which is called 'Benchmarking Lighting Design Software'.

Checking a lighting installation

When a lighting installation has been designed, the money spent and the installation completed, the most important factor is the opinion of the users. Do those for whom the installation is provided approve of the result? Do they like it? From the point of view of the lighting engineer, it is also always of interest to compare the achieved lighting levels with those predicted by the calculations.

It is necessary to ensure that an accurate lightmeter (illumination meter) is used to measure the performance of an installation in terms of the illuminance provided and that a sufficient number of illuminance readings are taken to give a correct indication of the practical performance of the installation.

The lightmeter

A good quality lightmeter usually has a silicon photocell fitted into a suitable head which provides an accurate response to light arriving at different angles (often called 'cosine correction'), and an accurate colour response so that similar illuminance levels produced by lamps of different colour (spectral distribution) give similar responses. The lightmeter should also have an appropriate electronic circuit that provides a satisfactory digital or analogue display of the illuminance values.

The lightmeter head should be connected by a suitable length of lead to the display unit so that there is little possibility of the operator casting a shadow on the photocell head whilst reading the display, thus giving a false reading.

The number of points required

Research has shown that the relationship between room dimensions and the number of measuring points required to calculate the average illuminance and give an error of less than 10% in a rectangular room with a regular array of luminaires at spacing no greater than 1.5–1.0 can be tabulated in terms of room index as shown below, where the room index is given by

$$RI = \frac{\text{Area of ceiling and floor}}{\text{Area of walls between the luminaires and the working plane}}$$

$$\text{So } RI = \frac{2l \times w}{2H\,(l + w)} = \frac{l \times w}{H(l + w)}$$

Therefore $RI = \dfrac{w}{2H}$ for a square room

where l = room length

        w = room width

        H = luminaire mounting height above the working
           plane

RI	Numbers of points
Below 1	9
1 and below 2	16
2 and below 3	25
3 and above	36

This is the minimum number and more can be used. The points should be laid out as a grid with half spacing at the walls. It is obvious that this grid must not coincide with the grid of the luminaires, since this would place each reading directly beneath a luminaire which would give large errors. In that case, the next higher number of points of measurement should be used.

    The installation should have run for 100 hours from new before the measurements are taken and this initial comparison of the calculated and measured average values should use a calculated value that does not include the maintenance factor. Later surveys to check when maintenance procedures should be applied should compare the measured value with the originally calculated value that did include the maintenance factor.

    The uniformity of the illuminance is usually expressed as the ratio of the minimum illuminance value divided by the average value. A value of $E_{min}/E_{av} = 0.8$ is usually considered appropriate for generally lit working areas such as offices. The minimum value used in this calculation should ignore readings within 0.5 m of the walls, since the illuminance often falls rapidly in this region and would give a false picture of the uniformity occurring in the general working area.

Question 9.1

An integrating sphere is painted with a finish of reflectance 0.8. Calculate the ratio of reflected illuminance to direct illumi-

QUESTIONS

nance within the sphere. If the reflectance was increased to 0.9, what would be the new value of that ratio?

What do these results indicate about the problems of using very high values of reflectance in integrators?

Question 9.2 A parabolic floodlight is tested at too short a distance so that only two-thirds of the reflector projected area is filled with the image of the small light source. Ignoring the size of the light source and any contribution from this source that is *not* reflected, what would be the difference in the measured intensity at this distance compared with the value measured at the correct distance? Consider only the intensity in the direction of the axis of the parabola.

Question 9.3 What is the maximum value of the vector scalar ratio that can be achieved?

Question 9.4 Can you suggest a simple test to determine the degree of disability glare present in an interior?

Question 9.5 If you were dealing with a complaint that the lighting was making it difficult to see pencil lines on drawings, or to see notes or a similar problem, how could you be sure that you had identified the source of the problem?

ANSWERS

Answer 9.1

$$\frac{E_R}{E_D} = \frac{1 - \rho}{\rho}$$

$$= \frac{1 - 0.8}{0.8} = 4$$

$$\frac{E_R}{E_D} = \frac{1 - 0.9}{0.9} = 9$$

A change of 12.5% in reflectance produced a 125% change in reflected illumination. At high reflectance values small changes can make large changes in the reflected illuminance. For this reason very high values of reflectance are avoided in integrators, since during use small changes in reflectance could occur unnoticed.

Answer 9.2 The intensity is equal to the luminance of the image multiplied by the projected area of the image. If this is only two-thirds of the total projected area when the reflector is filled with the image (fully flashed) then the intensity value obtained at the too short distance would be two-thirds of that measured at the correct distance.

Answer 9.3   A point source gives a maximum value of vector illuminance equal to the maximum illuminance that it produces at a point, so

$$E_{max} = \frac{I}{D^2}$$

In addition, the scalar illuminance produced by the same source at the same point is given by

$$E_S = \frac{I}{4D^2}$$

The maximum value of the vector scalar ratio is therefore 4.

Any other arrangement of light sources or reflection reduces the magnitude of the vector relative to the scalar illuminance.

Answer 9.4   Shade the eyes with the hand so that the light sources are not included in the visual scene. Any significant disability glare will become immediately obvious.

Answer 9.5   A simple test would be to replace the task with a mirror and then the light source creating the problem would be seen in the mirror.

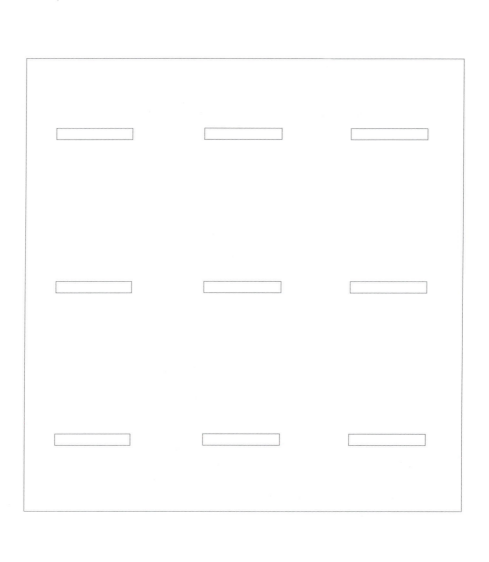

'Lumen' methods

Much general lighting design is now carried out with the aid of a computer, however it is still important to understand how to calculate illuminance levels. Sometimes there are projects where feeding the information required into a computer would be too time-consuming for the simple calculation required. Again, it may be necessary to check that the answer obtained using the computer is correct. The ability to both understand what is being done and to do it by hand, if necessary, promotes confidence.

The lumen methods of the chapter title represent an approach to lighting calculations which is based on some simple ideas that can be used for both interior and exterior lighting. It is a lumen- or flux-based approach rather than an intensity-based approach and relates in general to average illuminance values.

The average illuminance over an area is given by the luminous flux received on an area divided by the area $E_{av} = \dfrac{F}{A}$ where F is the required luminous flux and A the area. We then consider where the luminous flux comes from and what factors should be taken into account to ensure that over time the required average illuminance value is maintained. For simplicity, we will consider the illuminance of the working plane in a rectangular room (Figure 10.1).

The working plane is effectively at bench, desk or table level throughout the space. For example, it might be specified at 0.8 m above the floor. The idea is that a working surface might be placed anywhere in the room and still receive sufficient light. The area of the working plane is the 'A' value used in the illuminance equation. So,

$$E_{av} \times A_{wp} = F \text{ lumens}$$

Initially, these lumens are provided by the lamps installed in the luminaires. Therefore, we must take into account the

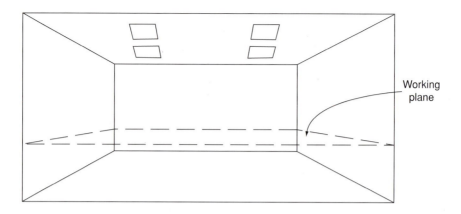

Working
plane

Figure 10.1

Illuminance on the
working plane in a
rectangular room

lumen output of each lamp F_L, the number of lamps in the installation n, the amount of light that *eventually* reaches the working plane and the allowance that is required for deterioration of the performance of the installation over time to arrive at the value of F.

Therefore, we replace F by $F = F_L \times n \times UF \times MF$ where F_L is the lamp flux, n the number of lamps, UF the utilization factor and MF the maintenance factor. The illuminance equation can now be written as

$$E_{av} = \frac{F_L \times n \times UF \times MF}{A_{WP}}$$

This can be used in various ways. For a defined installation E_{av} can be directly calculated. Often E_{av} is specified and so it is $F_L \times n$ that is required

$$F_L \times n = \frac{E_{av} \times A_{WP}}{UF \times MF}$$

where $F_L \times n$ are the initial lumens required for the installation to provide E_{av}.

If we wrote $\dfrac{n}{A_{WP}} = \dfrac{E_{av}}{F_L \times UF \times MF}$ we could calculate the number of lamps required per square metre of installation. This is sometimes a useful way of considering areas within a larger area and making minor adjustments to the area to be lit. The key to this apparently simple method lies in knowing the values of the utilization factor (UF) and the maintenance factor (MF) for a given scheme.

The utilization
factor

The light from the lamp passes through the optical system of the luminaire and in the process some light is lost. The factor by which to multiply to allow for losses due to the luminaire is called the light output ratio (LOR). A typical value of LOR for a fluorescent luminaire might be 0.7. When the light emerges from the luminaire some of it will go directly to the working plane, some may strike the ceiling and some the walls. The amount of light that is received on the working plane from the ceiling and the walls depends upon their reflection factors. A typical ceiling reflectance might be 0.7 and a wall reflectance 0.5. The utilization factor takes the luminaire LOR and the room size and reflectances into account. It is a sort of efficiency with which the luminaire and room combination work in a particular lighting scheme.

Over a period of time, the light output of the lamps falls, the lamps and luminaires gather dirt and dust, and the room surfaces deteriorate. The lamps may also fail. The maintenance factor is intended to allow for all these factors. By applying a maintenance factor the designer ensures that the initial average illuminance is significantly higher than the design value so that at the time when the maintenance procedures are carried out the installation will still just meet its illuminance specification.

The maintenance factor

The design illuminance is called the maintained illuminance, that is the value at which the maintenance procedures should be applied to ensure the illuminance falls no lower. The maintenance factor is made up as follows:

$$MF = LLMF \times LMF \times RSMF \times LSF$$

where LLMF is lamp lumen maintenance factor, LMF is luminaire maintenance factor, RSMF is room maintenance factor and LSF is lamp survival factor.

F_L, the LLMF and the LSF should be provided by the lamp manufacturer. The LMF should be provided by the manufacturer, but approximate LMF data are provided by CIE and CIBSE.

Data for lumen method calculation

RSMF data are provided by the CIE and the CIBSE includes data in its Lighting Code.

The utilization factor (UF) should be provided by the luminaire manufacturer.

Appendix 2 gives approximate maintenance factor data.

The tabulation of utilization factors makes use of a room index based upon the room dimensions. When light is emitted downwards from a lighting installation all of it will reach the

Tabulation of utilization factors

working plane unless it strikes a wall. If it strikes a wall, it will be redistributed and less will reach the working plane. Thus, the most efficient system for the distribution of direct flux to the working plane is one in which the wall area is small compared to the area of the working plane.

The room index classifies rooms in terms of the ratio of horizontal area to vertical area. The room index formula is given by

$$RI = \frac{\text{area of working plane} + \text{ceiling}}{\text{area of walls}}$$

$$= \frac{2 \times l \times w}{2lh + 2wh} = \frac{l \times w}{h(l + w)}$$

which for a square room becomes

$$RI = \frac{w}{2h}$$

An example of a lumen method calculation is given below.

Example 10.1   A general area requires a lighting level of 500 lux from a regular array of louvred luminaires. Given the following data calculate the number of luminaires required and arrange a suitable layout.

The room dimensions are: length 8 m, width 8 m, height 2.8 m.

Room reflectances: ceiling 0.7, walls 0.5, working plane cavity 0.2.

UF table for 0.7, 0.5, 0.2 reflectances

Room index

0.75	1.00	1.25	1.50	2.00	2.50	3.00	4.00	5.00
0.38	0.45	0.50	0.53	0.58	0.61	0.63	0.66	0.67

Maintenance factor 0.75
Maximum spacing to height ratio 1.75
Luminaire versions available:
2 × 1800 mm   70W (each lamp gives) 6550 lumens
2 × 1500 mm   58W (each lamp gives) 5400 lumens
2 × 1200 mm   36W (each lamp gives) 3450 lumens

(1)   Calculate room index and hence obtain *UF* value. Assume a working plane height of 0.8. So,

$$h = 2.0 \text{ m}$$

$$RI = \frac{w}{2h} \text{ for a square room}$$

$$= \frac{8}{2 \times 2} = 2.0$$

UF for RI = 2.0 is 0.58

(2) Calculate the total lumens required

$$E = \frac{F_L \times n \times UF \times MF}{A_{wp}}$$

$$F_L \times n = \frac{E \times A_{wp}}{UF \times MF}$$

$$= \frac{500 \times 8 \times 8}{0.58 \times 0.75}$$

$$= 73\ 563 \text{ lumens}$$

(3) Calculate the number of luminaires
The minimum number of luminaires will give the minimum number of electrical points and so the largest lamp size should be tried first. There are two lamps per luminaire: two 70W lamps give 2×6550 lumens = 13 100.

$$n = \frac{73\ 563}{13\ 100} = 5.6 \text{ luminaires}$$

This would be rounded up to 6 luminaires arranged in two rows of three.

Will the spacing for two rows exceed the maximum specified by the manufacturer?

Width of office 8 m, spacing between rows 4 m with 2 m to the wall at each side. The maximum spacing/mounting height ratio from the manufacturer is $S/h = 1.75$. $h = 2.0$ m, so allowable spacing is $S = 1.75 \times 2.0 = 3.5$ m.

It is necessary to have 9 luminaires in 3 rows to provide acceptable uniformity

$$\left(\frac{E_{min}}{E_{av}} \right).$$

Recalculate lamp output:

$$\frac{73\ 563}{9 \times 2} = 4087 \text{ lumens}$$

The only available lamp size that will provide 500 lux or more is the 58W lamp giving 5400 lumens. This solution will give a higher illuminance than that specified, but this is a common outcome and has to be accepted. The new illuminance value is

$$E = \frac{54\,100 \times 18 \times 0.58 \times 0.75}{64}$$

= 660 lux

The spacing for 9 luminaires would be 8/3 = 2.7 m with 1.3 m at the walls. $S/H = 2.7/2 = 1.35$, which is well within the 1.75 limit.

Room shape, uniformity requirements and the available luminaire/lamp combinations commonly dictate solutions that give a higher performance than the minimum recommendations (Figure 10.2).

Figure 10.2

Luminaire layout to achieve acceptable uniformity

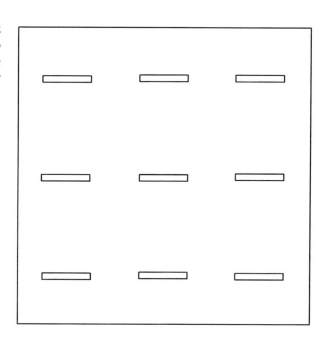

In this case, the fact that the room was square necessitated changing from 6 luminaires to 9. If the same area of room had been rectangular the original solution might have been acceptable, see below.

Area of room $8 \times 8 = 64$ m²

Spacing for two rows to meet uniformity requirements would not have to exceed $S/h \times hm = 1.75 \times 2 = 3.5$ m. The room would have to be 7 m wide to achieve this and to give the same area the length would need to be 64/7 = 9.1 m.

For three rows down this length the spacing would be 3.03 m, which is within the 3.5 m limit for uniformity.

Check that the room index has not changed significantly:

$$RI = \frac{7 \times 9.1}{2(7 + 9.1)} = 1.98.$$

Therefore, the original solution of 6 two-lamp 70W luminaires could have been used.

A further example is given in Chapter 15 and in Appendix 3, which also shows how to calculate the UF when only the polar curve scaled in cd/1000 lumens is available. It also includes determination of the maintenance factor.

Illuminance ratios

Illuminance ratios for walls and ceilings relative to the horizontal plane or working plane give an indication of the impression of brightness of the interior that is likely to be achieved. The final result will depend on the room reflectances (not always under the control of the lighting designer), but the wall and ceiling illuminances are a key element.

The SLL (CIBSE) Code recommends the following ranges of illuminance ratios and reflectances:

Walls $\left(\dfrac{E_w}{E_h}\right)$ 0.5–0.8

   R 0.3–0.7 (for a window wall 0.6)

Ceiling $\left(\dfrac{E_c}{E_h}\right)$ 0.3–0.9

   R 0.6 (min)

Floor R 0.2–0.4

Utilization factors for walls and ceilings can be calculated and illuminance ratios obtained. Examples of these calculations are given in Appendix 3.

Ratio of cylindrical to horizontal illuminance

The ratio of cylindrical to horizontal illuminance was mentioned in Chapters 8 and 9 and this ratio has been found to be related to the appearance of people within the illuminated space. The higher the ratio, the higher the level of user satisfaction tends to be.

In general lighting installations, the higher the ratio of wall to horizontal plane illuminance, then the higher the ratio of cylindrical to horizontal illuminance that can be expected. Figure 10.3 shows typical values of the ratio for the polar curves indicated plotted against room index.

Figure 10.3

Ratio of cylindrical to horizontal illuminance plotted against room index for a set of typical distributions

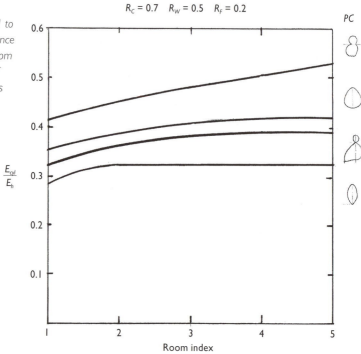

$R_C = 0.7$ $R_W = 0.5$ $R_F = 0.2$

PC

$\dfrac{E_{cyl}}{E_h}$

Room index

The other 'lumen' method

The method described in the previous section is appropriate when a general area is to be lit and the type of luminaire to be used has been selected. It starts from the light source and determines the effect it has in a given room. In some ways it is more logical to start with the overall lighting effect required within the room and work out what equipment is needed to achieve that aim.

In its 'pure' form, this method begins by specifying apparent brightness levels for the room surfaces and then relates these to the required luminances for all these surfaces. From these the direct average illuminances needed on each surface are calculated and hence the lumens required for each area of the room. Equipment and layouts are then chosen to meet these criteria.

The method is not as useful as might be thought for general lighting installations because there are a wide range of wall and ceiling brightnesses that have been found acceptable and when a choice is made it is sometimes found that the chosen brightness and the room reflectances are incompatible. By this is meant that when the calculations are carried out a surface sometimes is allocated a negative amount of direct illuminance to achieve the specification! In addition, when an array of similar luminaires is specified because of the general nature of the area, the specification for the light distribution from the luminaires sometimes cannot be met from the available luminaires. Hence, it is usually considered better to use a method that determines what effect an available luminaire will have in the given situation and, where necessary, change the luminaire or layout until a satisfactory scheme is achieved. However, there are some situations in which a modified version of this method is very helpful.

This method is particularly useful when a hierarchy of illuminances for various areas of a space can be established. A typical example would be a church and an example of a calculation for a church interior is given in Chapter 19. Here a very simple situation will be chosen to illustrate the method.

The illuminance specification method

Consider Figure 10.4. Here a simple rectangular room is shown, together with the surface reflectances and the specified illuminances. The information given in Figure 10.4 is entered on a spreadsheet:

Example 10.2

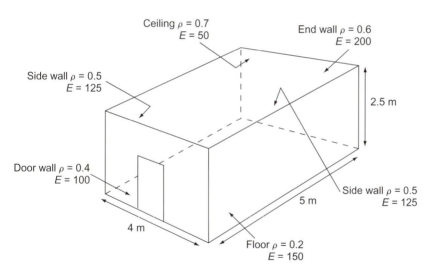

Location	E (lux)	A (m²)	r	E × A × ρ (lumens)
Door wall	100	10	0.4	400
Floor	150	20	0.2	600
Ceiling	50	20	0.7	700
Side walls	125	25	0.5	1562
End wall	200	10	0.6	1200
		85		4462

Figure 10.4
Room data for 'illuminance specification' example

$$\text{Interreflected illuminance} = \frac{4462}{85} = 52.5 \text{ lux}$$

The direct illuminances required on each surface are:

		Ed
Door wall	100 – 52.5	= 47.5
Floor	150 – 52.5	= 97.5
Ceiling	50 – 52.5	= –2.5
Side walls	125 – 52.5	= 72.5
End wall	200 – 52.5	= 147.5

The negative result for direct illuminance on the ceiling is so small that it can be ignored and the direct illuminance required on the ceiling taken as zero. Any large negative values would mean altering the initial specification.

The next stage would be to select the lamps and luminaires required to provide the direct illuminances. This is only a simple process if it can be assumed that each surface is lit by individual projectors that do not light the other surfaces directly. If this is true, then for any surface the basic relationship is as follows:

Number of lamps required =

$$\frac{\text{Direct flux required}}{\text{Flux for one lamp} \times \text{LOR of luminaire} \times \text{Maintenance factor}}$$

The direct flux = direct illuminance × area of surface.

QUESTION

Question 10.1 What is the main difference between the utilization factor method, which relies on UF values provided by the manufacturer, and the illuminance specification method?

ANSWER

Answer 10.1 In its simple form the illuminance specification method is a less accurate calculational method because it assumes the same value of reflected illuminance for all surfaces. However, it has the great advantage of giving a simple approach to the lighting of complex interiors. (See the example in Chapter 19.)

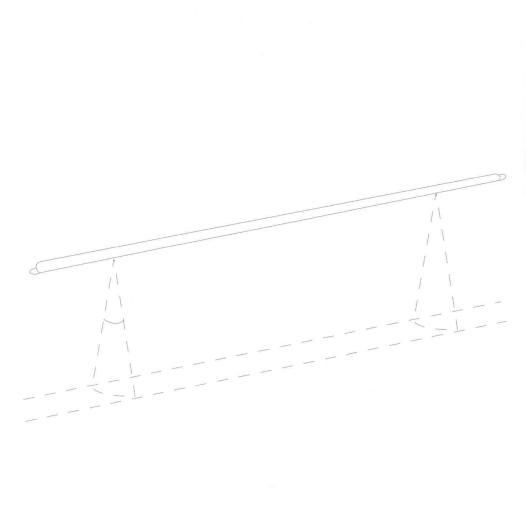

The significance of mounting height in an interior lighting installation

The mounting height of a luminaire can be considered in relation to the following effects:

1 The effect on the working plane illuminance and uniformity.
2 The effect on glare.
3 The effect on the appearance of the lighted space.

We have already established that the *direct* illuminance below a single small light source varies as the square of the distance. If the light source is raised to twice its original mounting height the illuminance will fall to one-quarter. If the original direct illuminance was 100 lux it would be reduced to 25 lux.

The effect on the illuminance

The point source

Consider Figure 11.1. The light flux passing through the sector denoted by a small angle $\delta\theta$ can be considered to be incident on the horizontal plane via an element of surface defined by $R\delta\theta$ and the length of the line source. For a fixed length of source the area is proportional to $R\delta\theta$ and for a fixed value of $\delta\theta$ only upon R.

The line source

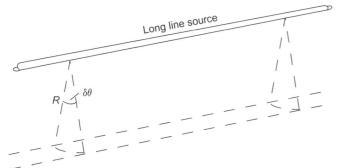

Figure 11.1

Variation of illuminance with mounting height for a long line source

The average illuminance at distance R directly beneath the source will vary as R, as long as the source is long compared with R. Thus, beneath a long line source, if the mounting height is doubled, the *direct* illuminance will be halved.

Large area source   The output of a large area luminous source can be considered in terms of the luminous flux emitted per unit of area; that is lumens per square metre. There is no special unit for this quantity, but it is called the luminous exitance. It gives an indication of the amount of light emitted, but it is not related to direction, as is luminance.

The luminous exitance is given by $M = \dfrac{F}{A}$, where F is the emitted flux and A the area of the source considered. In the special case of a uniform diffuser the relationship between luminance L and luminous exitance M is simple, $M = \pi L$.

In any region away from the boundaries of a very large area light source having a uniform value of luminous exitance, all the flux emitted by the light source can be assumed to reach the working plane. This means that the illuminance received will equal the luminous exitance of the source. This also means that as long as the space between the area source and the parallel working plane is small compared with the area of the source then the illuminance produced will be independent of the distance between the source and the working plane. The reason for this is that when the mounting height is increased, although the flux is lost to other areas of the working plane, the same amount of flux is gained from other parts of the area light source.

These three simple illustrations map out the progression from a single point source to a continuous line source or a row of point sources, through to a large area source or a large array of point or line sources, in terms of the effect of the mounting height on the direct illuminance.

As a row of point sources is increased in mounting height so the effect on the illuminance begins to be similar to that of a continuous line source. If a uniform rectangular array of point sources is raised in mounting height so the effect on the illuminance begins to be similar to a large area source. A similar effect occurs when continuous line sources in a regular array have the mounting height raised. This means that the larger the array of light sources the less the effect on the illuminance of changing the mounting height is likely to be, provided that the cut-off angles of the luminaires are such that the light from adjacent sources can overlap. In general, increasing the mounting height for a given area of working plane reduces the utilization factor because the walls interrupt more light.

Raising the mounting height relative to the spacing of the luminaires usually improves the uniformity, but special care must be taken with very sharp cut-off luminaires, where reducing the spacing to mounting height ratio could cause high illuminance points to overlap and reduce the uniformity.

In general, raising the mounting height of luminaires reduces the glare because the light sources are moved away from the horizontal line of sight.

The effect on the glare

The mounting height of the luminaires can have two effects upon the appearance of a lighted space. One is that of scale, for if decorative luminaires are mounted too high they can seem too small and if they are mounted too low they can seem intrusive. In either case, they have a disturbing effect upon the harmony of the space. The other effect is where an array of similar downlighting luminaires is suspended in a regular way across a space it can create an impression of a ceiling at the height of the luminaires. This can sometimes be used to advantage, where the room is too high or when it can be used to 'hide' unsightly pipework without the need for a false ceiling. However, it can also unintentionally make the ceiling appear oppressively low.

The third effect is on the shadows. As the mounting height is increased so the light from more of the luminaires overlaps and so shadowing is reduced. Additionally, when high bay luminaires are used with parabolic reflectors the angle of incidence of the light is closer to the normal at the working plane and the size of the shadows is reduced.

In addition to the above considerations, there is the important consideration of access to the luminaires for maintenance. Obviously, this is a consideration in atria and similar spaces and may have a strong bearing on the types of lamp and luminaires that are suitable for the location.

Question 11.1 In what way might a high value of inter-reflected illuminance modify the illuminance effects described within this chapter?

Answer 11.1 Interreflected illuminance superimposes an area source effect upon the direct light effects described and this usually reduces these changes, the reduction depending upon the relative magnitude of the direct/indirect components of illuminance.

ANSWER

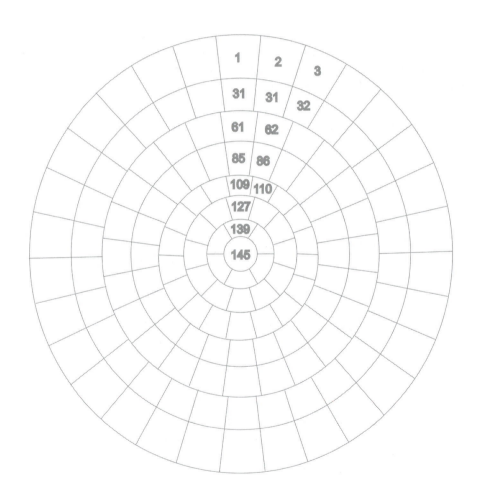

In Chapter 2 the concept of the daylight factor was introduced. The daylight factor (df) expresses the ratio of the illuminance at the point in the room as a percentage of the illuminance from the whole unobstructed sky and is based on the sky being overcast.

$$df = \frac{\text{indoor illuminance}}{\text{outdoor illuminance}} \times 100\%$$

In the UK it is found that if the *average* working plane daylight factor is 5% or more the room will look cheerfully lit during most of the day. If the daylight factor falls to 2% the daylighting will be such that the room occupants are likely to switch on the electric lighting. The use of an overcast sky for these calculations is based on the assumption that if the lighting is acceptable on an overcast day it is almost certain to be considered adequate on a bright sunlit day.

At the beginning of the design process it is useful to have an estimate of the area of glazing required to give a particular value of average daylight for a given room. This can be developed initially by using a modification of the formula developed for the integrating sphere in Chapter 9

$$F = \frac{F_D}{1 - R}$$

where F_D is the flux entering the room through the window, R is the average reflectance of the room surfaces and $F =$ the final flux received by all the room surfaces.

Dividing through by the total surface area of the room (A) gives:

$$E_{av} = \frac{F_D}{A(1 - R)}$$

It has been found that half the vertical angle in degrees of unobstructed sky measured from the middle of the window

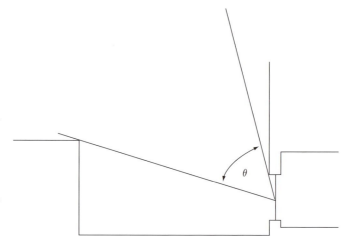

Figure 12.1

The vertical angle of unobstructed sky gives a reasonable approximation to the ratio of the window illuminance to that of an unobstructed overcast sky

(see Figure 12.1) gives a reasonable approximation to the ratio of illuminance on the vertical face of the window to that on the horizontal from an unobstructed overcast sky, expressed as a percentage.

So,

$$F_D = \frac{\theta}{2} \times \frac{E_{sky}}{100} \times T \times W$$

where T = transmittance of the glazing and W = window area. E_{sky} is the illuminance produced outside by an unobstructed overcast sky.

$$E_{av} = \frac{\theta}{2} \times \frac{E_{sky}}{100} \times T \times W \div A(1 - R)$$

$$\frac{E_{av}}{E_{sky}} \times 100\% = \frac{\theta TW}{2A(1 - R)}$$

= average daylight factor for the room (initial not maintained).

However, if the average daylight factor for the working plane is required, it has been found that the formula must be modified as follows:

$$df = \frac{\theta TW}{A(1 - R^2)} \%$$

Transposing the formula, we can obtain the area of glazing required for a given daylight factor:

$$W = \frac{df A(1 - R^2)}{\theta T} \text{ m}^2$$

A room has a window area of 3 m², a vertical angle of unobstructed sky of 60° and a room surface area of 80 m². The average reflectance of the room surfaces is 0.5. Is it likely that the electric lighting will *not* be switched on for much of the day, based on the average working plane daylight factor?

Example 12.1

$$df = \frac{\theta TW}{A(1 - R^2)}$$

The information given above does not include the transmittance of the glass. A suitable estimate would be 0.8.
    So,

$$df = \frac{60 \times 0.8 \times 3}{80\,(1 - 0.5^2)}\,\%$$

$$= 2.4\%$$

A daylight factor of 2.4% suggests that it is in fact *very likely* that the electric lighting *will* be in use for much, if not all of the day. Therefore, the answer to the question is No.

A major consideration in an example such as this is to ensure that the room is not too deep for the average daylight factor calculation to be inappropriate. A simple approach would be to assume that if the no-sky line cuts off a significant proportion of the room the daylighting will be inadequate (Figure 12.2).

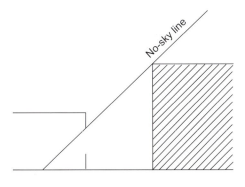

Figure 12.2
The 'no sky' line

    Where the windows are required for illuminance purposes only, that is, not for viewing out of, it is important to know which area of a window is most effective. An internationally agreed empirical formula for an overcast sky luminance distribution is the CIE formula:

$$L_\theta = \frac{1}{3} L_z \,(1 + 2\,\sin\theta)$$

where L_θ is the luminance of the sky at angle θ above the horizon and L_z the luminance of the sky at the zenith (Figure 12.3)

Figure 12.3
The CIE overcast sky luminance relationship

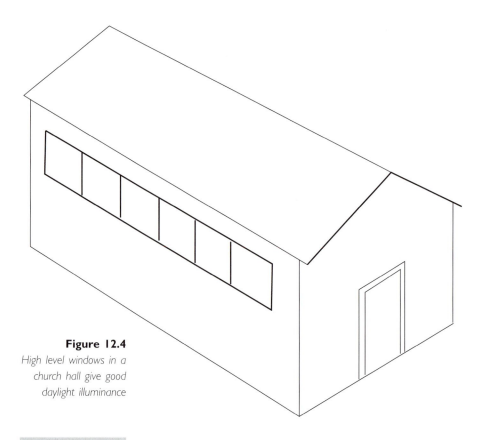

Figure 12.4
High level windows in a church hall give good daylight illuminance

If the window is unobstructed then this distribution of luminance shows that the greater the angle θ, the higher the sky luminance and so the greater the amount of light received from the sky per unit of window area.

Another factor is that at low values of θ the sky is often obstructed by buildings. Therefore, high level windows are far more effective than low level windows in admitting daylight into a room. Figure 12.4 shows a church hall where high level windows provide a good level of daylight, a reduced attraction to vandals and, for many activities, a reduced external distraction.

Daylight coefficients

Daylight coefficients enable a more detailed study to be made of the daylighting in a particular room. In Chapter 8 the inverse-square law cosine law formula was restated as:

$$E_p = L\omega\cos\theta$$

where L is the luminance of the light source and ω is the solid angle that the light source subtends at the point in question.

If a particular sky zone is considered, then the solid angle of that sky zone can be used as ω and if the luminance of the sky zone is known, then E_p can be calculated. One further change must be made, since the above expression is for angles measured from the downward vertical. If the angle is measured as an altitude or elevational angle, then the complementary angle is used, say γ, and the expression becomes:

$$E_p = L\omega\sin\gamma$$

In a practical room the daylight will have to pass through the window glazing and the transmittance T of that glazing will vary with the angle of incidence, both of altitude and azimuth so,

$$E_p = L\omega T_{\gamma\alpha}\sin\gamma$$

The daylight coefficient combines the last two factors so that

$$E_p = L\omega D_{\gamma\alpha}$$

Figure 12.5 shows a typical division of the sky into zones. The zones are based on 12 degrees of altitude; the azimuth angle depends upon the number of zones in the band.

The solid angle =
$2\pi(\sin\gamma_u - \sin\gamma_l)\backslash$number of zones in the band

This method can be further developed to take into account the interreflected component. It can also deal with direct sunlight. It has its greatest use where different distributions of sky

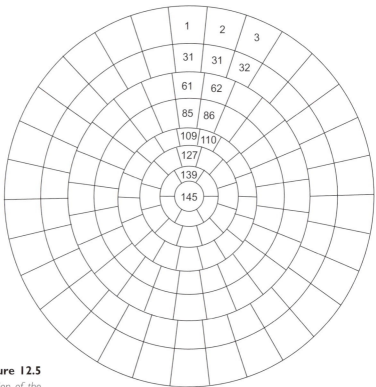

Figure 12.5
Typical division of the sky into zones

luminance are being considered, since D and ω do not change. This requires the use of a computer and numerical integration but, as shown above, it has a simple foundation.

QUESTION

Question 12.1 In these days when consultants often have global projects, what is the significant advantage of the daylight coefficient method of calculation compared with the average daylight factor approach based on integrating sphere type formulae?

Answer 12.1   The daylight coefficient method can deal with non-overcast skies which are conditions common in many countries. Sky luminance models have been developed for many areas and these enable more representative calculations to be carried out than those that would be produced using the formulae for UK overcast skies.

Energy management

In Chapter 8 it was suggested that during daylight hours, wherever possible, the major component of lighting should come from daylight. This was based on the preference of building occupants for daylit rooms. In this respect, occupant preference accords with the aim of good energy management, where daylight rather than artificial light is used wherever possible to save energy.

In recent times much attention has been paid to integrating electric and natural lighting by means of control systems, using photocells and dimmers. These can range from simple controls for small installations through to linking into a computer-controlled Building Energy Management System for very large building complexes. However, photoelectric control linking of natural and electric lighting must ensure that rapidly changing sky conditions do not result in unacceptable rapid changes in the electric lighting level. Another issue is the colour of electric light sources, which for linked systems should be about 4000 K.

The whole area of lighting controls has been developing very rapidly over the past decade. Initially, presence detection, using passive infrared sensors, was advocated for locations which were likely to have very intermittent use. However, with the development of high frequency control gear and easier dimming, together with digital ballasts and control, a whole array of systems and techniques have now become available.

These include:

1   Efficient local control of fluorescent luminaires, using a 1–10 V signal from a potentiometer combined with an on-off switch.
2   A combined presence detector and photocell system that switches the lights on when someone is present (except when the photocell detects sufficient daylight for this to be unnecessary).

3   A photoelectric system for adjusting the electric lighting relative to the available daylight to maintain a specified task lighting level. The photocell signal would operate with an appropriate timing delay to avoid rapid fluctuations due to sudden changes in daylight, e.g. movement of clouds.

4   A fully integrated photocell, dimming and presence/absence detection system with special pre-set programs according to the use of the space. An example might be where only one or two people are working late in a very large office. Scene-setting could be programmed for specific situations, such as a boardroom which is sometimes used for training sessions.

5   In considering these different levels of complexity, it should not be forgotten that a timeswitch is a simple, but effective, means of avoiding energy wastage. An obvious example is in the control of floodlighting, where a commonly used system is that of a photocell to switch on the floodlights as daylight fades and a timeswitch to switch them off when the lighting is no longer required.

An essential element in such control systems would be the provision of local override facilities to ensure user confidence.

Some experiments have been carried out involving the use of neural networks to monitor and 'learn' the lighting preferences of individual office workers in cellular offices. After an appropriate period this data was used to set the office lighting according to the daylight conditions and the previous user settings. Here, again, a manual override would be essential.

The commonly used sensors are:

PIR	Passive infrared – used in offices and smaller areas.
Microwave sensors	These find use in larger spaces, such as sports halls and warehouses.
Photocells	To monitor daylight levels.

Energy management of lighting is an area where the lighting engineering aspect of an installation, rather than the lighting design, comes to the fore, in terms of detailed lighting effects. Energy management is part of the overall consideration of the cost and efficiency of a lighting installation. In the past this was dealt with by considering the cost of the lighting equipment, the installation and the subsequent operating costs. Cost was the key element in the consideration. However, in recent years another factor has entered into the situation and that fact is the need to conserve energy. Where cost alone is no longer the sole issue, government agencies have to step in to ensure that financial aspects are not allowed to prejudice good energy management.

Although good energy management should promote long-term minimum cost, the key issue is who pays for the capital cost of the installation and who pays for the running costs. If the money comes from different purses then the installation that is cheapest may be chosen to the detriment of the energy use as part of the running costs.

At the present time Building Regulations, Part L give the provisions for the energy efficient lighting of buildings. These vary according to the type of building for which the installation is designed. This only applies where more than 100 m^2 is to be served by artificial lighting.

The provision for *offices, factories and warehouses* is that the overall luminaire efficacy should be at least 40 initial lumens per circuit watt. By relating the efficacy value to the circuit lumens rather than the lamp lumens the requirement takes into account the light output ratio of the luminaire. This includes any loss of lamp output produced by temperature changes caused by enclosure of the lamp in the luminaire, together with losses caused by the luminaire's optical system and the losses in any control gear for the lamp.

The luminaire efficacy is estimated in the following way:

$$\text{Luminaire efficiency} = 1 / \text{total circuit watts} \sum \frac{LOR.F_L}{CF}$$

LOR = light output ratio of the luminaire
F_L = initial lamp lumens
CF = Control factor (which takes into account switching or other mode of circuit operation)

Form of control	CF
Daylit space, luminaire is controlled locally by manual switching, photocell switching or dimming, with or without manual override	0.80
Intermittently occupied space with absence detection sensor to switch off the luminaire and manual switch on	0.80
Both of the above in combination	0.75
None of the above	1.00

Care must be taken that extinguishing lamps does not make circulation routes unsafe because safety is of primary importance. An allowance of an additional 500 W for display feature lighting can be made.

Example 13.1 In Appendix 3 there is a fully worked out calculation for lighting a waiting area. The area is 16 m^2. If it is part of an overall area that exceeds 100 m^2 then the requirements apply, but if the area is less than 100 m^2 then it is exempt.

Applying the formula:

$$\text{Luminaire efficiency} = 1/\text{total circuit watts } \Sigma \frac{LOR.F_L}{CF}$$

The installation comprises 16–18W fluorescent lamps operated on electronic control gear so that the total circuit watts are 16 × 20 W = 320 W. The lamps each emit 1400 lumens and the LOR of the prismatic luminaires is 0.47. Assume the CF value to be 1.00.

$$\text{Luminaire efficiency} = \frac{1}{320}\left[\frac{16 \times 1400 \times 0.47}{1.0}\right]$$

= 32.9 luminaire – lumens/circuit watts

This is below the limit of 40. If it is part of a larger area, exceeding 100 m^2, then other luminaire circuit arrangements must be designed to bring the average for the whole area up to the 40 limit. However, this room is only 4 m × 4 m and so if the waiting room has a window in one wall with a window glazing area which is 20% of the area of that window wall, then even though it has only manual switching a CF value of 0.8 can be applied (this is because no part of the space is more than 6 m from the window wall):

$$\frac{32.9}{0.8} = 41 \text{ which would meet the requirement.}$$

The main reason for the installation in this example being a borderline case is the choice of luminaire with an LOR of 0.47. A different luminaire with an LOR of 0.6 would have given a value of 42 with a CF of 1.0.

For other types of non-domestic buildings the requirement is in terms of a lamp circuit efficacy of 50 lamp lumens per watt. The difference here is that it does not include the light output ratio of the luminaire. This figure is for overall circuit efficacy; that is, not individual circuits.

Energy management is a broader concept than just energy conservation. It includes ensuring that the light energy is directed where it is intended and that it does not cause light pollution or sky glow.

In general, the more the light is optically controlled the lower the efficiency of the luminaire, so that a projector which has a light output profile, say, to light the front of a tower and little else may intrinsically be less efficient than another wide-angle projector with less control. However, there is little point in an 'efficient' projector that produces light pollution or sky glow to the visual detriment of the environment. In exterior lighting the beam angles of projectors should be chosen to match the area to be lit and in road lighting the emitted light should be below the horizontal, wherever possible.

Question 13.1 In recent times much more attention has been paid to the use of maintenance factors in calculations that seek to take into account more accurate estimates of the deterioration of room surfaces, lamp survival, the lumen depreciation of lamps and the effects of dirt on luminaires. What are the advantages of more precise estimates of light loss over a period of time?

QUESTION

Answer 13.1 Inaccurate maintenance factors mean that either the initial light levels are higher than they should be, with the consequent waste of energy, or that the lighting level falls below the recommended value before the maintenance procedures are carried out. Either of these outcomes is unsatisfactory and so improved accuracy in maintenance factors has the advantage of reducing these possible defects.

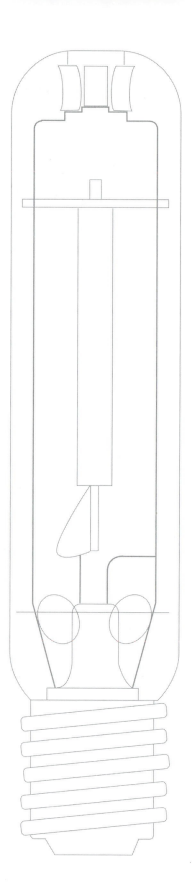

Chapter Fourteen

Electric lighting: light sources and luminaires (including emergency lighting)

Whether the electrical lighting installation is to be for the interior of a building or for exterior lighting, including road lighting, the first requirement is an adequate electrical power supply at the position where the luminaires (light fittings, street lanterns or floodlights) are to be used. This electrical power must then be converted into visible power of suitable quality; that is, light by an appropriate lamp. The lamp will require a means of support, connection to the supply and protection. In most situations the distribution of the light from the lamp alone will not meet the requirements of the installation designer. Therefore, some means of optical control of the light output of the lamp is usually needed.

The luminaire carries out all of these functions. It provides safe connection to the electrical supply. It may or may not contain any necessary current-limiting control gear or voltage-changing transformer. It will be intended to give a specified light distribution and have an appearance appropriate to the area being lit. Its construction and design will be intended to protect the lamp and ensure the safety of the users.

Two items have a major influence on the design of the luminaire. The first is the lamp chosen as the light source and the second is the desired light distribution.

The available light sources

Light sources are continually being developed and from time to time a major breakthrough is made which introduces either a new type of light source or a radically improved light source. An outline of the main types of light source presently available is given below.

Although Paris was lit by electric arc lamps as long ago as 1841, the real breakthrough in electric lighting came with the Edison/Swan invention of the incandescent filament lamp in 1878. The lamp has developed from the carbon filament vacuum lamp of those days through to the tungsten filament gas-filled lamp of today. Tungsten is used for the filaments because of its high melting point (3400°), low evaporation rate and because it emits more visible radiation at a given temperature than most other materials.

The general service lamp used today, particularly for home lighting, has a bulb of soda-lime silicate glass. The size of the lamp is dictated, in part, by the need to avoid excessive bulb and lamp cap temperatures. In early vacuum lamps it was essential to have a relatively large bulb to avoid excessive blackening from the evaporated tungsten from the filament, which would be deposited over the life of the lamp. An inert gas filling such as argon was introduced to maintain a pressure upon the filament and so reduce that evaporation. The filament was coiled to combat the cooling effect of the gas convection currents and in the lower wattage lamps that coil is itself coiled. Apart from the mutual heating of the coils a layer of hot gas is trapped in the coils and reduces the convection loss. In

Figure 14.1

The GLS incandescent lamp (note Dumet wire has a coefficient of expansion similar to the glass pinch through which it passes)

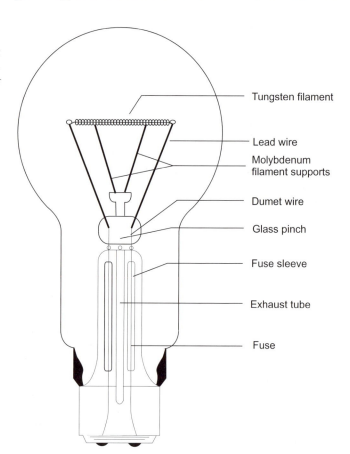

Tungsten filament

Lead wire

Molybdenum filament supports

Dumet wire

Glass pinch

Fuse sleeve

Exhaust tube

Fuse

addition, coiling the filament reduces the number of supports required for the filament and hence the conduction of heat down the supports from the filament. A small amount of nitrogen is introduced into the gas filling to improve the insulation properties and reduce the possibility of flash-over between the lead wires. Figure 14.1 shows the construction of a typical tungsten filament general lighting service lamp.

Safety is a high priority and, therefore, a fuse is fitted into one of the supply leads to break the circuit if an arc strikes between the ends of a broken filament at the end of life. The fuse itself is provided with a sleeve that fills the subsequent gap in the fuse to quench any secondary arc.

Table 14.1 Energy balance for 100W incandescent lamps with 1000 hour life (approximate)

Power distribution	Vacuum lamp straight filament	Argon filled coiled	Argon filled coiled coil
Visible radiation (%)	4	6	7
Invisible radiation (%)	88	71	78
Losses in holder and supports (%)	8	3	2
Losses in gas (%)	0	20	13

Table 14.1 shows the way in which the performance of a 100 watt general lighting service lamp is affected by introducing the gas and by coiling the filament. Introducing the gas enables the operating temperature of the filament to be raised for a given lamp life and this increases the light output. Coiling the filament and hence reducing the heat loss to the gas and supports enables a larger volume of filament material to be operated at the required temperature for a given wattage of lamp. An increased light output then results from this larger volume of incandescent filament material. The shorter and fatter the filament the higher the temperature at which it can be run for a given life (ratio of surface area to volume affecting the evaporation). The filaments become shorter and fatter as the lamp wattage increases or as the voltage decreases. Over the practical operating temperature range of 2600 K to 3400 K the proportion of visible radiation increases from 7 to 18%. The light output of a 100W GS lamp is about 12 lm/W and a 200W lamp 15 lm/W. The life of a general lighting service lamp is designed to be, on average, 1000 hours. This was based on calculations of the most economic operation of the lamps, in terms of cost of the lamp and the cost of electricity. The life of

these lamps depends upon them being run at the correct voltage. If the voltage is increased by 5% the life is reduced to half and if the voltage is reduced by 5% the life is doubled. The light output does not vary in such an extreme way, reducing the voltage by 5% reduces the light output by only 10%. This can enable double life lamps to be designed for a modest loss of output.

Tungsten halogen lamps

One of the dramatic steps forward in incandescent lamp technology was the introduction of the tungsten halogen lamp. The principle of the tungsten halogen cycle had been known for a long time, but it was only with the mass production of quartz tubing that the lamps became viable.

The tungsten halogen cycle stops the blackening of the lamp wall by the evaporating tungsten. This removes the need for a large bulb to allow for this effect. The use of quartz envelopes enabled the lamp wall to be brought much closer to the filament and its increased mechanical strength allowed higher gas pressures. This gave the lamp designers the possibility of increasing the lamp life for the same filament temperature, increasing the lamp output for the same life or a compromise improving both. The reduction in the volume of the lamp envelope, to about 1/100, meant that a more expensive gas could be used. Krypton, which is denser than argon, is more effective in reducing evaporation and also has a lower thermal conductivity than argon. Xenon may also be used. The most commonly used halogen is iodine and in the early days tungsten halogen lamps were often called tungsten-iodine lamps.

The tungsten halogen cycle

As already mentioned, the tungsten halogen cycle stops the blackening of the lamp envelope and, in so doing, it also prolongs lamp life for a given filament temperature by inhibiting the effects of filament evaporation.

The tungsten halogen lamp in its simplest form is a quartz tube enclosing a coiled linear filament. The tube is filled with an inert gas such as argon, krypton or xenon. Halogens are added to this gas – often iodine with methyl bromide (Figure 14.2).

When the lamp is switched on tungsten begins to evaporate from the filament. This evaporated tungsten, moving away from the filament, combines with the halogen to form tungsten halide. The tungsten halide has the property of non-depositing on the lamp wall. Those tungsten halogen molecules moving towards the filament dissociate due to the high filament

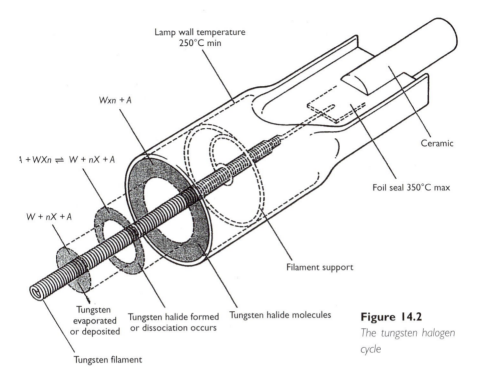

Lamp wall temperature
250°C min

Wxn + A

$A + WX_n \rightleftharpoons W + nX + A$

W + nX + A

Ceramic

Foil seal 350°C max

Filament support

Tungsten evaporated or deposited

Tungsten halide formed or dissociation occurs

Tungsten halide molecules

Tungsten filament

Figure 14.2

The tungsten halogen cycle

temperature and redeposit the tungsten onto the filament. If the tungsten always redeposited at the point where it was emitted the lamp filament would never fail due to evaporation. However, all filaments have hotter and cooler spots and the tungsten usually condenses onto the cooler parts of the filament. The hotter parts of the filament, therefore, gradually become thinner and hence hotter and this leads to eventual filament failure.

Characteristics

Lumen outputs from 15 lm/W to 25 lm/W are achieved from tungsten halogen lamps depending on the wattage and voltage at which the lamp is operated. Mains voltage lamps give about 15 lm/W at 75 W, whereas a similar low voltage lamp, at 12 V, will give up to 25 lm/W. This is because the low voltage lamp requires lower filament resistance and has a shorter, fatter filament and hence a lower ratio of surface area to volume compared to a mains voltage lamp. Since the evaporating surface is smaller, the lamp runs at a higher temperature for a given lamp life and this increases the light output per watt. Similar considerations apply to a mains voltage high wattage lamp, say 2000 W, where the surface area to volume is reduced to reduce the filament resistance and again 25 lm/W becomes possible.

Figure 14.3

Small tungsten halogen reflector lamp

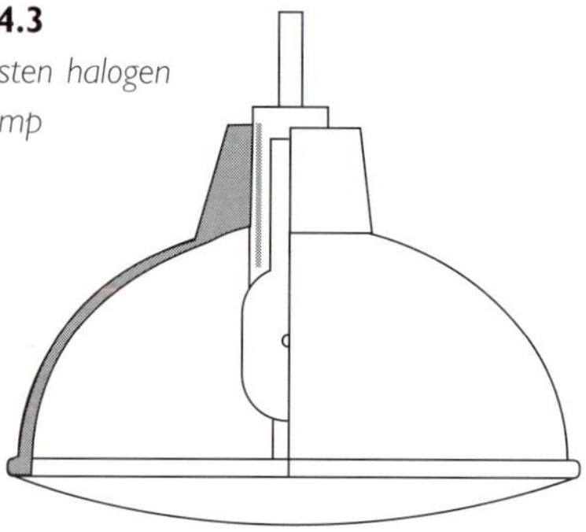

Many other types of tungsten halogen lamps have been developed for use in projectors and similar equipment, but perhaps the most common use is small capsule tungsten halogen lamps in a reflector form and particularly with dichroic reflectors, where the reflector absorbs the infrared radiation while reflecting the visible radiation. The cooler beams produced by these lamps are popular for display purposes (Figure 14.3).

Details of typical lamp types and performance are given in Appendix 1.

Discharge lamps: introduction

Gas discharge lamps provide a means of obtaining much higher efficacies than are available from incandescent lamps. Descriptions of the main types are given below. However, they require some form of current limitation to ensure stable operation. At mains frequency this is usually a relatively large induction choke. The lagging power factor produced by the choke then requires pf correction by means of a capacitor, which is usually placed across the supply.

With the advent of electronic control gear and high frequency operation the size of the control gear can be greatly reduced and, in some cases, built into the lamp cap. In addition, most discharge lamps require some starting aid. This may be in the form of a voltage pulse, an auxiliary electrode, earthed metalwork to increase the electric field strength or heated electrodes, or a combination of some of these.

Fluorescent lamps

Fluorescent lamps are extensively used in commercial, industrial and educational buildings. They have many advantages over other types of light source. One advantage is their low operating temperature, another is their high efficacy and a particular advantage is the wide range of colours and output spectrums that can be achieved. Their operation is based on using a low pressure mercury discharge to produce UV radiation from an efficient first energy level excitation (Figure 14.4).

The 254 nm radiation is absorbed by a fluorescent powder coating on the inside of the arc tube which, through further energy transition, acts as a wavelength converter and emits visible radiation. Figure 14.5 shows the construction of a typical fluorescent tubular lamp and Figure 14.6 illustrates, in a simple way, the light producing process.

Electrons emitted from the cathodes at the ends of the lamp are accelerated by an applied voltage down the tube until they collide with mercury atoms. If the collision is at an appropriate velocity an electron in the atom is raised to a higher orbit. After about 10^{-8} seconds the electron returns to its original orbit and, in doing so, gives up the energy received in the collision. The radiation emitted depends upon the energy level from which it returns. The fluorescent tube is designed to produce a large number of first energy level collisions producing 254 nm UV radiation. The exact spectrum of radiation produced depends upon the fluorescent powder used.

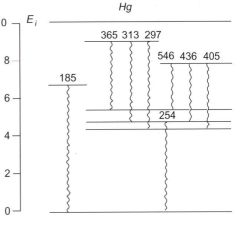

Figure 14.4
Simplified mercury vapour energy level diagram

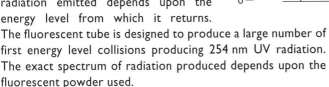

Figure 14.5
Construction of typical fluorescent tubular lamp

Figure 14.6
UV radiation from excited mercury vapour atom converted into visible radiation by the phosphor (fluorescent powder)

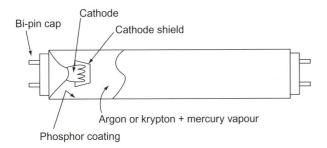

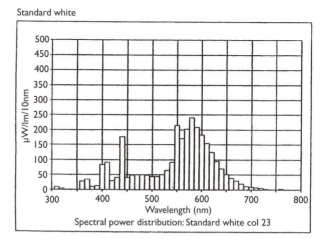

Colour ref: 23 CCT: 3400 K Ra856 (Group 3)
Chromaticity co-ordinates: $x = 0.439$ $y = 0.400$

For many years calcium halophosphate was the basic phosphor of fluorescent lamps and was made in a range of 'white' colours that all depended upon a large yellow component for their high efficacy. Where good colour rendering was important this could only be achieved by introducing other halophosphates which broadened the spectrum, but also reduced lamp efficacy (Figure 14.7)

Triphosphors   An important development occurred when it was discovered that lamps with emission peaks in the red, green and blue parts of the spectrum gave both good colour rendering as well as high efficacy. The lamps depended upon expensive rare-earth phosphors which could be used to produce these emissions. Sometimes triphosphors are used in conjunction with a calcium halophosphate background phosphor to improve overall distribution of spectral emission (Figure 14.8).

The fluorescent tube contains mercury at very low pressure, about 0.7 Pa and an inert gas, argon or argon–krypton mixture, at typically 200 to 300 Pa. The argon acts as a starting gas and as a buffer gas that modifies the path of the electrons through the discharge to produce the optimum number of excitation collisions. Collisions with the buffer gas also absorb energy, but this is reduced when a heavier gas is used, hence the use of krypton in some lamps.

Fluorescent lamps are temperature-sensitive and linear lamps usually give maximum light output when the ambient temperature is between 20 and 30 °C. If they are run much hotter or colder than this the performance suffers. Compact

LUMILUX® and LUMILUX® PLUS
Warm White

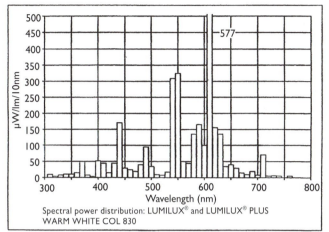

Figure 14.8
Spectral distribution from a triphosphor lamp

Spectral power distribution: LUMILUX® and LUMILUX® PLUS
WARM WHITE COL 830

Colour ref: 830 CCT: 3000 K Ra85 (Group 1B)
Chromaticity co-ordinates: $x = 0.439$ $y = 0.400$

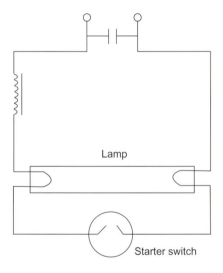

Lamp

Starter switch

Figure 14.9
Simple circuit for operation of a fluorescent lamp

lamps run at a higher temperature and hence need time to warm up.

A simple operating circuit for a fluorescent lamp is shown in Figure 14.9. The inductive choke in series with the lamp is required to avoid current run away once the lamp has been struck, since discharges have a negative resistance characteristic.

When the supply is switched on the voltage is insufficient to strike the lamp, but it is sufficient to operate the starter switch. The starter switch is a small glass bulb with open bimetal contacts in a suitable gas mixture including argon plus an ionizing agent. The bulb is enclosed in a small metal canister. When the supply is switched on an arc is created between the contacts and the heat from this causes the contacts to close, providing a path for current to flow via the lamp cathodes and it heats them. This then produces thermal emission of electrons into the tube. When the switch has closed the arc is extinguished removing the source of heat within the switch and the bimetal contacts snap open. This interrupts the current and causes the flux in the choke to collapse producing a voltage pulse sufficient to strike the lamp. Once the lamp has struck the lamp voltage is insufficient to continue to operate the starter switch. The capacitor shown is used to correct the power factor of the circuit to meet the requirements of the supply authorities.

In recent times there has been a strong move towards electronic control gear for discharge lamps and electronic starters and full electronic control gear are now available for fluorescent lamps.

Electronic control gear has very important advantages. It can be designed to give a much more controlled pre-heating cycle and precise application of the ignition voltage pulse which reduces the dependence of lamp life on the frequency of switching. Perhaps the greatest advantages stem from converting the mains 50 HZ frequency to about 30 KHz. The size of the choke depends upon the frequency of operation and, increasing the frequency by a factor of 600, makes a dramatic reduction in the magnetic circuit and the coil size of the choke. The basic method of design is to rectify the input to obtain DC and use an electronic inverter to obtain the high frequency AC current. The use of electronic control gear also gives opportunities for controlling the lamp circuits using low voltage digital signalling systems.

Both lamps and control gear are under continuous development and tubular fluorescent lamps are made in many diameters and lengths: 16 mm diameter lamps are typically made in lengths from 600 to 1200 mm, 26 mm diameter lamps from 600 to 1800 mm and 38 mm diameter lamps from 600 to 2400 mm.

In general, the greater the length a particular design of lamp is made the higher the efficacy. This is because the major losses occur in the cathodes at the end of the lamp. The lamp has only two cathodes regardless of length and so these losses become a smaller proportion of the lamp energy use as the length is increased. The 2.4 m limit was reached because of difficulties in lamp replacement.

With the advent of high frequency control gear the high voltages required to operate cold cathode lamps have become easier to produce. Fluorescent cold cathode tubes are now being used more often for interior lighting purposes. Cold cathode lamps have unheated electrodes in cylindrical form. Typical lamp data is length 2 m, 65 lm/W, CT 3500 K, life ~ 40 kh.

One consequence of the move to reduced diameter fluorescent lamps, which are becoming popular, is that for a given wattage the lamp wall must be brighter to produce the required light output. This increases the lamp luminance and hence the possibility of increased glare and particularly reflected glare from bright lamp images.

The introduction of smaller diameter tubes using the high efficiency triphosphors brought with it the possibility of folding the tubes to produce compact single ended lamps. The addition of electronic control gear built into the lamp cap has meant that these lamps have become popular for many situations as a replacement for incandescent lamps. A 12W compact fluorescent lamp gives the same output as a 60W tungsten GLS lamp and a 20W lamp has the same output as a 100W tungsten GLS lamp. There are also compact lamps without integral control gear of up to 36 W which produce nearly 3000 lumens. Apart from domestic use they are particularly useful in hotels, where the much longer life as well as lower energy consumption than incandescent lamps saves on running costs and maintenance (Figure 14.10a).

Compact fluorescent lamps

A further development of high frequency fluorescent lamps is the induction lamp. The main factor determining the life of a tubular fluorescent lamp is cathode failure. The induction lamp eliminates cathodes from the lamp design. Figure 14.10(b) shows the basic concept.

The induction coil is designed to provide a magnetic field with a frequency of 2–3 MHz. The magnetic field creates an electric field within the lamp which breaks down the gas and produces a circulating electric current. This current produces excitation of the mercury atoms and the UV radiation, which is converted into visible radiation by the fluorescent powder. Since there are no cathodes, the life of the lamp is mainly determined by the life of the RF coil and associated electronics. The life of such a lamp can be 60 000 hours, which represents many years' operation under normal conditions. These lamps are, therefore, very suitable for situations where maintenance is difficult; for example, some forms of atria. Efficacies of the order of 70 lm/W are achieved.

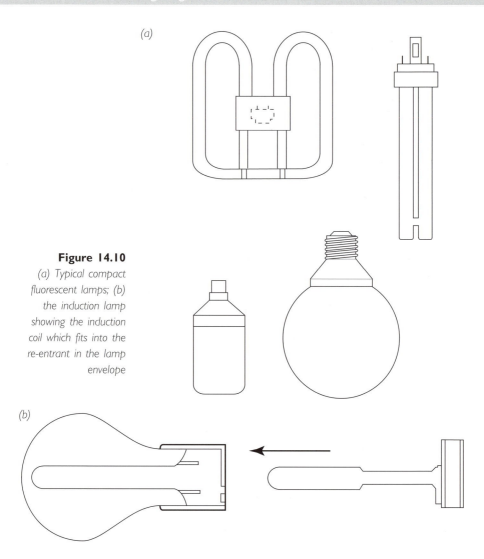

Figure 14.10

(a) Typical compact fluorescent lamps; (b) the induction lamp showing the induction coil which fits into the re-entrant in the lamp envelope

Low pressure sodium lamps At first sight the low pressure sodium lamp seems to be an ideal lamp, since it has the highest efficacy of all the available lamps. This is partly because its output is near the peak of the human eye response curve. Consequently, it can give up to 180 lm/W. However, the cause of its high efficacy is also the basis of its major drawback. Its colour rendering index is effectively zero. Low pressure sodium lamps are, therefore, used almost exclusively for road lighting, where their yellow light can be tolerated. Even in that field they are gradually being replaced by high pressure sodium lamps. Nevertheless, there are very large numbers of the low pressure lamps in use.

Another reason for the high efficacy of the low pressure sodium lamp is that the sodium atom has low values of first excitation and ionization potentials when compared with other gases or vapours. It is this combination of a low first excitation level and the 589.0 nm and 589.6 nm wavelengths radiation which has a $V\lambda$ value of about 0.76 that gives the lamp its high efficacy. Figure 14.11 gives a simplified energy level diagram for sodium.

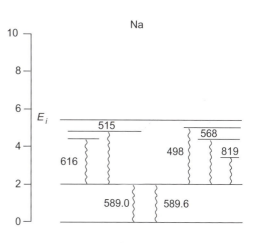

Figure 14.11
Simplified sodium energy level diagram

When the lamp is first switched on, the sodium is a solid deposit on the lamp wall and so an inert gas is introduced to initiate the discharge. The inert gas is neon, but a small amount of argon is also included to reduce the starting voltage. At first, once it strikes, the lamp has a low pressure, low brightness red neon discharge and the heat from this vaporizes the sodium. The sodium atoms then enter the discharge, giving the high efficacy yellow radiation. The lamp takes a few minutes to reach its full output.

The lamp is operated at a low sodium vapour pressure of about 1 Pa and the inert gas at about 1000 Pa. The arc tube temperature is about 260°C. At higher temperatures and pressures the radiation produced by the first level excitation is absorbed by other atoms, giving rise to other less efficient wavelengths of radiation. Even when operated under the appropriate conditions only the radiation for the outer atoms escapes to produce the light output.

The low pressure of the discharge means that energy density is low and the output per unit length of the arc tube is low. Therefore, the lamp requires a long arc tube to produce a useful output. The long arc tube is formed into a U shape and enclosed in a vacuum jacket. The mutual warming of the adjacent arms of the tube and the vacuum jacket coated with a heat-reflecting film maintain the lamp at its operating temperature. The arc tube is made from ply glass because ordinary silicate glass blackens rapidly under the attack of hot sodium vapour. The ply glass has a very thin layer of silica-free glass flashed onto the inside of the standard soda lime glass tube (Figure 14.12).

Like discharge lamps generally, the low pressure sodium lamp has to be operated in series with a ballast or choke to ensure that the arc current stabilizes at the design value, otherwise current run-away would destroy the lamp. In addition, the starting voltage required for the lamp is about

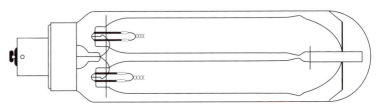

Figure 14.12

The low pressure sodium lamp

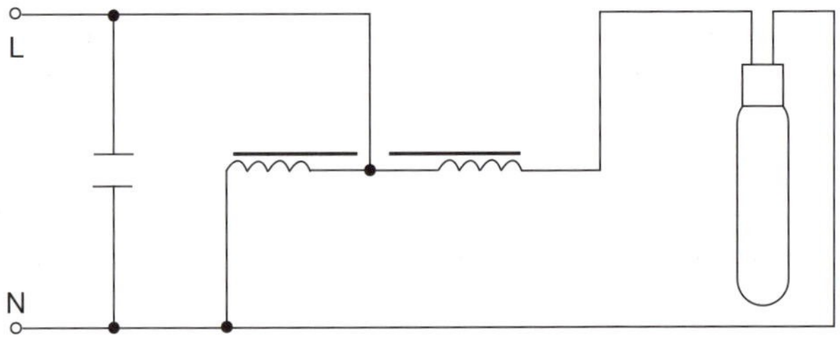

Figure 14.13

Leakage flux transformer circuit for a low pressure sodium lamp

500 V and so a means of transforming the mains voltage up to that level is required. The common solution is to combine both requirements in one device, the leakage flux transformer (Figure. 14.13).

In effect, this is a specially designed 'poor' transformer. By ensuring that a significant amount of the primary winding flux does not link with the secondary winding, it is possible to produce the required lamp starting voltage and ensure that, once the lamp has started, the flux that is *not* interlinked causes the transformer coils also to act as an inductive impedance. A parallel capacitor across the supply is usually employed to compensate for the lagging power factor produced by what is usually an autotransformer.

In common with some other discharge lamps, one problem with low pressure sodium lamps is that if the supply is momentarily interrupted, say the lights are switched off in error or the supply is otherwise interrupted, the lamp will not re-strike immediately, since the arc tube pressure is too high for the available starting voltage. This re-strike time can exceed the original run-up time with the low pressure sodium lamp. Therefore, any installation in a sensitive situation must be designed to take this into account.

The high pressure sodium lamp

Technical difficulties with the arc tube delayed the introduction of the high pressure sodium lamp for decades. The eventual solution to finding an arc tube that could withstand the high pressure sodium vapour was to use a translucent ceramic tube of alumina oxide (PCA).

If the vapour pressure of the sodium in the arc tube is raised to 10 000 Pa, then the low pressure lamp radiation is strongly absorbed and the efficacy is reduced. However, other lines in the sodium spectrum become more effective and the lines broaden due to interference between the atoms. The whole spectral output then widens to give a golden whitish light with fair colour rendering properties. The lumen output is in the region of 100 to 120 lm/W (Figure 14.14).

If the sodium vapour pressure is increased to 40 000 Pa, a very significant improvement in colour rendering is obtained at the expense of light output, which falls to the region of 70–90 lm/W. 'White' high pressure sodium lamps can be produced by raising the pressure further, but the output is reduced to about 50 lm/W. Mercury is included in the arc tube to act as a buffer gas, while xenon is introduced to act as a starting gas.

The circuit controlling a high pressure sodium lamp must produce a starting voltage pulse between 1.5 and 5 KV, depending upon the lamp rating and a choke ballast is also required. The high voltage starting pulse, for example, can be produced across the lamp once or twice per cycle, by the sudden discharge of a small capacitor into the primary winding of a pulse coil through a semiconductor switch controlled by a trigger circuit. Once the lamp has struck, the voltage on the trigger circuit falls below its operating level. A choke is required to limit the circuit current. Electronic control gear is becoming increasingly available and is in use for the lower wattage circuits at the time of writing. If the supply is interrupted and the lamp extinguished, it will not re-ignite until the lamp vapour pressure has fallen back to a suitable level and this takes minutes.

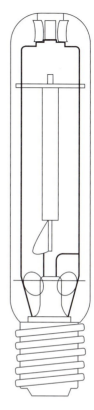

Figure 14.14
The high pressure sodium lamp

Mercury vapour and metal halide lamps

High pressure mercury vapour lamps find relatively little use today because of the development of the metal halide lamp from the ordinary mercury vapour lamp. The basic mercury vapour lamp had extensive use in street lighting and in its colour-corrected version found some use in factories. Before the advent of electronic starters the high pressure mercury vapour lamp had the advantage of not requiring a special starter. The arc tube is made from quartz (fused silica) and operates at temperatures in the region of 700°C. The filling is argon at 2000–5000 Pa and a mercury dose of 20–30 mg.

High pressure mercury vapour lamps give efficacies in the 40–60 lm/W region. The colour rendering is poor. Within the lamp envelope a resistor of about 30 KΩ is connected to one electrode lead and also to an auxiliary electrode inserted close to the other electrode at the other end of the arc tube. When the supply is switched on, the voltage is insufficient to strike the main arc, but it does strike a secondary arc between the auxiliary electrode and the adjacent main electrode. This small arc ionizes sufficient gas to reduce the required starting voltage to that available and the main arc strikes. The high resistance in the auxiliary electrode circuit ensures that excessive current does not flow in this part of the circuit when the lamp is switched on. The choke ensures that the supply voltage is shared with the lamp, so that stable operation is obtained.

The spectral distribution of the uncoated high pressure mercury vapour lamp consists of lines in the blue, green and yellow regions of the spectrum, which gives poor colour rendering. With a phosphor coating added to the outer bulb to convert the UV emission to red radiation the colour rendering is improved, but it is still not good.

The dissatisfaction with the spectral distribution of the high pressure mercury vapour lamp led to the idea of introducing other metals into the discharge to produce a more acceptable spectrum. The metals are added in the form of halides to avoid the additives attacking the arc tube wall and iodine is the preferred halogen.

Lamp designers choose a combination of metals to give the desired spectrum and provide stable operation over the

Figure 14.15

Spectral energy distribution for a metal halide lamp

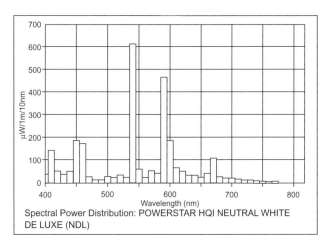

Spectral Power Distribution: POWERSTAR HQI NEUTRAL WHITE DE LUXE (NDL)

POWERSTAR® HQI NEUTRAL WHITE DE LUXE (NDL)
CCT: 4000 K/4200 K Ra: 85 (CIE Group 1B)
Chromaticity co-ordinates: $x = 0.380$ $y = 0.390$

life of the lamp. A typical spectral energy distribution is shown in Figure 14.15.

The introduction of the iodides into the discharge tube increases the required starting voltage and some form of electronic igniter is required to produce the high voltage starting pulse. Once the lamp has struck, the mercury spectrum is suppressed and as the temperature rises the metals dissociate from the halogen and enter the discharge. Typical constituents are metals such as sodium, thallium, dysprosium and indium.

Electronic control gear is becoming increasingly available for the lower wattage lamps. During the developmental period metal halide lamps gave problems with stability and the colour of the lamps. Eventually, for the lower voltages, a version called the CDM lamp, which incorporated a ceramic discharge tube similar to that used in high pressure sodium lamps, was introduced. This enabled higher pressures to be used, giving a warmer colour, 3000 K, and overcame the absorption problem which had caused colour change with life.

A wide range of metal halide lamps is now available (Figure 14.16), including reflector versions which have proved very popular because of the very good colour rendering achieved. The efficacies of these lamps are in the region of 70 to 100 lm/W.

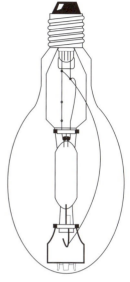

Figure 14.16
A metal halide lamp

LED (light emitting diodes) lamps

A light emitting diode is an electroluminescent p–n junction semiconductor. These have undergone considerable development over the past decades in terms of luminance, colour and output. Red, green and cyan LEDs have outputs of 10–40 lm/W and white lamps are also being developed. These lamps have a long life ~100 kh and a low operating voltage (2 V). They can produce significant light output when used in large arrays. An important feature is that by using microprocessor controls arrays of LEDs can provide special effects such as colour change by switching between colours (Figure 14.17).

Luminaires

Light distribution is of particular interest to the lighting designer, together with the 'efficiency' of the luminaire expressed as its light output ratio (LOR) or its performance in a room, expressed as a utilization factor (UF). The type of lamp determines the size of the luminaire and the degree of optical control that can be achieved.

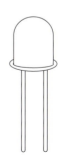

Figure 14.17
An LED

Figure 14.18

Control by obstruction –
a baffle used to
obstruct the direct view
of the lamp

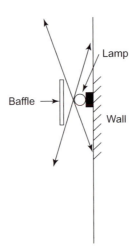

The simplest form of light control is obstruction; that is, placing something in the path of light travelling in an unwanted direction. A very simple example of this would be the use of an opaque lampshade on a table lamp. Light is allowed to pass through the top and bottom of the shade, but not through the sides. The use of a baffle is another obvious example (Figure 14.18).

A reflector is a development from this principle of obstruction. The obstructed light can be redirected by reflection to increase efficiency and so be added to the light of the bare lamp. The type of reflection will determine the effectiveness of this reflection. Sometimes scattered or diffuse reflection is required and sometimes specular reflection is more appropriate.

Figure 14.19

(a) Specular reflection:
(b) specular plus diffuse
reflection; (c) diffuse
reflection; (d)
preferential reflection

Types of reflection

Figure 14.19 shows different forms of reflection. Perfect specular reflection from a flat surface (*a*) produces a clear image of the source of light which appears to be behind the

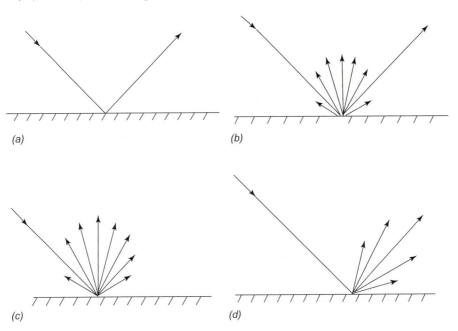

reflecting surface (mirror reflection). The angle of reflection is equal to the angle of incidence. Shiny surface reflection, where components of specular and diffuse reflection are present, is shown in (b). In (c) reflection from a perfectly matt surface produces uniform diffusion, so that the direction of the illuminance is not detectable from the luminance of the reflecting surface which is the same in all directions, i.e. the luminous intensity varies in proportion to the projected area of the surface. Therefore the

$$L = \frac{I_m \cos\theta}{A \cos\theta} = \frac{I_m}{A} = \text{constant}$$

(See Chapter 9, p. 84).

Figure 14.19(d) shows preferential reflection from a surface where the luminance is greatest at the specular reflection angle, but no image is present.

The degree of the obstruction provided by a reflector is determined by the cut-off angle of the luminaire, measured as shown in Figure 14.20. Alternatively, the complementary angle called the shielding angle is used.

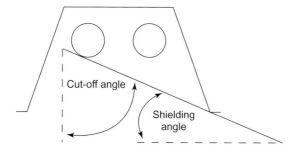

Figure 14.20

Cut-off angle and shielding angle of a luminaire

When specular reflection is employed then the reflector profile is of great importance in achieving the desired control. The cost of the reflector is a major factor in deciding the degree of sophistication to be employed in producing the reflector.

Three profiles are common:

1 spherical or cylindrical
2 parabolic
3 elliptical

(1) The simplest profile is that of part of a **sphere** or part of a cylinder, where a circular cross-section is used. Spherical profile reflectors can be produced from aluminium spinnings and cylindrical reflectors by rolling.

If the light source is placed, say, half way between the centre point and the pole of the mirror then rays close to the axis of the mirror would emerge almost parallel to the axis. This would be a cheap alternative to a parabolic mirror (Figure 14.21a).

Figure 14.21
(a) Spherical profile reflector; (b) parabolic profile reflector; (c) elliptical profile reflector

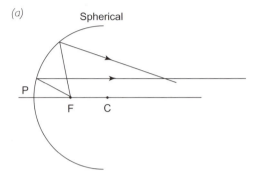

(a)   Spherical

(2) The **parabolic** profile can be used in a symmetrical reflector or a trough type reflector. A true parabolic profile is more difficult to produce accurately (Figure 14.21b).

Light travelling from the focal point to the reflector is reflected parallel to the axis, but since the light source must have size, rays from the points of source not at the focus will diverge, as shown.

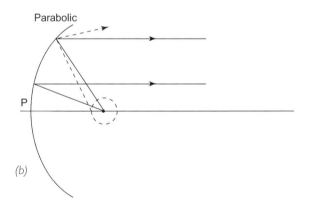

Parabolic

(b)

(3) The **elliptical** profile has the advantage that if the light source is placed at the first focal point all the light passes through the second focal point (Figure 14.21c). The elliptical reflector is sometimes used to concentrate light at a particular point or to pass light through a small aperture. Once again, the size of the light source causes a spreading of the area at the

(c)

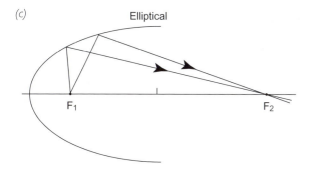

second focus receiving the light. A lens near the second focus can be used to further control the beam. A typical use of the specular reflector profiles is in the manufacture of floodlights.

The hyperbolic conic section finds less use in the reflector design than the other profiles because the second focus lies behind the reflector and gives a wide divergence from that focus, so that rays are more likely to strike the reflector housing and reduce efficiency. Where close control of downward light is required then specular louvres can make an important contribution. Figure 14.22(a) shows a parabolic specular louvre.

Here, in addition to restricting the light direction by the baffle effect of the louvres, locating the focal point of the parabolic surface at point A ensures that there is no inter-reflection between the louvre blades and so a specific shielding angle for the louvre can be achieved. The obstruction caused by the wideness at the top of the blade is overcome by stepping the profile, as shown in Figure 14.22(b).

It is possible to design specular reflector profiles for specific purposes, but most applications do not justify the

Figure 14.22
Parabolic specular louvre

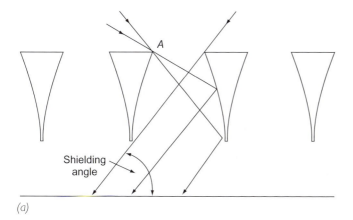

(a)

(b)

expense, except perhaps in specialist areas, such as car headlights.

Clearly, specular reflectors have greater use than simply obstructing light travelling in the wrong direction. If the light from the light source is masked so that only light that is reflected is included in the beam, a very good level of control can be achieved and this is seen in car headlights.

One approach to reflector design is to use flat sections or facets to form the reflector to give the desired distribution (Figure 14.23).

Figure 14.23

A faceted reflector

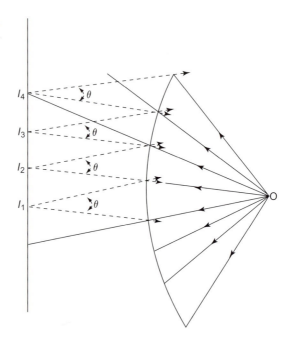

Each facet produces an image of the source in the desired direction and enables the intensity distribution to be built up. One difficulty is producing a reflector where each of the sections has the correct angle in respect to the axis of the reflector. With specular reflection the angle of reflection is equal to the angle of incidence and therefore an error of one degree in the angle of the reflector produces a two degree error in the deviation of the ray from the light source.

It was pointed out earlier that obstruction is the simplest form of light control and that from this reflectors are a natural progression. Another simple form of light control is diffusion, where a transparent medium, such as glass, is given a diffusing finish so that the light is scattered in all directions from the surface.

The advantages of diffusion are that it can scatter light into areas that would be unlit, it can reduce the perceived brightness of the source of light and, often, it gives a much more attractive appearance than a bare lamp. The simplest example is where the glass bulb of a filament lamp is given a diffuse finish, either by acid etching (the pearl bulb) or by a powder coating that could be coloured. In luminaires diffusing covers are most commonly used for decorative fittings. A classic design from early in the twentieth century that still finds considerable use is the opal sphere, where the globe enclosing the lamp gives a high degree of diffusion.

A simple approximation is to assume that the amount of light emitted by the diffuser in any direction will be proportional to the projected area of the diffuser at that direction (Figure 14.24).

Figure 14.24
Different shapes of luminaire diffuser

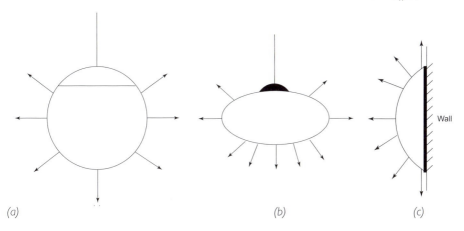

(a)   (b)   (c)

Wall

Refraction

Another technique for controlling the direction of travel of light rays is refraction, which is a more sophisticated version of control than diffusion or dispersion. This is bending the light by passing it from one transparent medium to another of different density. This phenomenon is caused by a change in the speed of the light as it passes from one medium to another. By shaping the denser material, such as glass, rays can be re-directed. The prism is a common example.

A lamp can be surrounded by a glass bowl or globe with banks of small prisms, which modify the angle at which the light is emitted by the luminaire. Prism banks are difficult to produce and require special tools. Therefore, they are only used where large numbers of luminaires can be produced to justify the cost of the tooling.

Prism design When the ray enters the denser medium it is bent towards the normal. When it leaves the denser medium at the other side of the prism it is bent away from the normal. Prism design is based on Snell's law:

$$\frac{\sin i}{\sin r} = \mu$$

where μ is the refractive index of the material.

As stated above the formula assumes that the light ray is passing through air and entering a denser medium, where it is refracted by angle *r* to the normal.

The angle *i* is the angle of incidence of the ray travelling in air to the normal at the surface of the denser medium, say, glass. When the ray is *leaving* the denser medium and returning to the less dense medium of air then the formula becomes:

$$\frac{\sin r'}{\sin i'} = \frac{I}{\mu}$$

(see Figure 14.25).

Figure 14.25

Deviation of light ray through a prism

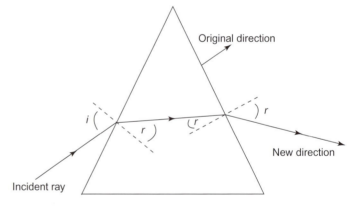

Detailed prism design is dealt with in the book *Lighting Engineering: Applied Calculations* (Simons and Bean, 2001).

In the past many street lighting lanterns (luminaires) employed prism banks to control the light from the long arc tube in low pressure sodium lamps, but with the requirement for the output to be kept below the horizontal to avoid sky glow, these have fallen out of favour, except for residential areas. Most new designs employ high pressure discharge lamps with small arc tubes which enable reflectors to give close control of the light distribution.

Prismatic diffusers find use in fluorescent luminaires in interiors, especially in schools and also for decorative lighting luminaires (Figure 14.26).

Figure 14.26

A prismatic diffuser

Prismatic front covers find use in floodlighting luminaires where a symmetrical reflector design can be used to provide a wide range of distributions when the appropriate refractor plate is used in conjunction with the basic reflector.

Total internal reflection

When light crosses a boundary between air and a denser medium it is not just refracted, some light is always reflected. This reflection increases rapidly after a certain angle of incidence is reached. For example, in the case of air to glass between 5° and 70° the reflectance increases from about 5% up to 15%, but thereafter increases rapidly towards 100% as 90° is approached.

Light travelling through glass to air has a similar reflectance for angles between 0° and 30°, but even more rapidly approaches 100% as the critical angle is approached. For soda glass this critical angle is 41°. The critical angle for the material can be calculated from the refractive index, since it is the angle at which the refracted ray is parallel to the boundary (Figure 14.27).

The angle can be calculated from Snell's law:

$$\frac{\sin r'}{\sin i'} = \frac{1}{\mu}$$

Let $r_a = 90°$
then $\sin r' = 1/\mu$ or the critical angle $= \sin^{-1} 1/\mu$
which for a material of refractive index 1.5 gives 41.8°.

Figure 14.27
Total internal reflection

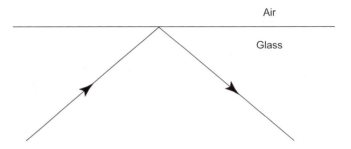

This property of internal reflection can be used to make reflecting prisms. A major use of total internal reflection is found in fibre optics.

Fibre optics

Essentially, a fibre optic lighting system is a luminaire designed to deliver the light at a considerable distance from the light source via fibre optic cables. Fibre optic cables use the phenomenon of total internal reflection to transmit light from the lamp to the point of use. Light is only transmitted efficiently when the light enters the cable at, or above, the critical angle for the material from which the cable is constructed. The maximum amount of light that could be transmitted by a cable will equal the luminance of the light source multiplied by the cross-sectional area of the cable. Fibre optics has certain valuable advantages, despite the fact that it is inefficient.

Advantages

1　Light can be transmitted over relatively long distances without electrical hazard at the point of use.
2　Heat or UV can be eliminated from museum cabinets so avoiding subjecting exhibits to possible degradation.
3　In flammable or explosive situations the light source and electrical supply can be remote from the hazardous area.
4　Light can be transmitted the full length of the cable or allowed to emerge from the side of the cable for decorative purposes.
5　A wide range of end attachments can be used to produce different lighting effects.
6　Motorized colour filters can be inserted at the input end of the cable to give colour changing.

A typical fibre optic system consists of:

1　a light box or projector housing an appropriate lamp
2　optical cable connected to the light box or projector
3　output ports or end attachments. (See Figure 14.28)

Figure 14.28

A fibre optic system

Luminaire construction

In general, luminaires are manufactured from metal, plastic or sometimes glass. An outline of typical materials and their uses is given below.

Sheet steel

Mild steel has good mechanical strength and ductility, but it is heavier than aluminium and because it is subject to corrosion it is normally painted. Typical uses are: battens, recessed box luminaires, control gear trays, coated reflectors and covers, etc.

Sheet aluminium

This is a popular material for reflectors and louvres. The reflector grades are 99.8% or superpurity at 99.9%. It is usual to anodize the reflectors which produces a thin protective oxide film on the surface. Problems can sometimes be experienced with iridescent effects and careful process control is required to reduce this. Coils or blanks are cut to size, pierced and then rolled into shape to produce a reflector for, say, a tubular fluorescent lamp, having fairly good control in the transverse direction but little axial control.

Axially symmetric reflectors are spun from circular blanks to an appropriate profile, for example, parabolic. Highly polished louvres used in some luminaires can be produced on automated machines, but louvre manufacture and assembly is often a labour-intensive business.

Aluminium castings

The LM6(12% silicon) alloy is most commonly used for castings because of its excellent corrosion resistance. Typical uses would be: street lighting luminaires, floodlighting bodies and interior spotlights. The corrosion resistant properties can be negated if other metals are brought into contact with it due to electrolytic action. Such metals are steel, stainless steel and copper. If these are to be used for components then they must be plated with zinc or cadmium (intermediate potential) or some other means of separation must be used, i.e. an appropriate plastic washer.

Plastics

The two main types of plastic in use are thermoplastics which can be re-melted and thermosets which cannot be re-melted once they have been cured. There are a wide range of materials available and their temperature range is a major factor in determining their suitability for use in a particular luminaire. Acrylics and polystyrene have been widely used for diffusers and refractors, but the new Building Regulations place some restriction on their use in interiors (see Approved Document B relating to the Building Regulations).

Polycarbonate is a material that is often used, partly because of its high impact strength and glass reinforced polyester (GRP) finds use in some luminaires, particularly road lighting lanterns.

Safety　An overriding requirement for any luminaire is that it must be mechanically, thermally and electrically safe in use. Tests to which luminaires should be subjected are laid out in BS4533101 and specific requirements to be met are found in BS4533102. These are connected to European Standards by also being numbered BSEN 60598.

An important consideration in selecting a luminaire is that it should have an appropriate electrical classification. Those allowed in the UK at present are:

- **Class 1:** A luminaire having basic insulation, where all metalwork is connected to an earth terminal and which is intended to be connected to the supply system earth.
- **Class 2:** A luminaire operated on a two-wire system, but with double insulation.

IP rating　Luminaires should also have an appropriate IP (Ingress Protection) rating. This rating is indicated by a two numeral code, for example IP20. Full details are given in BSEN 60598.

The first numeral relates to protection from the ingress of solid objects on a scale from '0', which is 'Non-protected' through to '6', which is 'Dust-tight'. The second numeral relates to protection from water. Again, '0' indicates 'Non-protected', whereas '5' indicates 'Protected against water jets'.

IP20, quoted above, would be for an indoor luminaire and '2' indicates that it is protected from 'Fingers or similar objects not exceeding 80 mm in length. Solid objects exceeding 12 mm in diameter'. In addition, '0' indicates that it has no special protection against the ingress of water. IP65 would be for, say, a bulkhead luminaire for external use that was both 'Dust-tight' and 'Protected against water jets'.

The IP rating will not be sufficient where the lighting equipment is required for use in an explosive atmosphere and the CIBSE Lighting Guide HHE (Lighting in Hostile and Hazardous Environments) should be consulted.

The equipment for such situations is classified according to the expected conditions as follows:

- **Zone 0**, in which an explosive gas is continuously present, or present for long periods of time.
- **Zone 1**, in which explosive gas-air mixture is likely to occur in normal operation.
- **Zone 2**, in which explosive gas-air mixture is not likely to occur in normal operation and if it does appear it is present only for a short period.

Emergency lighting

Emergency lighting is a safety system that ensures that when the electricity supply to the normal lighting system fails the emergency lighting provides sufficient light to enable the area to be evacuated safely and as quickly as possible.

Emergency lighting is not the same as standby lighting. Standby lighting is provided to ensure that work can be carried on when the mains electricity supply fails. Even where standby lighting is provided the requirements of an emergency lighting system must still be met.

Perhaps the most common hazardous situation is where a fire breaks out in a work place. The Fire Precautions (Workplace) Regulations 1997 state: 'Emergency routes and exits must be indicated by signs and emergency routes and exits requiring illumination shall be provided with emergency lighting of adequate intensity in case of failure of the normal lighting.'

The following points of emphasis need special attention when the design of a suitable layout of emergency lighting equipment is undertaken:

1 Emergency exit doors
2 Exit and safety signs (Figure 14.29)

3   Fire alarm call points
4   Staircases
5   Each change of floor level
6   Changes of direction
7   Fire fighting equipment
8   Intersections of corridors
9   Final exit doors inside and outside

General guidance is given in BS 5266 1999.

Figure 14.29

Emergency exit sign

It is important to ensure that no area or compartment is served by only one luminaire. There must always be at least two luminaires in case one fails and the area is then left in darkness.

Once the points of emphasis have been dealt with, it is necessary to ensure that all escape routes have the minimum level of illuminance required for them to be negotiated safely.

Figure 14.30

(a) Typical emergency lighting luminaire; (b) illuminance and spacing data for the luminaire shown in (a)

(a)

Photometric Data
Cat. No. EWB 3NM
Lamp: 8W T5 Non-maintained
Ceiling mounted
ULOR: 0.17 DLOR: 0.72 LOR: 0.89

2m Escape route

Min illum (lux)	Mounting height (m)	Max spacing (m) centre to end	Max spacing (m) between centres
1.0 trans	2.5	2.85	8.40
	3.0	2.65	8.30
	3.5	1.95	8.20
1.0 axial	2.5	1.55	4.70
	3.0	1.25	4.70
	3.5	0.70	4.40

Open area

Min illum (lux)	Mounting height (m)	Max spacing (m) centre to end Trans	Axial	Max spacing (m) between centres Trans	Axial
0.5	2.5	2.50	2.40	9.30	6.40
	3.0	2.50	2.40	9.70	6.70
	3.5	2.35	2.25	9.90	6.80

(b)

It is recommended that along the centre line of the route a minimum level of 1 lux is provided with 0.5 lux over a 1 m wide central band of the escape route. An escape route is taken as being 2 m wide. The illuminance can be reduced to 0.2 lux along the centre line and 0.1 lux over the 1 m central band for unobstructed routes of low risk.

In addition to designated routes, other areas, such as lifts, need emergency lighting. Although lifts are not part of the escape route under normal circumstances, they may well have occupants trapped by the power failure. Other areas requiring emergency lighting are large toilet areas, toilets for the disabled and, where necessary, other small toilets. In addition escalators, control and plant rooms and pedestrian routes in covered car parks require emergency lighting. The consideration must always be the safety of the users of the building.

A typical luminaire specifically designed for interior emergency lighting use might have the following features: white polycarbonate body with a clear polycarbonate prismatic diffuser, 8W T5 fluorescent lamp, IP40, maintained/non-maintained emergency lighting of 3 hours' duration (Figure 14.30a and b).

Non-maintained
In this mode of operation the luminaire only comes on when the electrical supply fails. When this happens the lamp lights under power from its built-in battery and when the supply is restored the lamp switches off and the battery is re-charged.

Maintained
In this mode of operation the luminaire can be switched on and used when the supply has not failed. In the event of mains failure the lamp either remains on or is switched on and powered by its internal battery, as with the non-maintained.

Modified standard luminaires

It is also possible to use some of the luminaires in the general lighting system as emergency lighting units. These luminaires are usually specially adapted by the manufacturer with an emergency lighting module incorporated into the circuit. Under normal operation the lamps operate from the main supply at full lumen output. When the supply fails one lamp usually continues to operate, but at a lower lumen output from the emergency lighting module.

A major issue is the proper checking of emergency lighting systems to ensure that each unit is working properly. This can be a significant task and so where large numbers of luminaires are involved a computerized automatic monitoring system becomes an attractive solution.

Question 14.1 In selecting a lighting system would you begin by considering the luminaire or the lamp?

Question 14.2 The Glare Index system (now Glare Rating) has had a great influence on luminaire design. What has this been?

Question 14.3 Why was the introduction of VDU or visual display screens a cause of major change in luminaire design? What was the negative consequence of this? Why has this situation begun to change?

Question 14.4 Why does a high bay luminaire used where there is a high ceiling often employ a parabolic reflector?

Question 14.5 Many low bay luminaires use high pressure discharge lamps mounted horizontally in the reflector. What would be the advantage of this?

QUESTIONS

ANSWER

Answer 14.1 The colour of the light and the efficacy and life of the lamp are usually the most important characteristics. The chosen lamp then has a major influence on the design of the luminaires available. Sometimes relatively inefficient lamps are chosen because of their decorative effect or size. Certain situations require particular types of luminaire or lighting system; for example, hazardous areas.

Answer 14.2 Manufacturers reduced the brightness of their luminaires in the direction of the observer by using prismatic controllers or louvres to ensure that the luminaires complied with commonly specified Glare Index values; for example, 19 for offices.

Answer 14.3 A major problem with VDU screens was the disturbing effect of reflections in the screen. In order to combat this, very sharp cut-off louvres were introduced for most commercial luminaires. The consequence was that wall and ceiling illuminances were greatly reduced, giving unsatisfactory visual conditions, except where the furnishings were very light in colour. There was also an increased use of high powered indirect lighting systems with the problem of ensuring that the ceiling luminance was not excessive.

The situation has changed because of the introduction of improved VDU screens and the use of positive screen software. This has greatly reduced the effects of screen reflections. In addition, a move to luminaires which provide more upward light, while carefully controlling the downward light, has created better visual conditions.

Answer14.4 A parabolic reflector concentrates the light downwards, so that the light reaches the working plane after travelling the shortest distance and less light is lost to the walls. In situations with an unclear atmosphere this also causes minimum loss of light by absorption.

Answer 14.5 Low bay luminaires need to spread the light across the horizontal plane to minimize the number of lighting points. A horizontally mounted discharge lamp directs a large proportion of its output in a wide downward direction without reflection.

Interior lighting

Lighting for offices

In most developed countries the balance between industrial work and administrative and sales-based work has dramatically changed over the past 50 years. The number of people in industry has fallen dramatically, while those in office-type environments has shown an equally dramatic rise.

Office lighting is now of great importance to the economy because it affects both the performance and the well-being of a large section of the working population. Good office lighting is not a matter of regulation, although regulation is required. It is a matter of good design. Good design takes into account the visual and psychological needs of the office occupants, as well as ensuring that energy is not wasted.

At different times during working hours the office worker has different needs. When concentrating on a particular task the lighting must make this as easy as possible. However, all workers need momentary or longer breaks between tasks and, unless unavoidable, it should not be necessary to leave the working area for the purposes of visual comfort only. The lighting of the office working area should be designed for the task activities, but also to meet the other interpersonal and psychological needs as far as possible.

These needs can be met when the lighting takes into account three factors of personal need. These are visual comfort, visual satisfaction and visual performance.

Whenever these three aspects become unbalanced dissatisfaction can arise, giving a feeling that the working environment could be improved. Such imbalance increases stress and the likelihood of workers taking time off or wishing to move to other employment. Although rapid job changing is becoming commonplace and even routine, it is still true that the best productivity usually comes from a keen, experienced workforce who feel well-disposed towards their employer. One factor in this equation is the quality of the lit environment.

Visual comfort   In Chapter 5 some attention was given to visual comfort and it was pointed out that this is mainly dealt with by removing the causes of visual discomfort. The UGR or Unified Glare Rating was introduced and the limiting value of UGR for general offices was mentioned. Ensuring that an installation meets this requirement deals with direct discomfort glare, but an additional phenomenon called 'overhead glare' is also worth taking into account. This type of 'glare' can occur when, according to the UGR, no significant glare is present. Overhead 'glare' has a disturbing or distracting effect, rather than a discomfort effect. It is due to the awareness of a very strong bright light directly above the head. The flow of this light gives a strong awareness of its presence and many people find it disturbing. This is probably due to the contrast between the bright lamp and its surroundings which becomes noticeable as the head is moved. This effect is most likely to occur when high efficiency specular louvre downlighters are used with high luminance lamps.

Visual satisfaction   The shape of large open plan offices is an important factor in visual satisfaction. If the office is very large and square then many of the occupants are a long way from any windows and an exterior view. In such a situation careful attention should be paid to providing adequate visual interest. Where large areas are long and relatively narrow the offices are usually much more satisfactory because many more of the staff are close to a window.

Visual satisfaction is related to the visual scene in general and particularly to the surroundings of the work area and the appearance of other workers. When looking round a room from a seated or standing position the eyes scan a vertical picture of the surroundings, which includes the faces of nearby colleagues. In a small space it is dominated by the walls; in a large open plan space the perspective of the ceiling plays an important role.

In an attempt to break with rigid lines of light, luminaires are sometimes arranged in square, star or other configurations. This should be done sparingly and only when the impression of orientation of the space has been considered in relation to the layout of desks or furniture. In addition, the ceiling pattern created by the unusual layout should be considered, not just the plan view, e.g. circle, square, star, etc. but also especially the perspective view of the ceiling.

Orientation is important for the avoidance of glare from daylight entering windows and it is most appropriate for the desks in the region of the windows to be placed at right angles to the window. For right-handed people the preferred direction of illumination is from left to right, since this avoids casting a shadow of the hand on the page when doing written work.

For those operating computers or doing word processing, it is equally important not to have distracting images of light sources or windows present on the display screen. Recent developments in screen surfaces and the use of positive background screens have greatly reduced this problem. However, care should also be taken with the orientation of the screen relative to windows to avoid both discomfort and disability glare from windows seen *beyond* the screen (Figure 15.1a), or distracting images in the screen from distant light sources behind the operator's back (Figure 15.1b). In smaller offices and particularly single offices, the problem is less difficult to solve because of the choice of desk orientation and the absence of distant light sources.

(a)

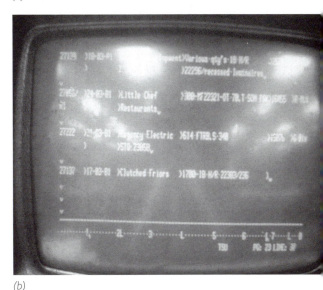

(b)

Research has shown that about one in ten of people working in an office can suffer from headaches that appear to be due to fluorescent lamps when these are operated on the 50 Hz supply. Therefore, high frequency control gear, where lamps operate at frequencies of the order of 30 kHz are to be preferred.

The ratio of mean vertical (E_c) to horizontal (E_h) illuminance has been found to be one of the indicators strongly associated with visual satisfaction and that is why so many lighting schemes designed to avoid reflections in display screen by directing the light strongly downward have proved less than satisfactory.

Figure 15.1

(a) Disability glare from windows beyond the display screen; (b) distracting images in the display screen from distant light sources

A high value of E_c/E_h ratio has been associated with satisfaction with the appearance of people's features. Values from 0.3 to 0.66 have been associated with increasing satisfaction. In addition, because in a generally lit area with a high proportion of downward light E_c is often found to be approximately equal to the wall illuminance, satisfaction with the appearance of the room has also improved as this ratio increases. Visual satisfaction will also be related to the interest of the visual scene generally. Most workers like the opportunity to look through a window from time to time during the daylight hours, since it gives a change of visual scene. It is possible to provide some visual interest and orientation within large open plan offices by providing different types of luminaires to light areas used for access or circulation. The use of wall washers, pictures, plants, etc. all have a part to play in avoiding the feeling of a bland and monotonous space.

Visual performance

Adequate visual performance can be ensured by providing the appropriate level of lighting on the task and its surrounds. Table 15.1 gives typical lighting requirements for various tasks.

Table 15.1 Typical lighting requirements

	E_{av}	URG	Ra
Reception desk	300	22	80
Filing, copying	300	19	80
Writing, typing, reading, data processing, CAD, meeting and conference	500	19	80
Technical drawing	750	16	80
Archives	200	25	80

There are a number of possible approaches to meeting this need.

1 Provide a general lighting level known to meet the needs of the majority of the office workers over the whole area.
2 Provide controls to enable individual workers to set their own lighting level. With the advent of electronic control gear the second option has become readily available. It is found that when the first option is adopted, some people feel that there is too much light. This is indicated by the

result of adopting the second option. It is found that a wide range of lighting levels are chosen, if the worker has control over their own lighting level.

There are some obvious reasons for workers choosing different lighting levels, such as age and eyesight. It would not be surprising to find that in a large open plan office with people in the 20–30 year age group working entirely from VDU screens most would be happy with a lighting level of 100 lux or less. Some call centres employ large numbers of such young people because of their quick reactions and their facility with computer systems operation. Office workers where the work is more varied and the average age is higher can be expected to require significantly higher illuminances.

A research study showed that where people were able to set their own illuminance levels values ranging from less than 100 lux up to 700 lux were chosen. However, 80% of the workers set values within the range from 0 up to 500 lux. This illustrates the point that ensuring that everyone in an office has *sufficient* light for the visual task requires a value in the region of 500 lux, which is the design value generally suggested for office lighting. Given the above facts, it is understandable that, in situations where the cost of the labour greatly outstrips the cost of the lighting, very sophisticated lighting systems are often employed to allow workers to control the lighting level under which they work. One of the problems related to giving this freedom of choice in open plan offices is that such free choice could result in creating a very unsatisfactory overall visual scene.

Below we consider three possible arrangements for lighting office working areas:

1 General lighting over the whole area; that is, similar lighting throughout the space (Figure 15.2).
2 Localized lighting, where the work areas are lit to a higher level than the access or circulation areas (Figure 15.3).
3 Local lighting, where there is an access or circulation area lighting level provided over the whole space with additional local lighting provided at each work station. This can be of a fixed value or locally controlled by the individual worker (Figure 15.4).

Method 1 gives the greatest flexibility in the location of work stations, but can be wasteful of energy.

Method 2 improves energy use, but can cause difficulties where working areas need to be moved.

Figure 15.2

General lighting

Figure 15.3
Localized lighting

Figure 15.4
Local lighting

Method 3 can be both energy efficient and convenient for movement, provided the underfloor electrical supply system to the work stations is well designed. However, it does require careful attention to the type of local lighting used.

Varied use of office space

Another important factor to be taken into account is the activity that takes place within the office space. In the modern office environment the activities are far more varied than in the past. For example:

- Small rooms where one or two people work
- Rooms used for team meetings and training sessions
- Large open plan offices with many people sharing the same space and sometimes even hot-desking to share the same desk on a shift or casual basis
- Spaces set aside for breaks where a more relaxed atmosphere is required
- Rooms dedicated to storage or filing of records
- Board rooms

The amount of time spent in the particular area will determine the type of lighting and control provided, together with the balance required between the three elements of good lighting design, namely visual comfort, visual satisfaction and visual performance.

A general office is to be lit. The office is 16 m long and 12 m wide, with a floor to ceiling height of 4 m. The room reflectances are $R_c = 0.8$, $R_w = 0.6$ and $R_F = 0.2$. It is proposed to use twin lamp fluorescent luminaires with satin finish louvres (Figure 15.5).

Example 15.1

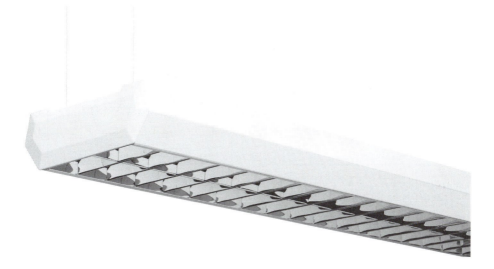

The relevant data sheet is given in Figure 15.6. Each of the two 58W, 4000 K lamps gives 5200 lumens.

The lumen method formula is used to determine the number of lamps and, hence, the number of luminaires required to provide an average illuminance of 500 lux.

Figure 15.5
A twin lamp fluorescent luminaire with a satin finish louvre

$$E_{av} = \frac{n \times F_L \times UF \times MF}{A_{wp}}$$

$$n = \frac{E_{av} \times A_{wp}}{F_L \times UF \times MF}$$

$$= \frac{500 \times 16 \times 12}{5200 \times UF \times MF}$$

$$= \frac{18.46}{UF \times MF}$$

We now need to calculate the UF value. This will depend on the mounting height of the luminaires above the working plane.

MODULIGHT 2000

Description: Satinbrite louvre with uplight
Luminaire maintenance category B
Conversion terms

Catalogue number	Lamp	DF,UF,PC	Glare	LD	Data code
FSNDIZ 258 SB	2 x 1500mm 58W 26Ø	1.00	0.0	1.00	R0019373 *

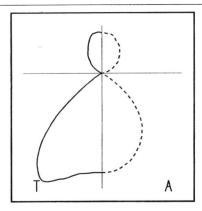

Light output ratio	Up 0.20	Down 0.52 Total 0.72
Max. spacing to height ratio	SHR MAX 1.90	

Utilization factors UF[F] SHR NOM 1.90

Reflectances			Room index				
C	W	F	1	2	3	4	5
0.8	0.6	0.2	0.60	0.69	0.73	0.75	0.76
	0.5		0.57	0.67	0.71	0.74	0.75
	0.3		0.53	0.64	0.69	0.71	0.73
0.7	0.6	0.2	0.58	0.66	0.69	0.71	0.72
	0.5		0.55	0.65	0.68	0.70	0.71
	0.3		0.52	0.62	0.66	0.68	0.70
0.5	0.6	0.2	0.54	0.61	0.63	0.65	0.65
	0.5		0.52	0.59	0.62	0.64	0.65
	0.3		0.49	0.57	0.61	0.63	0.64
0.0	0.0	0.0	0.41	0.46	0.48	0.49	0.50

DF[F]	0.41	0.46	0.48	0.49	0.50
DF[W]	0.11	0.06	0.04	0.03	0.02
DF[C]	0.20	0.20	0.20	0.20	0.20

UF ratios for reflectances C 0.7;W 0.5;F 0.2

UF[W]/UF[F]	0.34	0.33	0.33	0.33	0.33
UF[C]/UF[F]	0.54	0.50	0.48	0.48	0.47

Uncorrected UGR table (1:1 spacing)

Reflectances					
C	0.8	0.8	0.7	0.7	0.5
W	0.6	0.5	0.6	0.5	0.5
F	0.2	0.2	0.2	0.2	0.2

Room size		Viewed crosswise					ECT
X	Y						
2H	2H	2.3	2.8	2.6	3.1	3.9	+0.5
	3H	2.2	2.7	2.6	3.0	3.8	+0.4
	4H	2.2	2.6	2.5	2.9	3.7	+0.4
	6H	2.1	2.5	2.5	2.9	3.7	+0.4
	8H	2.1	2.4	2.4	2.8	3.6	+0.4
	12H	2.0	2.4	2.4	2.7	3.5	+0.4
4H	2H	2.1	2.6	2.5	2.9	3.7	+0.5
	3H	2.1	2.4	2.5	2.8	3.6	+0.4
	4H	2.1	2.4	2.5	2.8	3.6	+0.4
	6H	2.0	2.3	2.4	2.7	3.5	+0.4
	8H	2.0	2.2	2.4	2.6	3.5	+0.4
	12H	2.0	2.2	2.4	2.6	3.4	+0.4
8H	4H	2.0	2.2	2.4	2.6	3.5	+0.4
	6H	1.9	2.1	2.3	2.5	3.3	+0.4
	8H	1.9	2.2	2.3	2.5	3.3	+0.4
	12H	1.8	2.1	2.2	2.4	3.3	+0.4
12H	4H	2.0	2.2	2.4	2.6	3.4	+0.4
	6H	1.9	2.2	2.3	2.5	3.3	+0.4
	8H	1.8	2.1	2.2	2.4	3.3	+0.4

Figure 15.6

*Data sheet for the
luminaire in Figure 15.5*

The manufacturer recommends a length of suspension between 0.3 and 1 m. 1 m is chosen to give a fairly uniform ceiling luminance. The mounting height above the floor is 3 m and so above a 0.8 m working plane it is $3 - 0.8 = 2.2$ m.

The room index

$$RI = \frac{w \times l}{H(l + w)}$$

$$= \frac{12 \times 16}{2.2\,(12 + 16)}$$

$$= 3.1$$

If the luminaires had been mounted directly on the ceiling we could have now entered the UF table. However, suspending the luminaires by 1 m has created a ceiling cavity above the luminaires. Light will be interreflected within this cavity and some will be absorbed, effectively reducing the ceiling cavity reflectance. An allowance can be made for this by using the equivalent cavity reflectance formula (see Appendix 3).

$$R_E = \frac{R \times S_2}{R \times S_2 + S_1\,(1 - R)}$$

where R is the average reflectance of the cavity, S_1 the total internal surface area of the cavity and S_2 is the area of the cavity opening.

$$R = \frac{\text{Area of ceiling} \times \text{ceiling reflectance} + \text{wall area within the cavity} \times \text{wall reflectance}}{\text{Total cavity area}}$$

$$= \frac{16 \times 12 \times 0.8 + (2 \times 16 \times 1 + 2 \times 12 \times 1)\,0.6}{16 \times 12 + 2\,(16 + 12)}$$

$$= 0.75$$

So,

$$R_E = \frac{0.75 \times 16 \times 12}{0.75 \times 16 \times 12 + 248\,(1 - 0.75)}$$

$$= 0.7 = R_c$$

We can enter the table at $RI = 3$ and $R_c = 0.7$

$$UF = 0.69$$

$$n = \frac{18.46}{0.69 \times MF}$$

$$MF = LLMF \times LSF \times LMF \times RSMF \text{ (see Chapter 10)}$$

These factors relating to lamps, luminaires and room surface definitions can be obtained from Tables A2.1, A2.2 and A2.3 in Appendix 2. LSF is taken as 1.0, since lamps will be replaced on failure.

LLMF = 0.86 (8000 h), LMF = 0.86 (normal 1 year cleaning), RSMF = 0.88 (normal, 1 year cleaning). Thus,

$$MF = 0.86 \times 1.0 \times 0.86 \times 0.88$$
$$= 0.65$$

Finally,

$$n = \frac{18.46}{0.69 \times 0.65}$$

$$= 41$$

Twin lamp luminaires

$$\frac{41}{2} = 20.5$$

Twenty twin lamp luminaires in 4 rows of 5

$$500 \times \frac{40}{41} = 488 \text{ lux}$$

The same room reflectances, size and maintenance factor data were fed into a computer program and the summary sheet, layout and point by point results are shown below (Figures 15.7 and 15.8). The value calculated by hand lies between the computer lumen method and point by point method results. Examination of the point by point values shows slight departure from the symmetry that would be expected from a symmetrical luminaire layout. This is explained by the fact that an I table for an actual luminaire was used for the calculations.

In Appendix 3 a full calculation of the ceiling and wall to horizontal illuminance ratios is given. This shows that these ratios can be calculated easily, provided that the UF(C)/UF and UF(W)/UF ratios are provided by the manufacturer. These are available on the data sheet (Figure 15.6) used for the Example,

$$\frac{E_C}{E_{av}} = \frac{UF(C)}{UF} = 0.48$$

which agrees with the computer calculation

$$\frac{E(W)}{E_{av}} = \frac{A_{WP}}{Aw} \times \frac{UF(W)}{UF}$$

$$= \frac{12 \times 16}{2 \times 2.2 \,(12 + 16)} \times 0.33$$

$$= 0.51.$$

This value is much higher than that shown on the computer printout. The reason for this is that the computer does not use the cavity method for this calculation. Therefore, the wall area is not taken as that between the luminaires and the working plane, but that between the ceiling and the working plane, i.e. 3.2 m instead of 2.2 m

$$\frac{E(W)}{E_{av}} = \frac{12 \times 16}{2 \times 3.2 \,(12 + 16)} \times 0.33$$

$$= 0.35$$

which is much closer to the computer value of 0.38.

Results summary

Figure 15.7
Summary sheet from the computer calculation

Lumen method

| Luminaire: | 20 off | FSNDIZ258SB |
| Lamp flux: | | 5200 lumens |

Average illuminance: 517 lux

		Across	Along
Minimum luminaires for 0.7 uniformity:		3	3
Chosen luminaires:		4	5

Point by point calculation

| Luminaire: | 20 off | FSNDIZ258SB |

	Working Plane
Average illuminance:	480 lux

| Uniformity (min/ave) | 0.60 |
| Diversity (min/max) | 0.47 |

Task uniformity: 0.75

| Average ceiling luminance | 58 cd/m^2 |
| Maximum ceiling luminance | 146 cd/m^2 |

| Total power: | 2080 W | 10.83 W/m^2 |
| Total lumens: | 20800 lm | 100.00 lm/W |

Illuminance ratio

| Ceiling/working plane | 0.48 |
| Wall/working plane | 0.38 |

Figure 15.8

Point by point calculation results

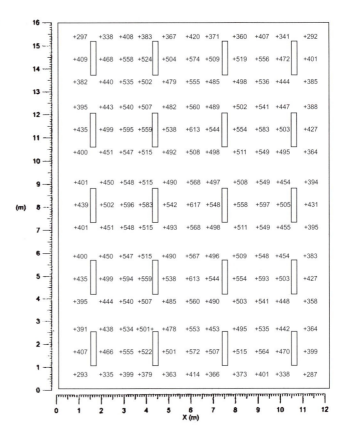

Unified Glare Rating (UGR)   The data sheet given in Figure 15.6 includes uncorrected UGR values so that a check can be made to ensure that the installation has a glare rating within the Code limit of 19. In the table the size of the room is expressed in terms of the height of the luminaires above the observer's eye height, taken as 1.2 m.

The luminaires are mounted at 3 m above the floor and so H = 3 − 1.2 = 1.8 m. The room dimensions are then taken as X = 12/1.8 = 6.7 and Y = 16/1.8 = 8.9.

Putting the values read from the data sheet into a simple table enables the uncorrected UGR value to be determined.

Y	X →	4H	8H	6.7
↓	8H	2.6	2.5	
	12H	2.6	2.4	
8.9H			2.51	= uncorrected UGR

Viewed crosswise

A correction has to be made for the actual lumen output of the luminaire (since the table is based on 1000 lumens). This is obtained from the formula:

Correction term = $8 \log_{10}$
[Total flux of lamps in the luminaire/1000]

The luminaire has 2 58W lamps each giving 5200 lumens. The luminaire lumens are 10 400:

$CT = 8 \log_{10} [10\ 400/1000]$

$= 8.14$

This gives a UGR value of $2.51 + 8.14 = 10.6$. For endwise viewing the end correction term is +0.4, giving a UGR of 11.0. Both values are well below the limiting value of 19.

Example 15.2

A rest room is to be lit by two uplighters suspended from the ceiling at a height above the floor of 2.2 m. The room is 3.2 m high, 5 m long and 3 m wide. The reflectances are ceiling 0.8, walls 0.5, floor 0.2 (Figure 15.9a and b).

Calculate the average illuminance and the illuminances at the working plane height of 0.7 m midway between the luminaires and the centre of one of the short walls.

The assumption is made that all the upward light from the luminaires is directly incident on the ceiling. The utilization factor is therefore

$UF_F = ULOR \times TF_{CF}$

Where TF_{CF} is the ceiling to floor transfer factor which includes interreflection (see Table A3.3 in Appendix 3).

To enter the table we need the room index (RI) based on the height of the ceiling above the working plane:

$h = 3.2 - 0.7 = 2.5$ m

$RI = \dfrac{3 \times 5}{2.5(3 + 5)} = 0.75$

From the table,

$TF_{CF} = 0.406$

$UF_F = 0.62 \times 0.406$

$= 0.25$

Figure 15.9

(a) A rest room lit by two uplighters; (b) data sheet for uplighter in (a)

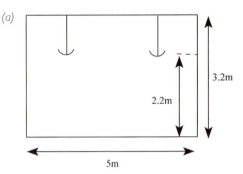

(a)

2.2m

3.2m

5m

(b)

MRG

Description Pendant uplight
Luminaire maintenance category F
Conversion terms

Catalogue number	Lamp	LOR	ULOR	Ho(min)	Data code
J139895	2 x 55W 2L	0.65	0.62	0.57	R0024221*

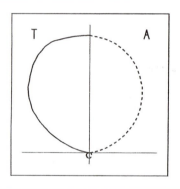

Illuminance curve in lux / 1000 lm

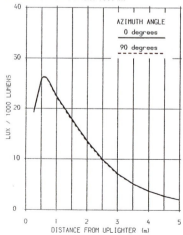

DISTANCE FROM UPLIGHTER (m)

AZIMUTH ANGLE
0 degrees

90 degrees

Luminous intensity in cd / 1000 lm

Elevation angle	Azimuth angle			
	0	30	60	90
90	1	1	0	0
95	3	3	4	5
100	10	9	18	14
105	28	28	39	31
110	50	50	61	49
115	75	74	83	68
120	100	99	102	86
125	125	122	120	104
130	144	140	137	120
135	161	155	153	135
140	173	169	166	150
145	186	182	176	162
150	197	193	185	174
155	205	201	193	184
160	210	205	198	192
165	210	208	203	199
170	210	208	206	204
175	210	210	209	207
180	210	210	210	210

The lumen method formula requires the maintenance factor:

$MF = LLMF \times LMF \times LSF \times RSMF$

$= 0.87 \times 0.86 \times 1.0 \times 0.9$ (from Appendix 2)

$= 0.67$ (lamps changed on failure)

$$E_{av} = \frac{2 \times 2 \times 4850 \times 0.25 \times 0.67}{15}$$

$= 217$ lux

The illuminance at the point between the two luminaires has two components – a direct component and an interreflected component.

The direct component can be calculated from the illuminance curve given on the data sheet. This curve is based on a mounting height of the luminaire of 1 m above the working plane and a distance from the luminaire to the ceiling of 1 m. Since the distance from the luminaire to the working plane is different, the curve must be re-scaled for the point on the working plane under consideration. This re-scaling is based on treating the reflected light as coming from a point source located above the ceiling at the same distance as the real luminaire is below the ceiling. (This method is explained in Appendix 3; see Figure 15.10.)

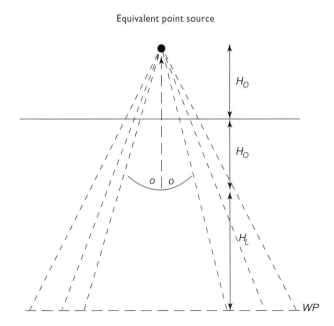

Equivalent point source

Figure 15.10
Diagram for point by point calculation of uplighter illuminance

The correction factors are a correction for illuminance given by $(2H_0 + H_L)^2/3^2$ and a correction factor for the distance scale given by $(2H_0 + H_L)/3$. $H_0 = 1$ m, $H_L = 1.5$ m.

The illuminance correction factor (ICF) is therefore

$$ICF = \frac{(2 \times 1.0 + 1.5)^2}{9} = 1.36$$

The distance correction factor (DCF) is

$$DCF = \frac{(2 \times 1.0 + 1.5)}{3} = 1.167$$

The midpoint between the luminaires is 1.25 m. The illuminance value before adjustment is read off at 1.25/1.167 = 1.07 m. The unadjusted value is 21 which is adjusted to 21/1.36 = 15.4 lux per 1000 lumen. The output of one luminaire produces 15.4 × 9.7 lux of direct illuminance. The two luminaires are the same distance from this point and so the final direct illuminance is 2 × 15.4 × 9.7 = 299 lux initial and 299 × 0.67 = 200 lux maintained.

To this must be added the interreflected component. The first 'bounce' flux from the ceiling to the floor has been taken into account in the direct illuminance and so interreflection factors (IF) that only take the second and subsequent reflections are used for this purpose (Figure 15.11). For a room index of 0.75 the IF value is: IF = 0.150.

INTERREFLECTION FACTORS (IF)

Reflectances			Room Index								
C	W	F	0.75	1.00	1.25	1.50	2.00	2.50	3.00	4.00	5.00
0.8	0.5	0.2	0.150	0.160	0.165	0.167	0.168	0.169	0.168	0.166	0.164
	0.3		0.077	0.086	0.094	0.099	0.107	0.113	0.118	0.124	0.128
	0.2		0.025	0.032	0.039	0.045	0.056	0.066	0.074	0.087	0.096
0.7	0.5	0.2	0.125	0.133	0.135	0.136	0.136	0.134	0.132	0.130	0.128
	0.3		0.064	0.072	0.077	0.080	0.086	0.090	0.092	0.096	0.099
	0.2		0.021	0.027	0.031	0.036	0.045	0.052	0.057	0.067	0.073
0.5	0.5	0.2	0.081	0.083	0.084	0.083	0.080	0.078	0.076	0.072	0.069
	0.3		0.042	0.045	0.048	0.050	0.050	0.051	0.052	0.053	0.053
	0.2		0.011	0.016	0.019	0.020	0.024	0.028	0.031	0.035	0.037

Figure 15.11

IF values for uplighter

The interreflected component to be added to the direct component is given by

$$\frac{IF \times F_L \times n \times ULOR \times MF}{L \times W}$$

$$= \frac{0.150 \times 4 \times 4850 \times 0.62 \times 0.67}{5 \times 3}$$

$$= 81 \text{ lux}$$

The total illuminance midway between the uplighters is 200 + 81 = 281 lux. At the middle of the wall, ignoring the direct light from the distant uplighter, the value would be 100 + 81 = 181 lux.

The maximum and average ceiling luminance needs to be checked for compliance with the limits (average 500 cd/m^2, maximum 1500 cd/m^2), but the method given in the Code does not directly apply to this luminaire because the distance between the uplighter and the ceiling must be at least three times the maximum dimension of the uplighter optic. In this case it would be $0.6 \times 3 = 1.8$ m. Fortunately the manufacturer gives the distance at which this uplighter would comply; that is 0.57 m. Since the uplighter is 1 m below the ceiling, it is sure to comply.

Finally, a very small amount of light is emitted through the slotted base diffuser, but it is not significant except in improving the appearance of the uplighter.

QUESTIONS

Question 15.1 An office space is lit satisfactorily by a direct/indirect general lighting luminaire, except that there is excessive contrast between the windows and the window wall during daylight hours. Suggest a solution.

Question 15.2 An office with an existing lighting system that provides the recommended task lighting level produces complaints that it is gloomy. What addition to the lighting system could be made to ameliorate the situation?

ANSWERS

Answer 15.1 The solution will depend upon the spaces between the windows. If these are not too wide then spotlights recessed into the ceiling and directed at the walls between the windows is an option.

If the spaces between the windows are relatively wide the linear fluorescent wall washer luminaires designed to 'wash' the window walls with light are probably most appropriate.

Answer 15.2 Suitably placed uplighters and wall lighting would almost certainly improve the situation. Illuminated features such as pictures and plants would also add further visual interest.

Industrial lighting

The distinguishing feature of industrial lighting is the great variety of tasks and situations to be accommodated. The large range of illuminance levels, limiting glare index values and special requirements, such as colour discrimination, make careful examination of the visual tasks important. To this is added the different types of building structure encountered which are sometimes dictated by the machinery, materials and manufactured products that must be handled. In some areas large machines or travelling cranes, moving heavy objects, are present, whereas in others there is close work by teams of operators working at long, well-illuminated benches. In order to meet these needs a variety of techniques are used, such as high bay lighting, low bay lighting, low mounted continuous rows of fluorescent luminaires (Figure 16.1a–c) as well as individual luminaires for work benches or inspection areas. In certain areas special lighting is often required for inspection purposes and machines for metal processing frequently require local lighting to produce high levels of local shadow-free lighting.

The move to high powered discharge lighting to reduce costs and save energy can re-introduce some problems that were virtually eliminated when fluorescent lighting was widely used. The first of these is shadows. The small size of discharge lamps means that shadows can be much sharper and stronger and with fewer luminaires, the reduction in the number of directions from which light is received can further increase the problem of shadows.

Sometimes it is worthwhile to use lower powered discharge lamps in a larger number of luminaires to reduce these shadowing problems.

Another problem that can be encountered with the use of small arc tube high pressure lamps (HPS and MBI) is the excessive brightness of the images produced in specular materials such as sheet metal and this can make working visually very difficult.

Figure 16.1

(a) High bay luminaires

Figure 16.1

(b) low bay luminaires

Figure 16.1
(c) continuous rows of
fluorescent luminaires

Where the roof height allows it, high mounted luminaires can provide uniform lighting and with sufficient luminaires can be arranged so that the overlap from different luminaires softens shadows. The light intercepted by the walls reduces the utilization factor, but can produce a more pleasant visual environment.

High bay lighting

Restricted ceiling height demands a larger number of lower powered luminaires to ensure satisfactory uniformity and to avoid deep shadows.

Low bay lighting

Fluorescent industrial luminaires have many advantages. They provide lighting which has soft shadows with good uniformity and when operated on high frequency control gear can eliminate stroboscopic effects and reduce the problem of excessively bright reflections in metal parts. Compact fluorescent lamps are particularly suited to local lighting for machine tools.

Fluorescent lighting

Where working zones are clearly defined and access ways are fixed, then the use of different types of luminaire to define these areas can give a sense of orientation and organization which adds to the satisfaction of workers with their environment. The task illuminances can be provided at the appropriate level, while the access and circulation lighting can usually be at a lower illuminance level, provided that the contrast is not too great. For detailed recommendations the CIBSE Lighting Code should be consulted, but an indication of lighting levels for different situations is given below:

Working zones

> 100 lux – circulation areas
> 300 lux – tasks with simple visual requirements
> 500 lux – tasks with medium visual requirements
> 750 lux – tasks with demanding visual requirements
> 1000 lux – tasks with difficult visual requirements
> 1500 lux upwards – tasks that are very exacting

Illuminance levels in adjacent areas should not vary by more than 5.0 to 1.0 and preferably 3.0 to 1.0.

In many industrial situations the vertical surfaces are as important as the horizontal surfaces and so attention should be paid to the lighting of these surfaces. In seeking good lighting on vertical surfaces it is important to achieve glare ratings within the specified limits.

Storage areas   Storage areas with high racks require special consideration to be given to the lighting on the vertical surfaces of the racks. A lower level of lighting for the aisles between the racks could be used, where a high rate of access is not required. This could be supplemented by lighting switched on locally to identify and illuminate particular sets of racks.

Obstructions   In some industrial areas there is a high degree of obstruction, which precludes a general lighting system. This may be due to very large machines or adjacent storage areas. In such circumstances, the approach should be to carefully place the lighting points to illuminate the key task areas to enable the work to be performed efficiently and safely. Once this has been done, further lighting points should be added to allow for movement and access to complete the scheme.

Light source position   The position of local light sources should be such as to ensure a correct evaluation of the object, tool or machine to be made and the avoidance of confusing shadows. This is particularly important for bench work, where a light placed behind the worker could cause a head or body shadow to fall on to the task. For many tasks light coming from a luminaire mounted in front of the worker can cause visual disability from reflections in specular materials or reduction of contrast for semi-specular surfaces. Light from the sides is preferred.

      Special lighting for critical inspection tasks always merits trials before adopting a particular system.

Table 16.1   Utilization factors UF(F)

| Reflectances | | | Room index | | | | |
C	W	F	1	2	3	4	5
0.8	0.6	0.2	0.76	0.87	0.91	0.93	0.95
	0.5		0.73	0.85	0.90	0.92	0.93
	0.3		0.68	0.81	0.87	0.90	0.92
0.7	0.6	0.2	0.75	0.86	0.89	0.91	0.93
	0.5		0.72	0.84	0.88	0.90	0.92
	0.3		0.68	0.80	0.85	0.88	0.90
0.5	0.6	0.2	0.73	0.83	0.86	0.88	0.89
	0.5		0.71	0.81	0.85	0.87	0.88
	0.3		0.67	0.79	0.83	0.85	0.87

Answer 16.1   Utilization factors are tabulated against room index, which is the ratio of horizontal to vertical surface area. The introduction of obstructions effectively reduces this ratio and lowers the utilization factor.

If the change in UF value from RI = 5.0 to RI = 1.0 at the lowest reflectance values is taken as an indication of the possible effect of obstruction then using UF values from Table 16.1 this can be estimated as

$$\left(\frac{0.87 - 0.67}{0.87} \right) = 0.23 \text{ or } 23\%$$

The number of luminaires could be increased by this amount to allow for obstruction. The closer spacing of the luminaires would lessen the effects of the obstruction and the higher initial illuminance would mean that, except in extreme cases, the reduction in illuminance should not be too severe.

The lowest reflectances have been used in this solution, but if the unobstructed area would have higher values then a case could be made for subtracting the lower UF values from a value based on the higher reflectances. For example, if the higher reflectances were $R_C = 0.7$, $R_W = 0.5$ and $R_F = 0.2$ the allowance would become

$$\frac{0.93 - 0.67}{0.93} = 28\%$$

If the obstruction is known to be severe then portable lighting or other solutions would be adopted.

ANSWER

Question 16.1   A large industrial interior is to have high bay lighting. However, the nature of the work means that very high obstruction may occur at almost any part of the working area for a few days at a time. Consider the utilization factor table (Table 16.1) and suggest how some adjustment could be made to the lighting system to reduce the effects of this obstruction, while using the same luminaire and mounting height.

QUESTION

Lighting for educational buildings and sports halls

The primary purpose of face to face teaching is the generation of enthusiasm for the subject being studied, since an enthusiastic student will learn more effectively. Good teaching can make what is thought of as a dull subject interesting. The lighting provided should assist the teacher or lecturer to communicate easily with the pupils or students to achieve their objective.

The atmosphere created by the lighting, both natural and artificial, can help to sustain interest and attention and make the carrying out of book work or display screen work easier. Good lighting does this without those using it having to think about it and, in general, only bad lighting is noticed.

The psychological value of daylight illumination has a particular role to play in the lighting of day schools. A bright and cheerful environment is difficult to create without the presence of daylight. School architects are fully aware of this and pay great attention to the placing and sizing of windows and roof lights (Figure 17.1).

Light room surfaces and furniture also add to the general brightness of the interior and careful use of colour adds to both the interest and stimulation provided in classrooms.

The electric lighting needs to be designed to fit in with the overall concept of the architect and to ensure that there is not just adequate electric light, but also lighting that adds to the architectural interest and functional effect of the building. In general, fluorescent lighting is to be preferred, both for the avoidance of harsh shadows and also the colour quality available. The linear nature of fluorescent tubes often enables the luminaires to blend appropriately with the rectangular nature of most teaching spaces.

Compact fluorescent indirect luminaires can often provide added brightness interest to the walls in high-ceilinged rooms. Correlated colour temperatures in the region of 4000 K are considered most suitable because the lighting will have to blend with daylight.

Figure 17.1

A bright and cheerful environment is required in a day school for young children

Table 17.1 Recommended illuminance levels for schools

	Standard maintained illuminance (lux)	Uniformity ratio	Limiting glare index
1 General teaching spaces	300	0.8	19
2 Teaching spaces with close and detailed work, e.g. craft and art rooms	500	0.8	19
3 Circulation spaces – stairs and corridors	80–120	–	19
lobbies, waiting areas and entrance halls	175–250	–	19
reception areas	250–350	–	19
4 Atria	400	–	19

The recommended illuminance levels for schools are given in Table 17.1, which is taken from the Department for Education and Employment Building Bulletin 90. These lighting levels are sufficiently high to ensure that, in general, fluorescent lamps are used. However, tungsten halogen spotlights have their place for some display purposes.

It is important to arrange the switching of the electric lighting so that lights close to the windows, where electric lighting is not required for much of the day, can be switched off separately from the rest of the classroom. The luminaires used for classroom lighting should be chosen to give a good level of lighting to the walls and ceiling to provide cheerful conditions.

Prismatic controllers used with fluorescent tubes are appropriate in many situations, provided the installation meets the glare rating of 19.

Where visual display screens are in use, care has to be taken to ensure that there are no veiling reflections on the screens from either windows or luminaires. When only one or two display screens are in use careful positioning can usually ensure this, but a room devoted to VDU use should have appropriate lighting, often louvred luminaires and window blinds. Classroom walls are often used for display purposes and fluorescent tubes placed behind pelmet-type baffles can provide an attractive means of lighting displays and providing visual interest by giving an acceptable variation of wall brightness.

Of particular importance in more senior teaching spaces is the lighting of chalkboards, of either the high or low reflectance type. Fluorescent tubes concealed behind suitable reflectors are frequently used for this purpose and a most important requirement is to ensure that reflected images of the lamp and luminaire do not cause problems for the students, especially those closest to the board. Figure 17.2 shows how this can be avoided by the correct positioning of the luminaire. For a dark board of reflectance no greater than 0.1 an average illuminance of 500 lux is recommended, but with a white board 250 lux would be appropriate.

Classrooms are sometimes used in the evenings for part-time students and since these are frequently older members of the community thought should be given to ensuring that the lighting available is appropriate to the activity and the degree of visual difficulty. Some forms of craft or art work require higher illuminances than those provided during normal daytime classes.

Special consideration should be given to areas where those with visual impairments may be present. A simple

Figure 17.2

Avoiding reflections in the chalkboard or whiteboard

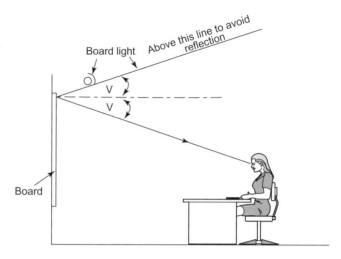

example would be the necessity to ensure that the lights in corridors are not switched off when it is essential that they should remain on. Key switches can be used to ensure that this does not happen. The equipment of classrooms for the visually impaired is a specialist subject and, therefore, is not dealt with here.

Lecture theatres with banked seats require lighting that ensures good vision of the front areas for all students, while being free from glare. The lighting level needs to be high enough for note-taking and 300 lux is generally the recommended level, but the facility for dimming should be provided for viewing visual aids such as slides. Care should be taken to ensure that lecturers can see their notes and local lighting in some form is appropriate for this purpose. A flow of light downward and towards the front of the lecture theatre is appropriate and a simple baffle system would provide this. High mounted louvred luminaires are also often used (Figure 17.3).

Figure 17.3

A simple baffle system used to control glare

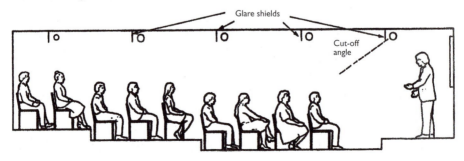

These are an important element in many schools and academic establishments and contribute a great deal to the well-being and enthusiasm of many students. They are sometimes windowless to avoid problems created by daylight conditions. Therefore, a good level of lighting is required, both for creating a pleasant atmosphere and to enable a variety of sports to be accommodated. A general lighting level of 300 lux is commonly recommended. Luminaires that give both upward and downward light are preferred and the interior surfaces of the hall should be light in colour and provide a good inter-reflected component. The mean vertical illuminance (cylindrical illuminance) should be at least 30% of the horizontal illuminance. The uniformity of the cylindrical illuminance is also important; too large a variation of the cylindrical illuminance can cause a fast-moving projectile to exhibit a flicker which makes judging its speed difficult. Where high intensity discharge lamps are used it is advisable to distribute the luminaires across the three phases of the supply to avoid stroboscopic effect on fast-moving objects.

Sports halls are of necessity high-ceilinged and the luminaires are mounted close to the ceiling, so that the full height can be utilized without obstruction. Even so, it is important that luminaires should be given protective guards (Figure 17.4).

Sports halls

Figure 17.4
A school sports hall

Other areas Sometimes it is necessary to use assembly halls, canteens, etc. for other purposes, such as examinations. The lighting should anticipate this variable function, wherever possible.

QUESTION Question 17.1 What is the main difference between spaces designed for infant school teaching and those designed for secondary schools, where academic topics related to examinations are being taught? How should this be accommodated by the form of electric lighting?

ANSWER **Answer 17.1** In infant schools the approach is usually very informal with the children often sitting around tables and working on simple projects supervised by the teacher who moves about the space from table to table. In secondary schools the teaching is usually much more structured and direction-orientated – for example, towards the front of the classroom and the board or overhead projector screen.

In infant schools the lighting would usually be multi-directional with fluorescent luminaires and sometimes spotlights to highlight displays. In a senior classroom adequate task illuminance and board illuminance is important, with a sense of focus created either by the orientation of the luminaires or the illuminance pattern.

Lighting for shops and stores

Shops and stores have a common purpose in the desire to sell their merchandise. How they endeavour to do this depends upon the sort of goods on offer. If they are selling essential goods such as food, household cleaning products, etc. then much of their attraction is likely to be in the prices they charge. The lighting required in such a shop or store needs to be businesslike, i.e. bright and well organized to indicate the route through the premises and to make it easy for customers to identify the product they require. A good high level of general illuminance throughout the store from luminaires that do not cause glare is required and 750 to 1000 lux is common. Hardwearing, light-coloured, diffuse surfaces to walls and floors are particularly important to provide a good reflected component to light (Figure 18.1).

Figure 18.1
Light-coloured diffuse surfaces provide a good reflected component of light

Figure 18.2

Warehouse type stores often use high bay luminaires

Some of the cut price stores are situated in warehouse type buildings with a high illuminance provided by lighting from high wattage metal halide lamps with parabolic style high bay luminaires (Figure 18.2).

In all these premises the lighting of the walls is important, since the boundaries of a space often have a significant effect on the perception of the cheerfulness of a space.

Special lighting can be provided for particular areas, where colour rendering is important in promoting a sale, such as meat or delicatessen counters, etc. Additional lighting is frequently provided at one end of the store at the point of sale, where rows of tills are located. This can be provided by special fluorescent luminaires mounted at a lower height than the general lighting.

In specialist shops and stores, where customers can be expected to spend more time appraising the merchandise, lighting levels in the region of 500 lux are common and extensive use is made of spotlights to emphasize displays of shoes and clothing, etc., especially where models are used to display goods (Figure 18.3).

Figure 18.3
Extensive use is made of spotlights to emphasize clothing displays, especially where mannequins are used

In very exclusive boutiques and shops selling designer clothing, shoes and jewellery a different atmosphere is required and subtle general lighting is supplemented by extensive use of carefully designed display lighting. In such shops indirect fluorescent lighting as a background to tungsten halogen spotlighting is often used. The atmosphere is designed to be comfortable and unhurried, with staff always near at hand for consultation. Specialist shops tend to use window displays to attract customers and use theatrical style lighting for that purpose. Diachroic reflector spotlights which have reduced reflected heat enable very high levels of illuminance to be achieved and to draw attention to dramatic displays (Figure 18.4). Department stores have similar displays, but tend to use metal halide reflector lamps because of the much larger windows areas to be covered.

Figure 18.4
Theatrical style lighting

Metal halide spotlamps find extensive use inside department stores for highlighting particular areas. The idea of a shop within a store is sometimes promoted by using canopies and counters that form a boutique-like area and in such an area localized spotlighting is usually incorporated. For example, an area selling wedding dresses within a particular part of the store might be treated in that way.

The CIBSE Lighting Code has suggested the following relationship between the display effect and the illuminance incident on the display. It is expressed in terms of the ratio of the illuminance on the object plane to the general horizontal plane illuminance.

Effect	Illumination
Subtle	5:1
Moderate	15:1
Strong	30:1
Dramatic	50:1

This table takes into account the law of diminishing returns mentioned in Chapter 3; hence ten times as much illuminance is required to have a dramatic effect compared with that required for a subtle effect.

Shop lighting in general and display lighting in particular is an area in which the prospective lighting designer can rapidly gain valuable experience by viewing and thinking about the lighting of shops and stores in any large town.

Question 18.1 In Chapter 6 the importance of illuminance variation as a means of creating the appropriate luminous field was emphasized. In the lighting of shops and stores this is the essential element in good display. How would the display of jewellery differ in its lighting requirements to that for the display of large metal objects such as stainless steel sinks?

QUESTION

Answer 18.1 Jewellery often requires illumination from bright point sources of light to produce bright reflected images and sparkle from the facets of cut stones or small polished metal surfaces. Large area reflecting objects produced from materials such as stainless steel often reveal their shape best under linear diffused lighting without the images of the light sources being too bright.

Lighting for public buildings and atria

Places of worship and hospitals, as well as civic buildings and libraries, are included under the heading of public buildings.

When entering a large public building, such as a town hall, the two main elements are impression and direction. The architecture is usually designed to reflect the sense of the power of a community working together for a common aim which is characterized by large spaces with lifts and wide staircases and the scale of the general lighting must be in sympathy with that aim (Figure 19.1).

Figure 19.1

The scale of lighting must be in sympathy with the purpose of the space

The second element is to enable the public users of the building to easily identify where the information they require can be found and, once that has been ascertained, the route to that information. There is usually a prominent reception desk(s) and the lighting should both indicate these areas clearly and also enable those working at the desks to carry out their tasks. The form of general lighting will depend upon the age of the interior and the ceiling height available. Where ceiling height allows, large suspended luminaires designed to fit in with the architectural style of the interior are suited to this task; the high mounting height and size of the luminaires adding to the feeling of civic authority, whilst at the same time providing lighting over a wide area. Such luminaires require raising and lowering gear to facilitate cleaning and lamp replacement. Where large suspended luminaires are used it is essential to ensure that they do not present a glare hazard to people descending staircases into the entrance hall.

Reception desks often have local canopies to give a more intimate atmosphere to the area and compact fluorescent lamps in cylindrical luminaires, or something similar, are used to provide illumination on desk areas while delineating the shape of the information area (Figure 19.2).

Where the open area has a lower ceiling height large recessed fittings can provide a satisfactory solution, especially in modern buildings. Compact fluorescent indirect wall lights and illuminated pictures or notice boards, placed as appropriate, add interest or directional information. If the open space is in the form of an atrium, either as part of the entrance hall to the building or as a central court within the building which rises through several floors, special lighting is usually required.

Maintenance is obviously a major issue in the design of an atrium lighting scheme. If the maintenance of the lighting can be related to the cleaning of the interior of the atrium windows then an effective system is to use high bay luminaires with high intensity discharge lamps. The good colour properties of metal halide lamps make them particularly suitable for this situation.

Another approach is to light the space rather like an outdoor pedestrian area, using post-top lanterns placed either down the centre of the atrium or mounted on brackets at the walls. Wall mounted luminaires on the side walls between the different levels of the floors opening onto the atrium is another method which has proved a good solution. Some upward light is desirable, but, in this case, care has to be taken to ensure that the luminaires cannot be looked into from the higher levels of the atrium.

The general working areas in public buildings, such as offices, are dealt with in the same way as those for other

Figure 19.2
*An information desk
should be obvious and
well lit*

buildings. However, there are other areas, such as council
chambers, that required special consideration. Again, the age
of the building and its architectural style must be taken into
account if the lighting is successfully to fulfil its dual function of
adequately and sympathetically revealing the interior and its

users, while providing good light for reading meeting agendas and other papers and note-taking. Facilities for dimming the lighting where visual aids are used should also be provided.

A dual lighting scheme consisting of general lighting to reveal the interior and the occupants with additional lighting to provide good working conditions should be considered.

Places of worship

One of the most significant functions of a place of worship is inspiration through things that are seen, things that are said and things that are done and the lighting of any worship area should assist in meeting these needs. Two of the main factors to be considered in the lighting of places of worship are the age of the building and the form of the worship.

One of the most interesting challenges to the lighting designer is to light an ancient church, using modern lighting equipment. The simplest solution is to seek to make the equipment as unobtrusive as possible, so that the lighting effect is perceived without the lighting equipment dominating the visual scene. Very successful schemes have been produced following this principle (Figure 19.3).

Figure 19.3
Unobtrusive lighting equipment can provide a good solution

The most sensible approach is to first of all consider each space separately; chancel, nave, aisles, etc., and to evaluate the most appropriate lighting levels and lighting systems for each. Once this has been done the relationship between these areas should be considered and, where necessary, adjustments to the design should be made. For example, it might well be considered that with little loss a common type of luminaire or lamp could be used in two areas, which would simplify maintenance.

For this example we use the specified illuminance method introduced in Chapter 9 (The Other Lumen Method).

Example 19.1: Calculation from specified illuminance values

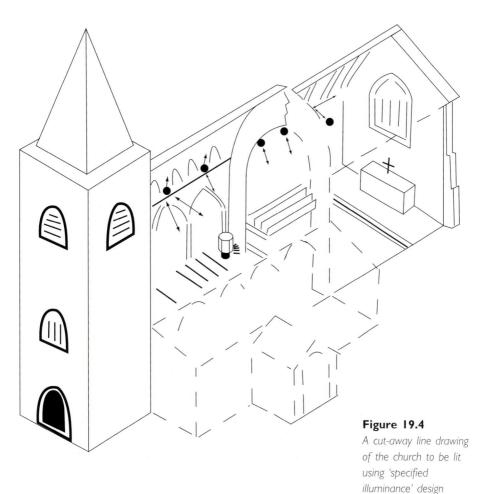

Figure 19.4

A cut-away line drawing of the church to be lit using 'specified illuminance' design

Spreadsheet calculation for a typical parish church

Location	Area A (m²)	Reflect-ance R	Specified illuminance E (lux)	Reflected flux ARE (lumens)	Direct illuminance $E_D = E - E_R$	Direct flux F $= E_D A$
Chancel						
Altar	2	0.3	600	360	551	1102
Altar panel	7	0.6	300	1260	251	1757
East wall	35	0.6	200	4200	151	5285
Ceiling vault	84	0.3	100	2520	51	4284
Walls	180	0.6	100	10800	51	9180
Floor	46	0.3	200	2760	151	6946
Choir	20	0.3	300	1800	251	5020
						33 574
Nave						
Chancel arch	9	0.7	150	945	101	909
Arcades	50	0.7	100	3500	51	2250
West wall	50	0.4	75	1500	26	1300
Pews and floor	84	0.2	200	3360	151	12 684
Ceiling vault	79	0.3	100	2370	51	4029
Pulpit and lectern	2	0.3	300	180	251	502
						21 674
Aisles						
Ceiling	111	0.4	50	2220	1	111
Walls	126	0.5	100	6300	51	6426
Pews and floor	76	0.2	200	3040	151	11 476
						18 013
	961			47 115		

$$\text{Reflected illuminance } E_R = \frac{\text{Reflected flux}}{\text{Total area}}$$

$$= \frac{47115}{961}$$

$$= 49 \text{ lux}$$

Each part of the church, chancel, nave, aisles is now allocated the appropriate number of lamps and luminaires. As a first step, since there are so many separate features a relatively low wattage projector is selected. A 35W metal halide lamp with a colour temperature of 3000 K and lumen output of 3300 is chosen in a projector with an LOR of 0.7. The maintenance factor is specified as 0.75.

Number of lamps (n):

$$\text{Chancel} \quad n = \frac{33574}{3300 \times 0.7 \times 0.75}$$

$$= 19.4 \qquad \text{say } 20$$

$$\text{Nave} \quad n = \frac{21674}{3300 \times 0.7 \times 0.75}$$

$$= 12.5 \qquad \text{say } 13$$

$$\text{Aisles} \quad n = \frac{18013}{3300 \times 0.7 \times 0.75}$$

$$= 10.4 \qquad \text{say } 10$$

This set of calculations gives a broad framework within which to work. The projectors are allocated according to the direct fluxes required by different parts of the church. The assumption of an LOR of 0.7 is simply an average value. The beam angles of the projectors will be selected according to the areas to be covered and, where it is appropriate, two 35W projectors will be replaced by one 70W projector.

Consider the altar and altar panel. Together they require 2859 lumens. One projector will provide 1732 lumens (3300 × 0.7 × 0.75), so two projectors must be used to cover that area. By overlapping in the altar area they will provide the emphasis that is required there. Another projector is allocated to the pulpit area, but it will also light part of the chancel arch.

In each area projectors must provide upward and downward components of the illuminance. This will require careful consideration and attention to their aiming.

The value of this approach is that it ensures that each area is considered individually and the projectors are selected accordingly. Overall, one or two more projectors than the calculations call for are usually needed to cover particular requirements. It may be decided that glare control louvres will reduce the LOR in some projectors, etc. when the fine details of the scheme are worked out.

In a modern building special lighting features can be part of the design and indirect lighting, wall washers, spotlights and even decorative suspended luminaires can all be considered.

However, the lighting equipment must be subservient to the main function of the building and the lighting designer must establish a hierarchy of brightnesses that are required to focus the attention of the members of congregation and enable them to read hymn books, etc. Depending on the form of worship, the main focus of attention is likely to vary. Where ritual is very important the lighting of the altar and its surrounds may be considered of greatest importance and, therefore, a high lighting level will be desired, say, 400–700 lux. Where the worship is dominated by the preaching, then the pulpit becomes the focus of attention. However, in all churches there are usually other areas to which, from time to time, the focus of attention is directed. It is essential that the designer consults with clergy and church officials to ensure that he/she fully understands how the church functions, which areas are the focal points of action and the direction of movement during services.

In some denominations multipurpose buildings provide for both weekday activities and Sunday worship. These spaces are usually very simple in design and require an overall lighting system suitable for the different church and community activities that take place there. The worship area is denoted on Sundays by moving a simple communion table, a preaching lectern and portable organ/keyboard instrument into place. The congregational seating is usually in the form of chairs that are easily stacked away at one side of the space when not required. A very suitable lighting scheme for such a space, which has only a moderate ceiling height, would be louvred fluorescent luminaires to provide the general lighting and track-mounted spotlights could provide the necessary emphasis for the worship area and any display areas on the walls.

Where gospel choirs or dance are a major feature of the worship then a more stage-like arrangement and theatrical-type lighting and sound systems may be appropriate. Switching is an important aspect of the lighting design and should be located conveniently for the users, minister, caretaker, officials, etc. Some two-way switches are appropriate in spaces that people pass through in a sequence simply as a means of carrying out some secondary activity, such as organ practice.

Where switches are mounted in banks they should be located so that they are easily accessible so that the lighting can be adjusted, if necessary, during worship without causing disruption. Dimming can be employed, if desired, but any major scheme should be thoroughly investigated and costed before proceeding in that direction, in order that costly mistakes can be avoided.

Hospitals have a number of very important features that need to be borne in mind when designing the lighting, one of which is that most of the people inhabiting the space are either ill or dealing with people who are ill. The consequence of this is that stress is a common ingredient and so the lighting must be designed to enable the work to be carried out quickly and efficiently while, as far as possible, seeking to provide a reassuring visual scene. This visual scene begins at the reception desk and the waiting area. A bright and cheerful atmosphere can be created by a good level of glare-free general lighting and adequate light for reading in the waiting area with good illumination on the walls. A simple system of fluorescent lighting arranged to preserve a sense of orientation and spacial purpose usually meets this need.

Hospitals

Most reception areas require good shadow-free lighting for dealing with appointment cards and avoiding reflections in display screens. Coloured lines on the floor can be very helpful in enabling patients to find their way to the right department easily, especially on a first visit. This is particularly so in older hospital buildings which often have many changes of direction en route.

Hospital corridors should be well lit since, during times of emergency, patients may have to wait on trolley beds in the corridors. A single continuous row of fluorescent luminaires mounted close to one wall and running the length of the corridor has been found to be a satisfactory arrangement. This avoids patients looking directly up at the lights as they are moved in bed or on a trolley down the corridor. It is unsatisfactory to mount fluorescent luminaires widthways across corridors because patients being moved are then subject to a view of alternate patches of bright and dark ceiling (Figure 19.5).

On wards the lighting must not cause discomfort or distraction to patients confined to bed. Someone who is sick and lying in a fixed position for long periods of time may be particularly affected by the lighting. At night it is important that staff can see sufficiently well to monitor patients in their care, but low lighting levels are required to allow patients to sleep. Local lighting is necessary at the bedhead, both for patient

Figure 19.5

Fluorescent luminaires in a hospital corridor which are mounted off-centre to avoid discomfort to patients being wheeled on trolleys along the corridor

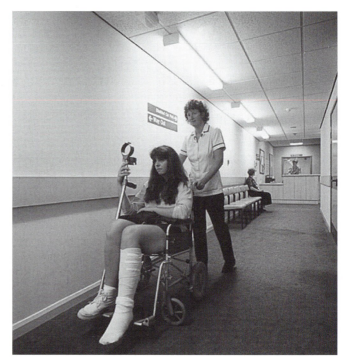

examination and to allow patients to read, write, etc. (Figure 19.6).

Throughout the whole hospital emergency lighting is required in public areas, and in many situations, such as intensive care units, treatment rooms and operating theatres etc., standby lighting to maintain the lighting level is vital.

The lighting of operating theatres requires specialized luminaires which provide very high illuminance values and shadow-free lighting for surgeons to work by. Lighting levels for this purpose can be of the order of 50 000 lux over the critical operating zone. The background lighting must be sufficient for the theatre staff to operate support equipment, and values of about 500 lux are often used. The general lighting also has to provide good shadow-free lighting for cleaning up the

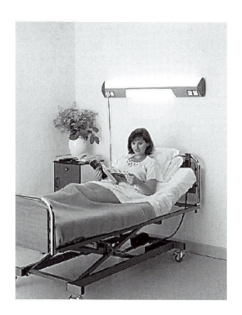

Figure 19.6
Hospital ward lighting

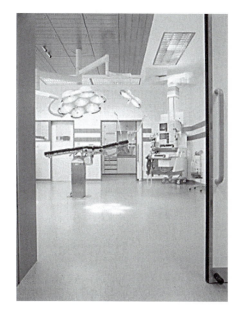

Figure 19.7
Specialized operating theatre luminaires backed up by good background lighting

operating theatre. The colour rendering properties of the lamps must meet clinical requirements (Figure 19.7).

The light source used in these areas should have a colour appearance of a full radiator at 4000 K and a clinical colour rendering capability. This colour rendering requirement applies to the emergency or standby lighting as well. Ancillary areas to the operating theatre also require this clinical level of colour rendering, i.e. in intensive care units and delivery rooms.

Libraries　In general, library lighting must facilitate three main tasks. First, it should enable users to view and identify books on the book stack shelves; secondly it should facilitate students and others working at study desks and thirdly it should enable the library staff to carry out clerical duties. In some libraries the lighting must also take into account the antiquity and the vulnerability of the documents on display and this will have a major effect of the type of lighting that is suitable.

Fluorescent lighting is very suitable for most libraries because the linear nature of the tubes and the diffuse nature of the light help to reduce shadows between the book stacks and those shadows caused by people looking at the books on the shelves. If the book stacks are fixed permanently then lighting placed centrally between the rows and running parallel to the book stacks can be very effective. Louvred luminaires designed to give good sideways illumination onto the stacks, while reducing the luminance of the luminaires towards those walking between the stacks, are desirable (Figure 19.8).

It is possible to incorporate the lighting into the book stacks by bracketing luminaires from the top of the stack, but it is difficult to get a suitable level of illuminance at the bottom of the stack unless the lower shelves are sloped to accept the light at a more effective angle.

Where shelves are likely to be moved then a good system of lighting is to run the luminaires in continuous lines at right angles to the book stacks; since moving the book stacks in the direction of the lines of luminaires should still leave them adequately illuminated (say, 150 lux or more).

The lighting for study areas needs to have higher values (300 lux or more) than that between the book stacks. If study areas are between bookshelves then additional local lighting, which can be switched off when not required, can be used to increase the lighting level.

Many libraries now have much material available on computer display screens and care must be taken to avoid distracting reflections in the screens from the lighting.

Figure 19.8
Lighting mounted parallel to book stacks, where book stacks are unlikely to be moved

High frequency control gear is advisable for the fluorescent lamps to avoid flicker, improve energy efficiency and to ensure that the control gear does not produce any disturbing humming noise.

Fibre optic lighting is sometimes used where ancient manuscripts are displayed to ensure that the light source is remote from the illuminated material and that it is not subject to heat or ultraviolet light (see Chapter 14).

QUESTION

Question 19.1 This chapter has dealt with public buildings, but has not specifically dealt with art galleries or museums. In one sense this is because they have much in common with some shops and stores because they are devoted to displaying exhibits and drawing attention to them. In what ways are these areas quite different to shops and stores?

ANSWER

Answer 19.1 Shops and stores are devoted to attracting customers to purchase the items on display and usually allow the customer to handle the merchandise. Museums and art galleries seek to attract the viewing public while ensuring that they do not handle the exhibits. Many of the artifacts on display are fragile or easily damaged and so it is often important not to overlight or allow exposure to IR or UV radiation. Hence, the lighting levels are often kept low and the light sources remote: for example, the use of fibre optic lighting. For this reason, although the principles of display are the same as for shops and stores, in museums and art galleries the contrast is often achieved by generally low lighting levels with moderate levels on the objects displayed.

Domestic lighting

Everyone is involved with the use of domestic lighting and so it is a subject of universal importance, yet many suffer from poor home lighting without taking action to rectify it. This is mainly because of inflexibility in the electrical wiring installation.

Certain areas such as kitchens (Figure 20.1) and bathrooms (Figure 20.2) require carefully placed permanent lighting to make the use of the space both convenient and safe, while not being unattractive. Other areas such as lounges and

Figure 20.1
Kitchen areas with under cabinet lighting

Figure 20.2
Bathroom with over mirror lighting

dining rooms require an element of artistic design to suit the occupants, as well as adequate lighting for their leisure time pursuits. The ability to use the lighting to change the mood of a room is very desirable in the main living room. A simple rule is to light objects of interest within the room first and then consider the ambient lighting level.

The use of a central light fitting is often abandoned for the more interesting effects created by wall lights, but the ability to switch on a central light for some purposes is always useful. A room designed to appear as a film set may not be so helpful if someone drops a contact lens or a piece of jewellery on the floor and a higher lighting level is needed to find it. A central light is also helpful when the room needs to be cleaned. However, the lighting of, say, a living room is a matter of taste as well as utility, but the universally effective system is to have more than one source of light in the room and if possible many more. Switching on table lamps, spotlights, standard lamps, walls lights or luminous sculptures can dramatically change the 'feel' of a space and enable it to be fitted to the current activity. The side lighting produced by wall lights can give good facial appearance (Figure 20.3).

Even when careful attention has been paid to the general lighting, it is always worthwhile to have the possibility of switching on a table lamp or a standard lamp. With regard to watching television, it is also important to be able to switch off a light causing reflections in the screen (often the central light) without putting the room into darkness except for the light from the television screen. Some low level of light on the wall behind the television helps to reduce the contrast. This could be from hidden lights, but a table lamp with a suitable shade placed nearby, or an uplighter, will often suffice.

Figure 20.3
Lighting of plants, pictures etc. also adds interest

The positioning of table lamps should be considered not just in terms of their appearance in daylight or as a piece of furniture, but also for their effect at night. Carefully positioned table lamps on coffee tables beneath paintings or pictures can create interest.

The lighting of a dining room where guests are entertained is important. A common method is to place an attractive luminaire at a fairly low level over the table to form a centrepiece to the gathering, although this can restrict the table position. More distant lighting around the room or a close ceiling light that can be switched off can allow the full effect of a table candelabra centrepiece to be appreciated. There is no adequate replacement for a well-candlelit dinner.

Bedrooms are particularly important spaces, in that they must function as utilitarian areas for getting ready for work or for a function, as well as being restful and romantic places. Here again, attractive ceiling lighting supplemented by dressing table lamps, bedside lamps or indirect wall lights provides a good solution. Cleaning also requires a good lighting level, particularly in the winter months (Figure 20.4).

En-suite bathrooms with appropriate wash basins/vanity units are increasingly being installed in new houses. A very good lighting method for such a space, where possible, is to take the mirror up to the ceiling and place an attractive linear luminaire (say, with a set of small circular louvre apertures) very close to the top of the mirror. The luminaire is then reflected as though it is the on other side of the mirror, which is a good direction from which to receive the light onto the person standing before the mirror. Obviously, this would work equally well in a family bathroom.

Staircase lighting is also important in the home and an approach to stair lighting is included in Chapter 6 under discussion of the role played by shadows.

Kitchen lighting is different to other domestic lighting in that it is essentially a place where many tasks are carried out and where mistakes could be dangerous. Shadow-free lighting with good colour rendering is required and this can best be provided by fluorescent lamps. A number of appropriately placed circular recessed compact fluorescent lights with diffusing or prismatic front covers are a good solution in that situation.

Domestic lighting often has to cope with a wide range of situations and occupants often with widely differing visual capabilities. Older family members can require as much as three times the illuminance level of that required by the younger family members to perform similar visual tasks. Therefore, the ability to change the lighting level in living

Figure 20.4

Bedside lamps add to the decor

rooms is desirable. Sometimes dimming can be the answer, but many luminaires that look attractive at full brightness often look less satisfactory when dimmed. Appropriately placed reading lights can be a welcome addition to a living space, but care must be taken to ensure that there is not excessive contrast between the reading material and the background because of an imbalance in the lighting levels, since this can rapidly lead to headaches.

Exterior lighting

Displaying a building after dark

There are a number of reasons for wishing to illuminate a building after dark. Where a town hall or other public building is lit, a major reason is civic or national pride. A mixture of civic pride and the desire to remind the local populace of its presence is frequently the reason for floodlighting a church. A further reason for floodlighting suitable national and local buildings and statues is to make a town or city more attractive to visitors. In addition, a building can be lit externally for commercial reasons and sometimes this actually detracts from the area's attractiveness.

This chapter deals with lighting designed to display a building as an object of interest and architectural merit because of its function or age. The art of floodlighting of such buildings usually depends upon illuminance variation to achieve its objective. Good floodlighting does not seek to reproduce a daylit appearance, but rather to show the structure in a different but recognizable and attractive way. To this end it is important to realize that when displaying a building after dark the shadows created can be as important as the areas illuminated, and therefore, in a way, the term 'floodlighting' is inappropriate, since merely flooding a building with light produces a very uninteresting result.

Careful thinking about the purpose of the building, its location in the community and the view of those who own the building, should be undertaken before an attempt at external lighting of a building is made. This is particularly true with regard to the colour of the light to be employed.

There is a temptation to use coloured light to obtain a dramatic effect. This can be very successful, but only in very specific and appropriate circumstances. A classic case is the statue shown in Figure 21.1 (see back cover for colour reproduction), where it is immediately obvious how appropriate the use of coloured light is in this case.

Figure 21.1

A situation where the use of coloured light is obviously appropriate (see back cover for colour reproduction)

In general, a building usually benefits from the unifying effect of a single colour of light or, occasionally, a subtle change of colour with direction. It is the revealing power of the lighting that should be harnessed in the scheme's design.

Light from a prominent direction can display a building very successfully by allowing the varying orientation of the building's surfaces to create the shadows necessary to reveal its features.

Lighting designers have found that, as far as possible, the direction of the lighting should not be from the same direction as the main direction of view of people looking at it, since when both coincide the effect produced can be flat and uninteresting.

One of the most important considerations when designing floodlighting for a particular building is the possible siting of the floodlights. If there is sufficient space around the building to light it either from close to or at a distance, then both of these possibilities are worth considering.

However, in somewhere like a town centre only close proximity floodlighting is sometimes possible. Close proximity or close offset floodlighting is most effective where there are horizontal features or curved arches that benefit from a specifically upwards flow of light (Figure 21.2).

Figure 21.2
Close off-set floodlighting

Where the features of the building are mainly vertical ones then close offset floodlighting requires skilful attention to the preservation of the sense of the building's form. Vertical features are best revealed when the light flows across the building from a prominent direction, so that their shape is clearly revealed.

Close offset floodlighting usually requires a large number of low powered floodlights, whereas at a greater offset distance a smaller number of powerful floodlights produces the best result.

The most important characteristic of a floodlight is its intensity distribution, since this determines both its illuminating power and directional control. There are three common forms of intensity distribution for floodlights:

- Symmetrical
- Asymmetrical
- Double asymmetrical

These are illustrated graphically in Figure 21.3 in terms of isocandela lines and a common angular system: H for horizontal angles and V for vertical angles.

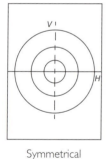
Symmetrical

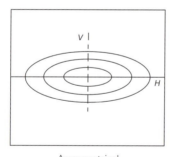
Asymmetrical

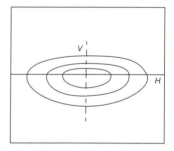
Double asymmetrical

Figure 21.3

Forms of intensity distribution

A particular floodlight will have a basic shape, but a specific angular distribution would be defined by the V and H angles.

A symmetrical distribution would be specified as having, say, a 70° beam angle. This indicates a 35° angle either side of the beam axis (direction of peak intensity) in both the H and V directions.

An asymmetrical distribution would be described by two angles, say 80° horizontal (40° + 40°) and 30° vertical (15° + 15°).

In the case of a double asymmetrical distribution there would be one horizontal angle, say, 90° (45° + 45°) and two vertical angles, one above the peak and the other below, say, 15° above and 40° below (15° + 40°).

A list of typical floodlight data is given below:

Beam angles (from axis to 0.1 peak)
Beam angles (from axis to 0.5 peak)
Cut-off angles (to 0.01 peak)
Beam factor (flux in beam to 0.1 peak/lamp flux)
Peak intensity

An example of another form of floodlight data sheet is given in the sports lighting example in Chapter 22.

The first step in determining the approximate number of floodlights required across the facade of a building is to obtain an estimate of a suitable average illuminance. Table 21.1 gives approximate values of average illuminance for the preliminary design.

Table 21.1 Average illuminances (lux) found satisfactory in practice

$R = \dfrac{M}{E}$	Rural	Suburban	Town centre
0.8	15	25	40
0.6	20	35	60
0.4	30	50	85
0.3	40	65	110
0.2	60	100	170

The values are based upon experience and are related to building reflectance. An estimate of the surface reflectance of a building can be obtained on site by measuring the illuminance of an unobstructed part of the building under overcast daylight, then measuring the reflected illuminance from that surface at a distance close enough for the surface to be considered as an approximation to an infinite area source without the light-meter photocell casting a shadow.

Then

$$\rho = \frac{E\ (\text{reflected})}{E\ (\text{direct})}$$

Example 21.1

Figure 21.4 shows a photograph (a) and a plan view (b) of a church built from the twelfth century onwards which has some very interesting features. These include a very attractive white boarded spire and a west porch that is canted relative to the

Figure 21.4

(a) Church to be floodlit; (b) plan view of the same church

(a)

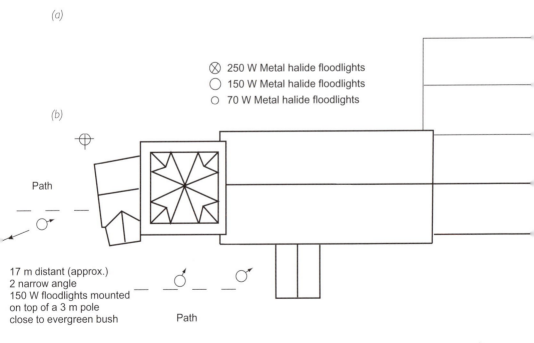

(b)

- ⊗ 250 W Metal halide floodlights
- ⦿ 150 W Metal halide floodlights
- ○ 70 W Metal halide floodlights

Path

Path

17 m distant (approx.)
2 narrow angle
150 W floodlights mounted
on top of a 3 m pole
close to evergreen bush

tower. The porch has an upper floor called the 'priest's chamber' reached by a staircase housed in a projection on the right-hand side of the porch. This church was floodlit as part of the Millennium celebrations. The most important aspects in the design were considered to be the west porch, tower and spire, together with the south side of the church and the clock installed to commemorate the coronation of King George V. It is these aspects that will be considered in this example.

The church is set at one end of a large village high street, with an open aspect to the south side. Metal halide lamps were chosen as the light source because of the range of different materials from which the church is constructed. A value of 40 lux was selected as a target average illuminance from Table 21.1, taking into account the location of the church and the various reflectances from the different building materials. Actual illuminance values will vary considerably at different parts of the building, but setting an average value is always a good starting point.

The total area of the west front and the south side was determined as 554 m². The final lumens required for an average of 40 lux are $40 \times 554 = 22\,160$.

Assume 0.3 as an estimate of utilization factor and maintenance factor.

Lamp flux required $\dfrac{22160}{0.3} = 73\,866$ lumens

Assume lamp efficacy of 80 lm/W = 923 watts required

Detailed consideration is now given to the types of floodlights that will be needed to floodlight such a building efficiently and a mixture of narrow angle and wide angle floodlights is required.

The maintenance factor will apply to all calculations

$MF = LLMF \times LMF$

$= 0.96 \times 0.8$ $LLMF$ (Manufacturer's data, 1000 hours PA)

$= 0.77$ LMF nomogram (upwards facing in clean
                      area, 12 months cleaning; see Figure 22.7)

The plan view of the church (Figure 21.4b) shows an asymmetry to the west porch which could cast distorting shadows on the tower, possibly giving it an odd appearance from a distance. In order to avoid this problem, reduce the number of ground mounted floodlights and simplify the lighting of the spire and upper tower, two narrow angle floodlights are located on a

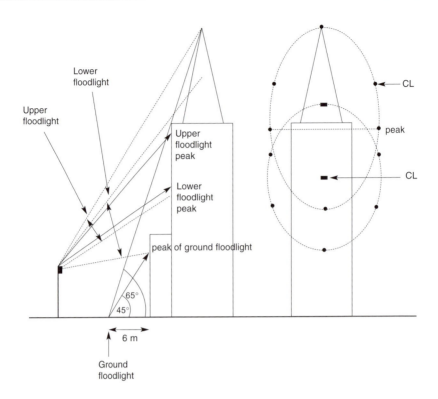

Figure 21.5

Aiming of the floodlights on the west side of the tower

3 m pole about 17 m from the west porch. These are screened by the high bushes shown in Figure 21.4(a). The west porch is lit with a ground mounted, low powered, wide angle double asymmetric floodlight. The top of the south side of the tower is lit by a narrow angle floodlight. The west side of the south porch and adjacent wall, together with the lower part of the south side of the tower are lit with similar low powered flood-lights. The nave and chancel on the east side of the porch are lit by a large wide angle asymmetric floodlight.

Figures 21.5 and 21.6 show the aiming of the floodlights on the west and south sides of the tower. The types of flood-lights and their photometric details are as follows:

Lamp type and size	Beam angles Horiz	Vert		Beam factor	Maximum intensity cd	Lamp lumens
MH 250 W	100°	40°		0.53	18 000	19 000
MH 150 W	23°			0.3	35 200	11 250
		Above peak	Below peak			
MH 70 W	90°	20°	45°	0.55	5180	5500

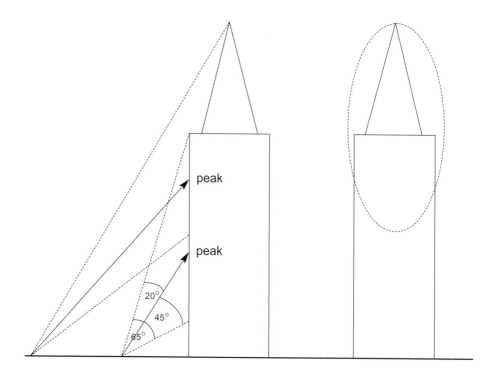

The number of floodlights used will be:

$3 \times 150W = 450\ W$
$3 \times 70W = 210\ W$
$1 \times 250W = \underline{250}\ W$
$\underline{910}$

Calculations

(1) West side:

Pole mounted narrow angle 150W floodlights

Upper floodlight (150W)

Peak intensity illuminance

$$E = \frac{IR}{D^3} \text{ (from Chapter 9)}$$

$$E = \frac{35\ 200 \times 20.5}{(23.5)^3} = 56 \text{ lux (initial)}$$

$56 \times 0.77 = 43$ lux (maintained)

Figure 21.6
Aiming of the floodlights on the south side of the tower

Lower floodlight (150W)
Peak intensity illuminance

$$E = \frac{35\,200 \times 20.5}{(22)^3} = 68 \text{ lux (initial)}$$

$$68 \times 0.77 = 53 \text{ lux (maintained)}$$

Note: each of these floodlights would receive about 10% from the other floodlight at the peak because of overlap.

Ground mounted floodlight (70W)
Peak intensity illuminance

$$E = \frac{5180 \times 5.5}{(8)^3} = 56 \text{ lux (initial)}$$

$$56 \times 0.77 = 43 \text{ lux (maintained)}$$

When floodlighting a building, particularly a church tower and spire, some of the light will usually not fall on the building and will be wasted. An estimate is made of the waste light factor to account for this and to assist in making this estimate an approximate ellipse can be drawn when the distribution of the floodlight is symmetrical.

In Figure 21.5 six points can easily be marked to enable the approximate ellipse to be drawn. The upper floodlight covers the spire and part of the tower and so high precision is not achieved, but it is quite sufficient for the purpose.

Two obvious points are the top and bottom of the ellipse, where the beam strikes the building in the vertical plane. These are projected on to the front elevation. The centre of the ellipse and hence its widest point will be halfway between these two points. The width of the beam can be calculated for the point where the peak intensity is aimed on the building.

West side upper floodlight (150W)

Beam width = 2 × tan 11.5° × distance to building

= 2 × 0.203 × 24

= 9.8 m

This is marked on the front elevation firstly as two points on the line projected from the peak intensity point on the side elevation, which is below the ellipse centre line. The ellipse will have the same width at the same distance above the centre line and so two further points can be inserted. These six outer points can now be used to sketch an approximate ellipse on to the elevation. The waste light factor can now be estimated for this beam and two things are borne in mind in making this estimate:

1   Half the flux is below the peak and so more than half of the flux is aimed at the tower area with little light loss;
2   The illuminance in the beam is strongest at the centre, falling off to a low value at the edges and so the light loss will be less in the upper part of the beam than a comparison of spire area to upper ellipse area would suggest.

Taking these two factors into account, a waste light factor of 0.7 is chosen for this beam. The initial lumens to be taken into account can now be calculated for this floodlight:

$$\begin{aligned} \text{Initial lumens} &= \text{Lamp output} \times \text{Beam factor} \times \\ &\quad \text{Waste light factor} \\ &= 11\,250 \times 0.3 \times 0.7 \\ &= 2363 \text{ lumens (upper floodlight)} \end{aligned}$$

West side lower floodlight (150W)
Another ellipse is drawn in the same way for the lower floodlight and using similar considerations a waste light factor of 0.8 is chosen:

$$\begin{aligned} \text{Initial lumens} &= 11\,250 \times 0.3 \times 0.8 \\ &= 2700 \text{ lumens} \end{aligned}$$

West side ground mounted floodlight (70W)
The horizontal angle of this floodlight is 90°, but it is much closer to the tower and so a waste light factor of 0.7 is chosen.

$$\begin{aligned} \text{Initial lumens} &= 5180 \times 0.55 \times 0.7 \\ &= 1994 \text{ lumens (ground floodlight)} \end{aligned}$$

Total initial lumens from the three floodlights:

$$\begin{aligned} &= 2363 + 2700 + 1994 \\ &= 7057 \text{ lumens} \end{aligned}$$

Area to be lit:

Tower	16×6.5	$= 104 \text{ m}^2$
Spire	$8 \times 5 \div 2$	$= \underline{20 \text{ m}^2}$
		$\underline{124 \text{ m}^2}$

$$\text{Initial } E_{av} = \frac{7057}{124} = 57 \text{ lux} \quad 57 \times 0.77 = 44 \text{ lux (maintained)}$$

(2) South side:

The same procedure is repeated for the south side of the tower (Figure 21.6):

150W floodlight	peak intensity illuminance 91 lux (initial)
	70 lux (maintained)
70W floodlight	peak intensity illuminance 35 lux (initial)
	27 lux (maintained)

$$\text{Initial } E_{av} = \quad 37 \text{ lux}$$
$$29 \text{ lux maintained}$$

South side: between the tower and the south porch
A 70W floodlight similar to that used for the bottom of the tower is used here. There will be very little waste light.

South side: to the east of the porch
A 250W floodlight is directed at an angle to light the side of the porch, the roof of the nave and chancel and the nave and chancel walls (an area of 216 m^2); the waste light factor will be low and is taken as 0.9, with the beam factor is 0.53.

$$\text{Useful lumens} = 19\,000 \times 0.53 \times 0.9 = 9063$$

$$\text{Initial } E_{av} = \frac{9063}{216} = 42 \text{ lux}$$

$$42 \times 0.77 = 32 \text{ lux (maintained)}$$

Peak intensity illuminance

$$E \quad = \frac{18\,000 \times 8}{(12)^3}$$

$$= 83 \text{ lux (initial)}$$

$$83 \times 0.77 = 64 \text{ lux (maintained)}$$

The eaves are at about 5.5 m and aiming the floodlight at an angle just above the eaves would adequately light the walls and put sufficient light on to the roof to avoid any disembodiment of the structure.

Figure 21.7 shows the completed scheme at night.

Figure 21.7

The completed scheme at night (Courtesy of St Nicholas' Church, Great Wakering, Essex)

Some public buildings, including some classically designed churches, have pillared porticos. These can be difficult to light in a major town centre, where the problem of the siting of the floodlights can arise. A commonly adopted solution is to light the building surface behind pillars, so that these are then seen in silhouette. The floodlights can then be mounted behind the pillars.

Statues or similar features require special consideration, if they are intended to stand out from their surroundings. In general a statue requires a higher illuminance level than that used for floodlighting a building in the same area. The lighting level for a statue could be three times that of the floodlit building and even more in some circumstances. If the statue is of stone or a light material the direct illuminance is usually the appropriate form of lighting. However, statues of very dark material are better seen in silhouette against an illuminated background. A very simple, but useful, form of photometric data for lighting small areas, such as statues, is the cone diagram, an example of which is shown in Figure 21.8. If the maximum intensity of the floodlight is known then the maximum illuminance can also be calculated.

Statues, in particular, can benefit from using lamps of different colour from two opposing directions, but such a scheme should be subjected to a trial prior to permanent

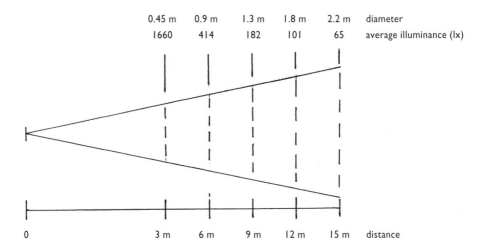

| 0.45 m | 0.9 m | 1.3 m | 1.8 m | 2.2 m | diameter |
| 1660 | 414 | 182 | 101 | 65 | average illuminance (lx) |

| 0 | 3 m | 6 m | 9 m | 12 m | 15 m | distance |

Figure 21.8

Cone diagram of illuminances

installation. In fact, it is well worthwhile undertaking a trial of some part of any floodlighting scheme before full installation to check its suitability, particularly with regard to the colour of the light source.

A practical challenge to the floodlighting art is to light a fountain. The basic technique is to pass the light through the water rather than to use it as a reflector. When light is passed through moving water it is re-distributed by diffusion and scattering and it can be one of the most interesting of decorative night-time scenes. This often requires waterproof submerged lighting just below the surface of the fountain.

Outdoor sports lighting

The term 'floodlighting' applies more obviously to many outdoor sports situations than to illuminating buildings or statues to reveal their architectural or artistic merit.

Sports fields for football, rugby, hockey etc. all require the whole area to be flooded with light. Night-time lighting of major sporting venues has become a very important lighting application with the advent of the television reporting of sport and its huge financial implications. The challenge to the lighting designer is to provide the appropriate light distribution and lighting level without causing excessive glare for spectators, as economically as possible in terms of capital costs, running costs and maintenance.

In a sporting activity the two major consideration are:

1 the ability of the players to see well enough to perform to a high standard, and
2 the ability of the spectators, both at the match and at home via television, to follow easily and enjoy the match.

In the majority of sports the illumination of the vertical plane is as important as the horizontal plane. It is also very important for the volume of space above the pitch to be illuminated, so that there is no possibility of a high travelling ball, etc. being lost to view by passing above the illuminated zone.

The most effective way of lighting a large area is to mount the floodlights as high as possible, so that the light spreads as far as possible over the ground. This also reduces the problem of glare for players and spectators alike. For this reason many of the largest stadia are lit from beyond the four corners of the playing area from high towers with large arrays of floodlights (Figure 22.1).

The floodlighting towers are placed well beyond the touchlines to ensure that the angle of incidence of the light is such as to give a good lighting level on the vertical plane, as

Figure 22.1

A large stadium lit from four corners

well as on the horizontal plane. The use of four towers also minimizes the number of directions in which floodlights come into the view of the players as they twist and turn on the pitch. Where high towers sited well away from the pitch are not a practical proposition, side floodlighting from floodlights mounted on or above the stands at right angles to the direction of play is often used. It is more difficult to achieve the required uniformity with this system and it gives more glare for the spectators. Some designers favour a continuous row of flood-lights from one end of the stand to the other on each side of the pitch. Interestingly, as the lighting levels have been greatly increased to accommodate colour television the raised adapta-tion level produced tends to mitigate against glare. In addition, in recent times spectator stands at major clubs have increased in height so much that both achieving good uniformity with

Figure 22.2

Continuous row of floodlights at right angles to the line of play

acceptable glare levels with stand mounted floodlights has become easier (Figure 22.2).

Amateur club pitches are given much simpler treatment because of cost. Floodlights mounted on poles are usually placed at appropriate intervals in the direction of play and well beyond the touchline, so that there is no possibility of play spilling off the pitch and causing a player to collide with a post.

A major scheme will have lighting calculations carried out by computer and previous scheme data will give a starting point. The calculations for outdoor areas are based on the use of point sources and so the detailed calculations are based on the point source formula. Initial estimates are often based on assuming a utilization factor of, say, 0.25 to 0.3 and then from this choosing the appropriate lamp size for the initial calculations. The absence of interreflections makes outdoor calculations simpler.

For simple installations, with few floodlights, a manufacturer's data sheet is available which allows both the utilization factor to be determined and some point by point calculations to be carried out. A scheme for a practice area is given in Figure 22.3 to illustrate its use. The data sheet is shown in Figure 22.4

Figure 22.3

A practice area lit by four floodlights

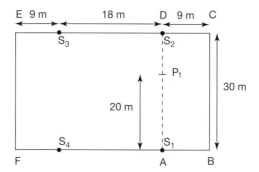

Figure 22.4

Floodlight data sheet

Areaflood 40

Description General area floodlight for stirrup mounting
Luminaire maintenance category IP65

Catalogue number	Lamp	Data code
AFBS250.T	1 x 250W SONXL-T	R0018740

Beam data

Peak intensity (I) cd/kdm		1110
Beam factor to 10% peak (I)		0.74
Beam angle to 10% of peak (I)	Horizontal	2 x 50°
	Vertical	36°/66°
Beam angle to 50% of peak (I)	Horizontal	2 x 39°
	Vertical	7°/13°
Beam angle to 1% of peak (I)	Horizontal	2 x 67°
	Vertical	49°/89°

θ = 21°

Isocandela and zonal flux diagram

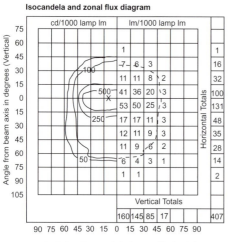

Intensity curve in cd/1000 lm

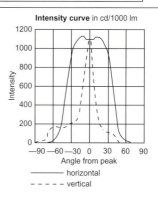

X-indicates the position of peak intensity. The pecked line shows 10% peak contour. The direction of the peak intensity in the vertical plane is 21 degrees above the normal to the front face of the floodlight.

In this data sheet two diagrams are combined. One is an isocandela intensity diagram while the other is a flux diagram. One half of each diagram is shown because they are symmetrical about the vertical axis. The vertical and horizontal angles are measured from the beam axis of the floodlight at 0,0. The angles must be calculated for individual floodlights, as indicated in Figure 22.5, to enter the diagrams.

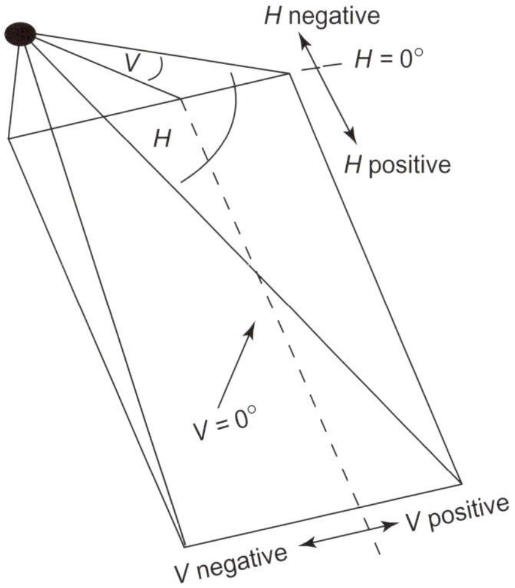

Example 22.1

Figure 22.5

Angles required to enter data sheet diagrams

It will be seen from the diagram that the vertical angles relate to planes, while the horizontal angles are angles on those planes. As will be seen, a *V* angle relates to planes above and below the peak; that is positive and negative angles on this diagram. The *H* angles are shown as positive to the right-hand side of the floodlight and negative to the left-hand side. The number in each square on the flux diagram relates to the lumens represented by that square per 1000 lamp lumens.

See Figures 22.3, 22.4 and 22.5.

The 250W SON floodlights are on 10 m poles. The floodlights at the top of the poles are marked S_1, S_2, S_3, S_4 and the relevant points on the ground A, B, C, D, E, F, P_1.

Since four similar floodlights are specified only one set of calculations is required because of symmetry. In the first instance the peak intensity is often directed to a point two-thirds of the distance across the area, marked P_1 and this relates to the peak intensity of floodlight S_1. There will be similar positions for the peak intensity directions relating to the other floodlights.

The first stage is to plot the outline of the right-hand side of the area onto the flux diagram which is done by calculating V angles in the direction of the line AD and H angles for the directions AB and DC.

The positive value for V is obtained by subtracting the angle from S_1 to P_1 (a negative or below the peak V angle) from the angle from S_1 to D.

$$\text{Angle } AS_1D = \tan^{-1} \frac{AD}{AS_1} = \tan^{-1} \frac{30}{10} = 71.6°$$

$$\text{Angle } AS_1P = \tan^{-1} \frac{AP_1}{AS_1} = \tan^{-1} \frac{20}{10} = 63.4°$$

the above the peak angle P_1S_1D = 71.6 - 63.4

8.16°

and the below the peak angle is 63.4°

For the right-hand side of the diagram both values of H are positive.

$$\text{Angle } AS_1B = \tan^{-1} \frac{AB}{AS_1} = \tan^{-1} \frac{9}{10} = 42°$$

$$\text{Angle } D\,S_1\,C = \tan^{-1} \frac{DC}{S_1D} = \tan^{-1} \frac{9}{\sqrt{10^2 + 30^2}} = 15.9°$$

The outline of the area relating to these angles is shown by the solid lines on the flux diagram in Figure 22.6.

From this figure the flux per 1000 lamp lumens to the right of the floodlight S_1 is obtained by summing across the squares horizontally, estimating where a whole square is not covered.

23 + 4 =	27
53 + 25 =	78
17 + 14 =	31
12 + 11 + 2 =	25
11 + 9 + 4 =	24
1 + 1 + 1 =	3
Total	188 lumens per 1000 lamp lumens

It is now necessary to calculate only the negative H values because the V values apply to both left- and right-hand sides of the floodlight.

The required angles are AS_1F and DS_1E:

$$\text{Angle } AS_1F = \tan^{-1} \frac{AF}{AS_1} = \tan^{-1} \frac{27}{10} = 69.7°$$

Areaflood 40

Description General area floodlight for stirrup mounting
Luminaire maintenance category IP65

Catalogue number	Lamp	Data code
AFBS250.T	1 x 250W SONXL-T	R0018740

Beam data

Peak intensity (I) cd/kdm		1110
Beam factor to 10% peak (I)		0.74
Beam angle to 10% of peak (I)	Horizontal	2 x 50°
	Vertical	36°/66°
Beam angle to 50% of peak (I)	Horizontal	2 x 39°
	Vertical	7°/13°
Beam angle to 1% of peak (I)	Horizontal	2 x 67°
	Vertical	49°/89°

$\theta = 21°$

Isocandela and zonal flux diagram

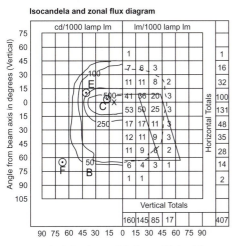

Intensity curve in cd/1000 lm

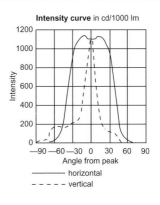

X-indicates the position of peak intensity. The pecked line shows 10% peak contour. The direction of the peak intensity in the vertical plane is 21 degrees above the normal to the front face of the floodlight.

$$\text{Angle } DS_IE = \tan^{-1}\frac{DE}{S_ID} = \tan^{-1}\frac{27}{\sqrt{10^2 + 30^2}} = 40.5°$$

Figure 22.6
Outline of the areas plotted on the flux diagram

The correct result will be obtained if the left-hand side or negative *H* angles are plotted on the positive side of the diagram because of the symmetry of the floodlight distribution.

The outline for the left-hand side angles is shown by the dotted line. The flux per 1000 lamp lumens is obtained by a similar summation as before:

$$23 + 20 + 11 = 44$$
$$53 + 50 + 25 + 1 = 129$$
$$17 + 17 + 11 + 2 = 47$$
$$12 + 11 + 9 + 2.5 = 34$$
$$11 + 9 + 6 + 2 = 28$$
$$1 + 1 + 1 = 3$$

Total   285 lumens per 1000 lamp lumens

Adding together the left- and right-hand side values gives 188 + 285 = 473 lumens per 1000 lamp lumens. The utilization factor is therefore 473/1000 = 0.473. The same value of UF can be applied to each of the floodlights because of the symmetry. If they were not placed symmetrically the lumens per 1000 lamp lumens for each floodlight would have to be calculated, the four values added together and divided by 4000 to obtain the overall UF.

We need the value of the maintenance factor to complete the average illuminance calculation:

$MF = LLMF \times LMF$ LLMF manufacturer's value for 8000 h

$= 0.9 \times 0.82$ LMF from nomogram (Figure 22.7)

$= 0.66$ ('fairly clean', 18 months cleaning)

$$E_{av} = \frac{F_L \times 4 \times UF \times MF}{A}$$

$$= \frac{27500 \times 4 \times 0.473 \times 0.66}{30 \times 36}$$

$$= 32 \text{ lux}$$

It is now necessary to determine the uniformity that is E_{min}/E_{av}. The minimum value can be expected to occur at the four corners of the training area. If the illuminance values at the four corners for one luminaire are calculated and added together this would be the value for the four luminaires because of the symmetry.

The angles to the corners are already known from the previous calculations and so if these values are plotted on the isocandela diagram the intensity per 1000 lumens can be obtained. These are shown on Figure 22.6.

The estimated values are:

$C = 500$ cd/klm
$E = 248$ cd/klm
$F = 0$ cd/klm
$B = 60$ cd/klm

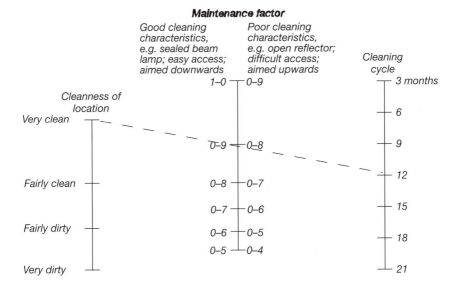

Figure 22.7
Maintenance factor
nomogram

The point source formula is used in the form:

$$E = \frac{I \cos^3\theta}{H^2}$$ H is the mounting height of the floodlight.

The calculation of the angle θ is the same as the horizontal angle for points B and F, but the values for points E and C require additional calculation. So, angle $AS_1 B = 42°$ and angle $A S_1 F = 69.7$.

$$\text{Angle } AS_1 C = \tan^{-1}\frac{AC}{AS_1} = \tan^{-1}\sqrt{\frac{9^2 + 30^2}{10}} = 72.3°$$

$$\text{Angle } A S_1 E = \tan^{-1}\frac{AE}{AS_1} = \tan^{-1}\sqrt{\frac{27^2 + 30^2}{10}} = 76°$$

For the four required values $E =$

$$\frac{(500\cos^3 72.3° + 248\cos^3 76° + 60\cos^3 42°) \times 27.5 \times 0.66}{100}$$

$$= (14 + 3.5 + 24.6) \times 27.5 \times 0.66/100$$

$$= 7.6 \text{ lux}$$

Uniformity $\dfrac{E_{min}}{E_{av}} = \dfrac{7.6}{32} = 0.24$

Another common sports area is a tennis court and three possible arrangements are shown in Figure 22.8. The double court has two floodlights per column; one narrow angle to light the area of the court opposite, but further from the pole, and one

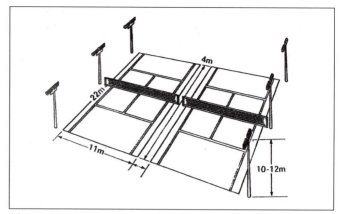

(a)

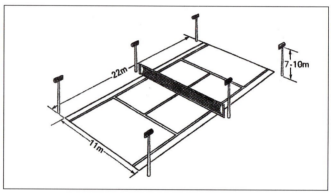

(b)

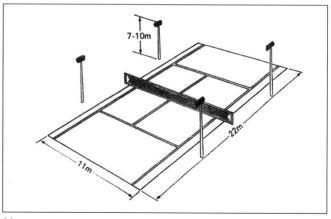

(c)

wide angle to light the area closest to the pole. In this way light from each side illuminates both the players and the balls as they are played. It is always important to ensure that players will not collide with the floodlight columns during play and, where three columns per side are used the middle one is sited conveniently opposite the end of the net. Illuminances for various levels of play are given in Table 22.1.

Table 22.1   Illuminances for various levels of play

	Level	E (lux) (horizontal)
Football	FA Amateur	120
	FA Conference	250
	Football League	350–500
	Premier League	800
Tennis LTA	Recreational	300
	Club	400
	Country	500

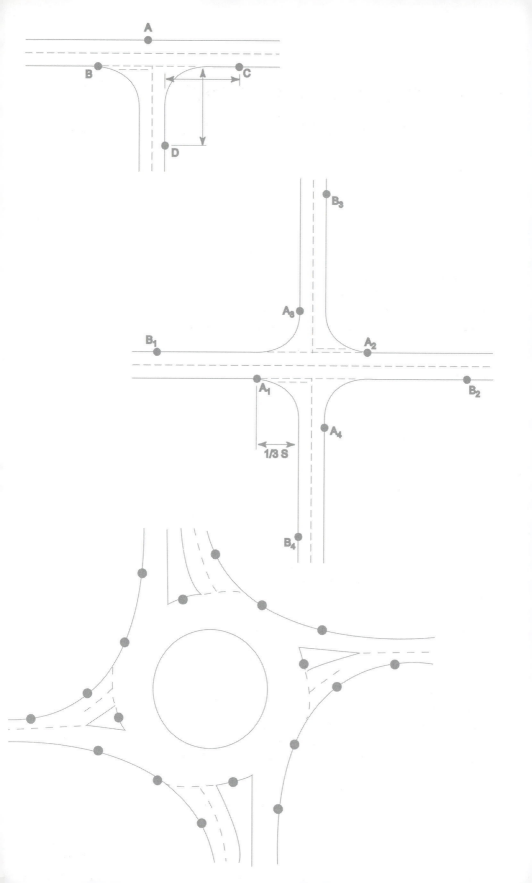

Motorway and high speed road lighting

The main economic justification for road lighting has been the reduction in road accidents. However, other factors such as the improvement of a town centre or the reduction in crime often come into consideration. The arguments for not providing lighting are often based on the obtrusiveness of such lighting in quiet rural areas, the need to conserve energy, the problem of sky glow and the cost.

There is a significant difference in the design approach for roads used by high speed traffic and those used by low speed traffic and pedestrians. A driver of a high speed vehicle must scan the road 60–100 m ahead to detect a hazard, decide what to do and take action in the time available. In low speed and pedestrian areas the viewing distance is much closer and the lighting is required to perform other functions than simply detecting hazards to be avoided by drivers. Since the two approaches are so different there will be intermediate situations where the two approaches come together and where special care must be taken.

The two approaches are respectively to design for a certain level of road luminance, as perceived by the driver of a vehicle travelling at high speed, or to design for a certain illuminance level on the road.

The luminance design approach was developed from the observation by J. M. Waldram in the 1930s that when a driver is viewing at distances of 60–100 m at those small angles from the horizontal the road surface reflectance towards the driver is high and produces a bright road surface due to light from distant luminaires. This luminance has far greater effect than the direct illuminance on the vehicles and so the vehicles are seen in silhouette. This fact can be easily established by driving along a long road which is lit and observing distant vehicles. Therefore, where lighting is provided on motorways and high-speed roads it is designed to provide a specified average road luminance towards the driver with a stipulated uniformity.

Luminance design is based on the perspective view of the road seen by the driver. The luminance distribution on the road in the direction of the driver is dictated by variation with the angle of view of the road surface reflectance, as much as with the light distribution of the luminaire. So, in effect, the luminaire and the road surface in use are one lighting system and must be considered together.

Unlike interior lighting, exterior lighting and particularly road lighting does not generally involve the consideration of interreflection. Therefore, the standard calculations to establish the appropriateness of a particular installation are based on the formula for point light sources. The large number of calculations required are conveniently carried out by means of an appropriate computer program. However, to indicate the sort of calculation required a calculation for a single point on a road is developed below (Figure 23.1).

Figure 23.1

Relationship in terms of angles for the luminaire, the illuminated point and the observer

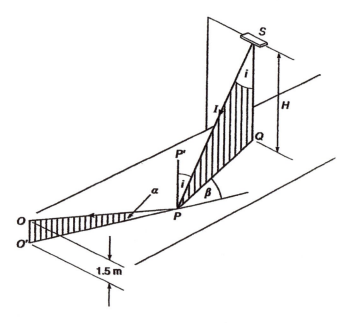

In Chapter 9 various forms of the point source formula are given. Since the mounting height of the road lighting luminaires is usually constant the cos³ version of the formula is used. At any point on the road

$$E = \frac{I\cos^3 i}{H^2}$$

where *I* is the intensity in the direction of the illuminated point, *i* is the angle of incidence on the road and *i* is also the angle of the emergent ray to the downward vertical of the luminaire which equals γ (on the C,γ system), when the luminaire is mounted at the angle for which the photometric data was obtained. H is the mounting height of the luminaire.

When the light strikes the road surface it will usually be scattered in many directions and the luminance seen by the driver will depend on how it is scattered by the particular road surface being used.

Samples of road surfaces are tested to obtain the ratio of road luminance to road illuminance at every relevant point on the road and for every relevant direction. This gives values of $L/E = q$ for the road surface in question. The formula can then be written in terms of luminance:

$$L = \frac{qI\cos^3 i}{H^2}$$

where q is called the luminance coefficient.

The calculation is further simplified by combining q and $\cos^3 i$, since a particular value of q will have an associated value of i. (Note q also depends on another angle, β; see Figure 23.1.)

So,

$$q \cos^3 i = r$$

where r is called the reduced luminance coefficient.

The final form of the formula becomes

$$L = r\frac{I}{H^2}$$

To calculate L, r is looked up in an r table, for the particular road surface in terms of i and β. I is looked up in an I table in terms of C and γ (related to i). The data for I is usually given in cd/1000 lamp lumens (Figure 23.2). For the example we will assume that the C plane is at 5° and γ is 45°. The horizontal angle on the road towards the observer is 10° and i is taken as the same as γ, that is, 45°. From the I table the intensity per 1000 lumens at $C = 5°$, $\gamma = 45°$ is 280.

To enter the r table we need tan i which in this case is 1.0, $\beta = 10°$

$$r = 354 \times 10^{-4}$$

$$L = r\frac{I}{H^2}$$

Assume that the mounting height H is 10 m and a 150W HPS lamp giving 14.5 klm.

So,

γ (deg)	Azimuth C (deg)						
	0.0	5.0	10.0	15.0	20.0	25.0	30.0
0.0	218	218	218	218	218	218	218
10.0	224	225	226	227	227	226	226
20.0	257	260	261	258	254	249	242
30.0	299	305	304	298	286	272	256
35.0	311	317	315	306	292	273	25?
40.0	297	304	303	294	277	256	23
45.0	275	280	278	267	249	227	2
47.5	277	283	279	265	242	217	
50.0	276	282	278	263	239	213	
52.5	274	282	279	263	238	211	
55.0	274	283	281	265	240	212	
57.5	268	278	275	259	234	206	
60.0	265	275	273	257	231	20	
62.5	261	271	270	253	228		
65.0	257	268	266	249	225		
67.5	247	257	255	240	216		
70.0	229	240	240	225	2		
72.5	204	218	219	207			
75.0	136	153	163	164			
77.5	77	87	91				
80.0	47	54	5O				
	26	31					

(a)

tan i	β (deg)							
	0	2	5	10	15	20	25	30
0.00	329	329	329	329	329	329	329	329
0.25	362	358	371	364	371	369	362	3
0.50	379	368	375	373	367	359	350	
0.75	380	375	378	365	351	334	31	
1.00	372	375	372	354	315	277		
1.25	375	373	352	318	265	221		
1.5	354	352	336	271	213	1		
1.75	333	327	302	222	166			
2.00	318	310	266	180	1			
2.50	268	262	205	119				
3.00	227	217	147					
3.50	194	168	1					
4.00	168	1						
4.5O								

(b)

Figure 23.2
(a) The I table (part);
(b) the r table (part)
(values are r × 10⁴)

$$L = \frac{354 \times 10^{-4} \times 280 \times 14.5}{10^2}$$

$$= 1.4 \text{ cd/m}^2$$

Obviously an array of such calculations is required to establish that the installation meets the stipulated requirements of the British Standard (BS 5849). Figure 23.3 shows a typical field of calculation.

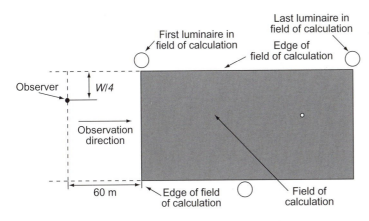

Figure 23.3
A typical field of calculation

Since the reflectance of the road in the direction of the observer depends on the position of the observer, this must be specified, and the convention is to take this position to be 60 m in front of the first luminaire in the field of calculation. As shown in Figure 23.3, the observer is assumed to be in the centre of the carriageway; that is one-quarter of the width of a two-direction road, at a height that subtends an angle of 0.5° to 1.50° at the point on the road under consideration.

The British Standard requires the following quantities to meet specified criteria:

Average luminance (L_{av})
Overall uniformity of luminance (U_o)
Longitudinal uniformity of luminance (U_L) (calculated for the centre of each lane as L_{min}/L_{max})
Threshold increment (TI). This is the measure of the disability glare caused by the luminaires

An expression for TI has been developed based on a standard curve of human contrast sensitivity and the age of the observer (assumed to be between 20 and 30 years old).

The formula is

$$TI = \frac{650 \times E_{vert} \times MF^{0.8}}{L_{av}^{0.8} \times \theta^2}$$

E_{vert} is the total illuminance in lux based on initial lamp lumens produced by new luminaires on a plane at the observer's eye normal to the line of sight. θ is the angle in degrees between the line of sight and the centre of each luminaire. MF is the maintenance factor and it is included to adjust L_{av} to its value when the installation is new, since this is the condition for which E_{vert} is calculated and which is when the lamps give their greatest output, so the value of TI is highest.

From the formula it will be seen that increases in the direct vertical illuminance from the luminaires is assumed to increase the disability glare and that, for a given value of E_{vert}, increases in $L_{av,}$ the background luminance, are assumed to reduce the disability glare.

Luminaire spacing and the layout of luminaires

The characteristic patch of light seen from the position of the observer if only one luminaire is alight would be roughly T-shaped (Figure 23.4). This is because light from the area of the road directly below the luminaire is diffusely scattered and this

Figure 23.4

(a) The patch from a single luminaire; (b) patches from a staggered arrangement; (c) the same installation when the road is wet; (d) patches for a single-sided arrangement on a bend

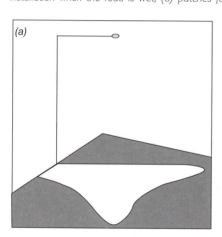

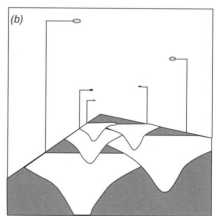

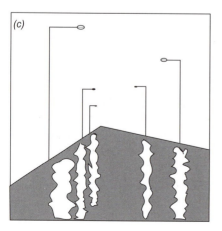

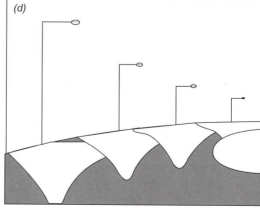

diffuse component is seen by the observer. Light from the luminaire that travels towards the observer at a high angle from the luminaire undergoes a more specular form of reflection and, in effect, produces a series of distorted images of the luminaire on the road surface towards the observer. This second effect produces the tail of the T. When the road is wet the diffuse reflection under the luminaire tends to be suppressed and the specular component sharpened to give a very narrow tail and a little head to the T; that is, the images appear as streaks.

The magnitude of all these effects depends on the type of road surface in use. Porous road finishes have been developed which can greatly improve the wet weather performance of installations.

The aim of the installation designer is to merge the T-shaped patches so that a uniform road luminance is achieved. For straight sections of road the computer program's calculation of the specified parameters ensures that this is achieved. However, when the road has a significant bend (radius less than 80 times the mounting height of the luminaires) a particular form of layout is favoured.

From the foregoing description of the T-shaped patch it will be appreciated that as the observer's position moves around a bend, as far as the patch tails are concerned, only the patch tails of luminaires toward which they are moving will be fully effective in helping to produce a bright carriageway and especially in wet weather. Therefore, the aim is to have the luminaires so placed that as the driver travels around the bend he is facing towards as many of the lanterns as possible. To this end, all the luminaires tend to be mounted on the outside of the bend.

If lanterns are mounted on the inside of the bend the tail of the T will not be towards the driver, but across the line of sight and so will not be very effective.

Special isoluminance templates for the luminaire and road surface in use are drawn to enable designers to ensure a suitable spacing for the luminaires on the outside of the bend.

Lighting arrangements on straight roads

Figure 23.5 shows typical luminaire layouts for straight roads in the UK. They are: (a) single sided; (b) staggered; (c) opposite; (d) twin central; (e) opposite for a dual carriageway. The most commonly used arrangement for lighting on straight roads is the staggered arrangement because it is economic and, provided that the road is not too wide, it can be designed to meet the relevant criteria. A single-sided arrangement can work on narrow roads or where there is an electricity supply

Figure 23.5

Luminaire arrangement on straight roads: (a) singled sided; (b) staggered; (c) opposite; (d) twin central; (e) opposite for a dual carriageway

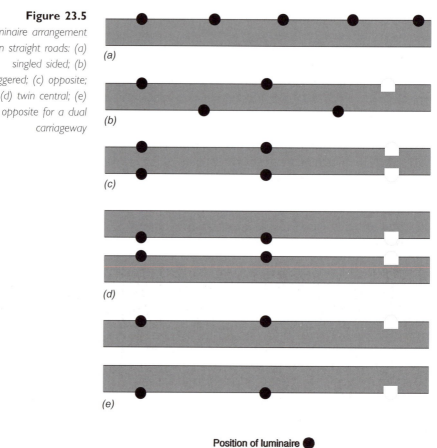

Figure 23.5

Luminaire arrangement on straight roads: (a) singled sided; (b) staggered; (c) opposite; (d) twin central; (e) opposite for a dual carriageway

Position of luminaire ●

problem, but it is more difficult to produce a suitable uniformity. Wide roads usually require an opposite arrangement of the luminaires.

Twin central mounting is common on roads with a suitable central reservation, since this gives savings in columns and electricity supply. However, it introduces the problem of difficult maintenance, since access usually requires the closure of traffic lanes. Opposite mounting on such roads is expensive, but it usually simplifies maintenance.

Mounting height

The range of mounting heights given below has been found to be satisfactory in practice. The actual mounting height chosen must take into account a number of considerations, such as the need to meet the requirements of the appropriate lighting class, the daytime appearance and the scale of any surrounding buildings.

Typical mounting heights would be:

5/6 m   Residential and subsidiary roads
8/10/12 m   Traffic routes
12/15 m   High speed dual carriageways and
               motorways

Column and luminaire assemblies 18 m or more high would constitute high mast lighting. There the intention is to light more than one road and its adjacent area from one or more columns, using a group of luminaires giving a widespread distribution (Figure 23.6).

This approach is often used at complex junctions to avoid an excessive and confusing number of lighting columns and luminaires.

Figure 23.6

High mast lighting to light more than one road and its adjacent area from a group of luminaires

A junction where two or more streams of traffic meet is an example of what is termed a 'conflict area'. It is a place where extra care is needed to ensure that drivers correctly interpret the situation ahead of them and are able to respond to it.

The lighting of junctions and roundabouts

Where two major roads meet in this way traffic signs, traffic islands and traffic lights are employed to ensure that traffic behaves in an orderly way and that drivers are given the infor-

The T junction

Figure 23.7

*Lighting layout when a
side road meets a
major road at a T
junction*

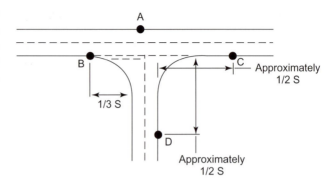

mation that they need to proceed safely. The street lighting, where it is provided, has an important role to play, but it is not the primary source of information. However, when side roads meet major roads at a T junction the layout indicated in Figure 23.7 is used wherever possible. The figure shows the suggested arrangement of the lighting columns and associated luminaires for such a junction.

Figure 23.8

*Side roads forming a
cross roads at a major
road*

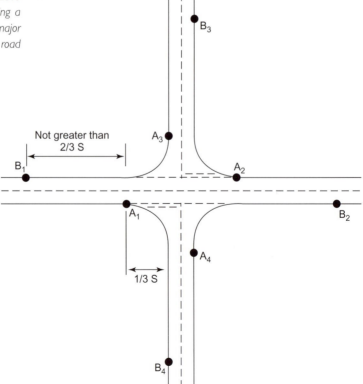

A lighting column and luminaire is placed on the major road directly opposite the nearside lane of the minor road. This in intended to indicate clearly to drivers on the minor road that the junction is being approached. A further luminaire is placed just beyond the junction on the same side as the junction to reveal the kerb of the side road to a driver on the major road. The luminaire situated on the same side, before the junction is reached, is placed at a greater distance from the junction, so that it does not mitigate the revealing effect of the other luminaire by overlighting the kerb riser. Similarly, the luminaire on the side road closest to the junction is kept at a distance that again stops it mitigating the revealing effect of the main road luminaire which is beyond the junction. At cross-roads similar arrangements apply, but of necessity the lanterns indicating the approaching junction are omitted (Figure 23.8).

Roundabouts

At one time roundabouts were treated in a similar manner to T junctions and a luminaire was placed on the central island opposite the nearside lane of the entry roads. However, this is no longer the practice because of frequent collisions with those lighting columns by cars travelling too fast. Obviously, when such a mistake is made the unobstructed width of the traffic island gives the driver a better chance of stopping safely.

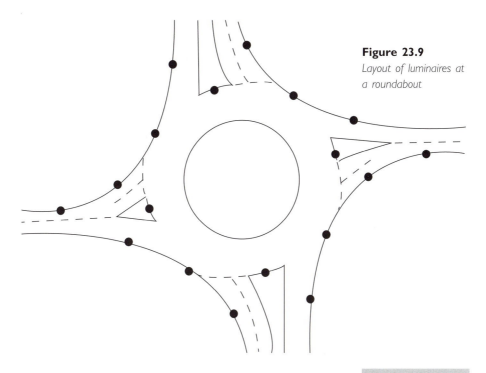

Figure 23.9

Layout of luminaires at a roundabout

The lighting for roundabouts consists of placing a ring of luminaires on the outside of the roundabout and placing them clearly to reveal the kerbs and the emerging traffic entering the roundabout (Figure 23.9).

The British Standard 5489 gives detailed guidance on these and more complicated conflict situations.

Two other matters are worthy of mention. One is the lighting of the sides of the roads just off the carriageways, so that anything that might come onto the carriageway from the side, particularly pedestrians, can be seen. The other is the lighting of pedestrian crossings.

The lighting of verges and areas adjacent to the roadway is dealt with either by providing a suitable value of surround ratio, or by applying one of the lighting classes associated with pedestrian or cyclist activity, etc.

The surround ratio relates the illuminance which falls on the road surround or verge to that on the edge of the carriageway itself, adjacent to the verge.

The illuminances are measured along 5 m wide strips of the roadside and the carriageway. The ratio is given by:

$$\frac{\text{Illuminance on the verge}}{\text{Illuminance on the road}}$$

The specified value of this ratio is usually 0.5.

When a pedestrian crossing is provided on a section of the road away from a junction, it is found best to place it midway between two luminaire positions with the luminaire on the nearside being beyond the crossing, so that people stepping onto the crossing are seen in silhouette against the bright road surface.

Where the crossing is close to a junction or where it is considered advisable, the crossing should be specially lit to a higher illuminance level by lights of suitable design mounted on poles, one at either side of the crossing. These poles would be lower than the normal street lighting columns and the lights would be shielded, so as to avoid glare to both pedestrians and drivers.

Table 23.1 gives a typical extract from the tables relating to luminance design in the British Standards.

At the present time a revised BS 5489 is in draft form. The principles of the design given in the present Standard are certain to be retained, but for residential and similar areas greater emphasis is likely to be given to vertical illuminance. The recommended luminance values for motorways and high speed roads are likely to show little change, although there will be some additional classes introduced, including those for wet roads.

Table 23.1 Typical extract from table relating to luminance design in the British Standard

Criteria	Motorways	High speed roads	Important traffic routes	Minor traffic routes
Average luminance (L_{av} cd/m^2)	2.0	1.5	1.0	0.5
Overall uniformity (U_o)	0.4	0.4	0.4	0.4
Longitudinal uniformity (U_e)	0.7	0.7	0.5	0.5
Threshold increment ($TI\%$)	10	15	30 or 15	30 or 15
Surround ratio (SR)	0.5	0.5	0.5	0.5

Source: BS 5489 Part 2 Table 1, Part 3 Table 1, Part 10 Table 1

There seems to be no provision for the use of manufacturer's design tables. This is only to be expected, since all significant designs would be produced with the aid of computer calculations.

For example 23.1 see overleaf.

Example 23. 1

Lighting of traffic tunnels

The lighting of roads at night is to a far lower value of luminance or illuminance than that obtained in daylight hours and traffic tunnels usually need lighting during the day as well as at night. So it is that the major problem with tunnel lighting is the level of lighting required during the day, when the driver may be travelling towards the tunnel at high speed and viewing a brightly lit road and tunnel surround before entering the tunnel itself and must then adapt to the tunnel luminance. As the driver begins to enter the tunnel they begin to adapt to the lower luminance level within the tunnel. In order that the driver may enter the tunnel safely they must be able to detect vehicles already within the tunnel and to do this the luminance within the tunnel entrance must be related to the luminance of the tunnel surround. This can be calculated approximately or measured and the lighting system within the tunnel designed to ensure safe visual conditions.

As an aid to design of tunnel lighting, a five zone approach to the problem has been adopted in the British Standard (Figure 23.10)

First, the **access zone** stretches from the tunnel portal back to the stopping distance of the vehicle from the tunnel entrance. This distance depends on the speed of the vehicle

street example
1

Page 1

OPTILUME Street and Amenity V3.21 © 2001 Thorn Lighting Limited

main traffic road

Scheme Geometry

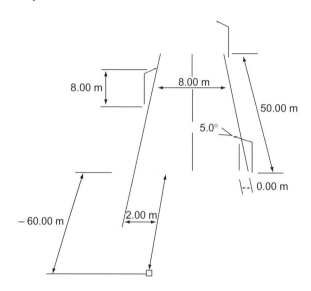

Luminaire details

Left row	QA8HNB1150.4 + QA8DHP0	Alpha Eight
(R = 0.00) (Rot. = 180.0)	LTI Road lighting lantern	
(S = 25.00) (Tilt = 5.0)	150 W HPS-T(HO)	17.50 (klm)
(H = 8.0)	Overall Maintenance Factor	0.89

Right row	QA8HNB1150.4 + QA8DHP0	Alpha Eight
(R = 8.00) (Rot. = 0.0)	LTI Road lighting lantern	
(S = 0.00) (Tilt = 5.0)	150 W HPS-T(HO)	17.50 (klm)
(H = 8.0)	Overall Maintenance Factor	0.89

Road Surface details
CII = Standard British Blacktop
Q0 = 0.070

Results

BS 5489 part 2 Grid

Grid start: R-Coord/Up	0.40	*Surface Name*
Grid start: S-Coord/Along	0.00	Main road
Grid end: R-Coord/Up	7.60	
Grid end: S-Coord/Along	45.00	

Average luminance (cd/m²)	1.83
Overall Uniformity	0.53
Longitudinal Uniformity	0.55
Threshold Increment (%)	14.43
Surround Ratio	0.65

street example 1

Page 2

OPTILUME Street and Amenity V3.21 © 2001 Thorn Lighting Limited

main traffic road

Grid Values

Luminance: BS 5489 part 2 Grid

S (m)	0.0	5.0	10.0	15.0	20.0	25.0	30.0	35.0	40.0	45.0
R (m)										
0.40	1.66	2.05	2.36	2.67	2.37	1.68	1.62	1.27	1.20	1.31
1.20	1.00	2.00	2.29	2.67	2.42	1.73	1.69	1.40	1.36	1.47
2.00	1.69	1.90	2.09	2.55	2.35	1.83	1.76	1.42	1.40	1.42
2.80	1.61	1.74	1.83	2.20	2.14	1.79	1.71	1.52	1.53	1.51
3.60	1.59	1.65	1.68	1.93	1.91	1.81	1.72	1.65	1.73	1.65
4.40	1.73	1.69	1.61	1.73	1.73	1.84	1.87	1.89	2.05	1.92
5.20	1.76	1.69	1.60	1.71	1.66	1.90	2.02	2.07	2.36	2.19
6.00	1.77	1.66	1.48	1.50	1.62	2.09	2.17	2.31	2.67	2.35
6.80	1.62	1.54	1.32	1.28	1.41	1.86	2.18	2.46	2.76	2.42
7.60	1.54	1.44	1.06	0.97	1.08	1.46	2.00	2.31	2.62	2.35

Example 23.1

Figure 23.10
The five zones relating to tunnel lighting

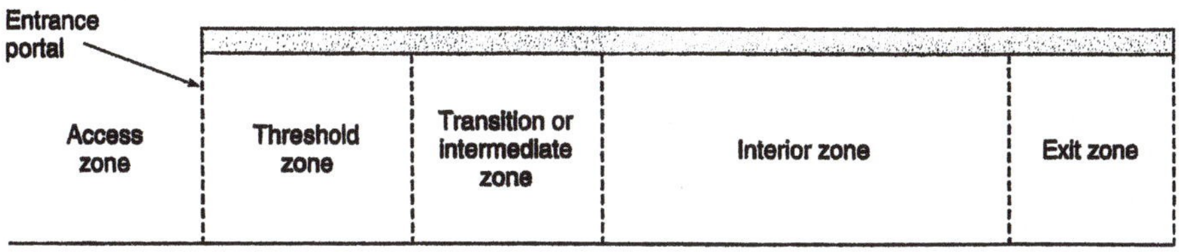

Part three

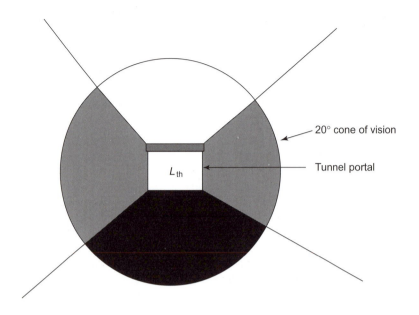

20° cone of vision

L_{th}

Tunnel portal

Figure 23.11

Luminance in the threshold zone calculated from the 20° surround luminance, L_{20}

and the time taken for the driver to detect the hazard, react to it and for the vehicle to stop. It is at this stopping distance that the average luminance of the surround to the tunnel entrance is evaluated. To do this a 20° cone is used with the origin at the driver, as shown in Figure 23.11.

The projected areas of the sky, road, surrounds and entrance portal are determined and luminances ascribed to allow the luminance required at the beginning of the tunnel, called the **threshold zone** to be calculated. This luminance is a fraction of the 20° surround luminance L_{20} and is given by

$$L_{th} = KL_{20}$$

The value of K depends on the stopping distance and can vary from 0.04 up to 0.10. A typical value would be 0.06.

A typical value of surround luminance would be 4000 cd/m^2 and so the threshold luminance would be calculated as

$$L_{th} = KL_{20}$$

$$= 0.06 \times 4000$$

$$= 240 \text{ cd/m}^2$$

This high luminance level is required to be maintained over at least half the threshold zone. This zone is also as long as the stopping distance. By the end of the threshold zone the luminance can be reduced to 0.4 L_{th} which, for the example given above, is 96 cd/m².

After the threshold zone, the **transition zone** is crossed. This zone varies in length and depends on the time taken to reach the interior zone with falling luminance levels until the appropriate steady luminance level for the **interior zone** is reached.

The interior zone has a steady luminance level depending on the tunnel class. The higher the class number the more difficult the driving task and the higher the specified interior luminance. As an example, the 0.06 value for K used above is associated with a stopping distance of 100 m for a class 4 tunnel. The relevant value of average luminance for the interior zone is specified as 6 cd/m².

From the interior zone the driver enters the **exit zone** and during daylight hours begins to rapidly adapt to the daylight beyond the exit. The high brightness of the exit aperture means that small vehicles behind large lorries may become inconspicuous. Therefore, the exit zone luminance must be the same as the interior zone of the tunnel, or for class 4 high speed tunnels the luminance should be increased linearly over a length equal to the stopping distance, up to a level five times that of the interior zone at a distance of 20 m from the exit portal. At night-time the additional lighting at the entrance and exit is not required and the lighting level should be reduced to that of the access road. The above is an outline of the main considerations for the lighting of long tunnels, but the Standard should be consulted for full details.

Tunnels shorter than 25 m do not need daytime lighting. Tunnels longer than 200 m always need some kind of additional lighting to avoid adaptation problems for the road users. Again, the Standard should be consulted for guidance.

Lighting for urban, amenity and residential areas

The previous chapter was devoted to the lighting needed to enable drivers to drive safely on high-speed roads. This chapter devotes itself to situations where traffic speeds are much lower and pedestrians and cyclists are likely to be present.

In urban areas where roads approach urban centres and the speed limit is gradually reduced, the needs of cyclists and particularly pedestrians become increasingly important and a major consideration as a town centre or amenity area is entered. Sometimes the pedestrian and cyclist areas are separated from the main traffic route and then luminance design for the road is still relevant. However, once pedestrian and cyclist traffic are also present then illuminance design should *also* be applied. Where roads run through major shopping and amenity areas then illuminance design would usually be used because the speed of traffic is so low that the viewing distances make luminance design inappropriate.

When urban centres are being considered the following issues become important:

1 The provision of lighting that will ensure safety from moving vehicles for pedestrians.
2 The provision of lighting that is appropriate for the type and volume of the vehicular traffic.
3 The provision of lighting designs and equipment appropriate to the architectural scene and the urban landscape. The intention is also to make the area attractive after dark when the amenities are in use.
4 The provision of lighting that will deter anti-social behaviour.

The lighting class chosen from the British Standard for mixed vehicular and pedestrian areas would normally be defined in terms of horizontal illuminance and uniformity. This would vary according to the situation, but a typical value would be 25

Figure 24.1
A residential area

Figure 24.2
A commercial area

lux with a uniformity of 0.4 (minimum to average). The standard allows for the whole area for vehicles and pedestrians to be treated as the same class where separate areas for vehicles and pedestrians are not well defined. Such considerations relate to items (1) and (2) above. Item (3) relates to the mounting heights chosen for the luminaires and the style of the luminaires in relation to the surroundings (Figure 24.1).

Where large pedestrian areas are involved the mounting height for the adjacent roadway lighting might relate to the height of the buildings, say 8 or 10 m; while that for the pedestrian areas would probably be significantly lower to harmonize with the layout and scale of the pedestrian area, say 5 or 6 m (Figure 24.2).

Example 24.1
(see pages 279 and 280)

In shopping areas and residential areas the visual task is usually at a distance of 5–10 m and includes viewing the footway, the road and other pedestrians. More time is available to make decisions and the assumption is that motor traffic and cyclists will have their own lights which will enable them to proceed safely and be seen by others using the roads.

In residential areas mounting heights are usually 5–6 m and the luminaires usually light the fronts of buildings or front gardens, which gives a much more pleasant environment and a greater feeling of security. Street lighting in a mainly residential area improves the amenity of the area and can result in more people using the streets after dark.

It has been found that improved lighting can reduce the fear of crime and, to some extent, crime itself. In some cases, it has been found that *daytime* crime when the street lights are not lit is also down. However, it is possible that some types of crime are simply dispersed to other areas.

Where illuminance is the criterion the calculations are simpler because the road surface reflectance is no longer a factor in the equation and the calculations are based on the point source formula:

$$E = \frac{I\cos^3\theta}{H^2}$$

the value for E being summed for all contributing luminaires.

Table 24.1 gives a typical extract from tables relating to illuminance design in the British Standard.

Table 24.1 Typical extract from tables relating to illuminance design in the British Standard: minimum requirements for road verge, footway or footpath

	Average illuminance (lux)	Minimum point illuminance (lux)
Roads where night-time public use is liable to be high	10.0	5.0
Roads where night-time public use is likely to be moderate	6.0	2.5
Roads where public use is minor, crime risk low, traffic use equivalent to a residential road	3.5	1.0

Source: BS 5489 Part 2 Table 1, Part 3 Table 1, Part 10 Table 1

**street example
2**

Page 1

OPTILUME Street and Amenity V3.21 © 2001 Thorn Lighting Limited

subsidiary road

Scheme Geometry

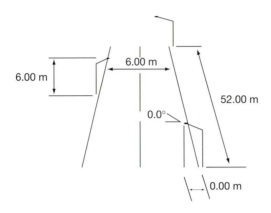

Luminaire details

Left row
(R = 0.00) (Rot. = 180.0)
(S = 26.00) (Tilt = 5.0)
(H = 6.0)

QR70N.4(VOL1)
70W SONXL-T lamp, position 1
70W HPS-T(HO)
Overall Maintenance Factor

Riga

6.50 (klm)
0.89

Right row
(R = 6.00) (Rot. = 0.0)
(S = 0.00) (Tilt = 0.0)
(H = 6.0)

QR70N.4(VOL1)
70W SONXL-T lamp, position 1
70 W HPS-T(HO)
Overall Maintenance Factor

Riga

6.50 (klm)
0.89

Road Surface details
CII = Standard British Blacktop
Q0 = 0.070

Results
BS 5489 part 3 grid

Grid start: R-Coord/Up	0.40	*Surface Name*
Grid start: S-Coord/Along	0.00	Main road
Grid end: R-Coord/Up	6.00	
Grid end: S-Coord/Along	52.00	

Average Illuminance (lux)	13.13
Minimum Illuminance (lux)	6.15
Max. Intensity @ 80° (BS 5489 Pt3)	34
Max. Intensity @ 90° (BS 5489 Pt3)	5

Figure 24.3a

*Typical extract from tables relating to
illuminance design in the British Standard*

**street example
2**

Page 2

OPTILUME Street and Amenity V3.21 © 2001 Thorn Lighting Limited

subsidiary road

Grid Values

Luminance: BS 5489 part 3 Grid

S (m)	0.0	5.2	10.4	15.6	20.8	26.0	31.2	36.4	41.6	46.8	52.0
R (m)											
0.00	9.73	8.58	7.49	6.16	8.92	28.59	8.92	6.16	7.49	8.58	9.73
1.00	14.77	10.87	8.30	6.99	10.85	30.37	10.85	6.99	8.30	10.87	14.77
2.00	21.07	12.94	8.70	7.85	14.33	26.83	14.33	7.85	8.70	12.94	21.07
3.00	25.54	14.62	8.55	8.55	14.62	25.55	14.62	8.55	8.55	14.62	25.54
4.00	26.03	14.33	7.85	8.70	12.94	21.07	12.94	8.70	7.85	14.33	26.83
5.00	30.37	10.85	6.99	8.30	10.87	14.77	10.87	8.30	6.99	10.85	30.37
6.00	28.59	8.92	6.15	7.49	8.58	9.73	8.58	7.49	6.15	8.92	28.59

Figure 24.3b

Typical extract from tables relating to illuminance design in the British Standard

Glare control   In the present Standard for these roads glare is controlled by limiting the luminaire intensities at 80 and 90 to the downward vertical to less than 160 cd/klm and 80 cd/klm respectively at any angle of azimuth. In the revised Standard, in addition to intensity restriction to control disability glare, a glare index is expected to be included to control discomfort glare.

Appendices

Typical lamp data

Table AI.I Typical lamp data (approx.)

Lamp	Power (W)	Initial lumens	Colour temp.	CRI	Life/h
GLS tungsten	60	720	2700	99	1000
	100	1300	2800	99	1000
	200	3000	2800	99	1000
Tungsten halogen	100	1700	2850	99	2000
	200	3500	2900	99	2000
Tungsten halogen (low voltage)	75	1500	2900	99	3000–5000
Fluorescent lamps					
Halophosphate	36	2900	3-6500	55	10000
	58	4500	3-6500	55	10000
Triphosphor	18	1400	3-6500	85	16000
	36	3500	3-6500	85	16000
	58	5200	3-6500	85	16000
	70	6500	3-6500	85	16000
Compact fluorescent	18	1200	3-6000	85	10000
	26	1800	3-6000	85	10000
Induction	55	3500	3-6000	85	60000
Cold cathode	50	3000	3-5000	60	40000
Metal halide	70	5500	4000	80	9000
	150	11250	4000	80	9000
	250	19000	4000	80	9000
	400	45000	4000	70	15000
Metal halide (CDM)	70	6000	3000	80	6000
	150	13000	3000	85	6000
HP mercury	50	2000	3500	57	12000
	125	6700	3400	55	20000
	250	14200	3300	57	20000
HP sodium SON	70	6600	1950	23	25000
	150	16500	1950	23	25000
	250	32000	1950	23	25000
SON improved colour	150	13000	2150	65	14000
	250	23000	2150	65	14000
LP sodium SOX	35	4600			16000
	180	32000			16000
SOX E	36	5800			16000
	131	25000			16000

Typical maintenance factor data

Table A2.1 Lamp lumen maintenance factor (LLMF) and lamp survival factor (LSF)

	Time in operation (h)*			
Type of lamp	6000	8000	10 000	12 000
Fluorescent LLMF	0.87	0.86	0.85	0.84
Triphosphor LSF	0.99	0.95	0.85	0.75
Metal halide LLMF	0.72	0.69	0.66	0.63
LSF	0.91	0.87	0.83	0.77
HP sodium LLMF	0.91	0.89	0.88	0.87
LSF	0.96	0.94	0.92	0.89

*Manufacturer's data preferred.

Table A2.2 Luminaire maintenance factor

	Cleaning interval and situation								
	1 year			2 year			3 year		
Type of luminaire	Clean	Normal	Dirty	Clean	Normal	Dirty	Clean	Normal	Dirty
Open top reflector	0.90	0.86	0.83	0.84	0.80	0.75	0.79	0.74	0.68
Enclosed luminaire IP20X	0.88	0.82	0.77	0.83	0.77	0.71	0.79	0.73	0.65
Uplighter	0.86	0.81	0.74	0.77	0.66	0.57	0.70	0.55	0.45

Table A2.3 Room surface maintenance factor

Room size	Luminaire distribution	Cleaning interval and situation								
		1 year			2 year			3 year		
		Clean	Normal	Dirty	Clean	Normal	Dirty	Clean	Normal	Dirty
Small	Down	0.97	0.94	0.93	0.95	0.93	0.90	0.94	0.92	0.88
	Down/up	0.90	0.86	0.82	0.87	0.82	0.78	0.84	0.79	0.74
	Up	0.85	0.78	0.73	0.81	0.73	0.66	0.75	0.68	0.59
Medium to large	Down	0.98	0.96	0.95	0.96	0.95	0.94	0.96	0.95	0.94
RI > 2.5	Down/up	0.92	0.88	0.85	0.89	0.85	0.81	0.86	0.82	0.78
	Up	0.90	0.82	0.77	0.84	0.77	0.70	0.78	0.72	0.64

Example A2.1

Calculate the maintenance factor (*MF*) for an installation of HP sodium lamps in open top reflectors in a normal environment with luminaire and room cleaning every three years and lamps changed after 6000 hours.

$$MF = LLMF \times LSF \times LMF \times RSMF$$

LLMF	at 6000 hours	0.91
LSF	at 6000 hours	0.96
LMF	at 3 years	0.74
RSMF	at 3 years	0.95
(medium size room)		

$$MF = 0.91 \times 0.96 \times 0.74 \times 0.95$$
$$= 0.61$$

Illuminance, illuminance ratios, cavity reflectance, glare: examples and observations

A hospital waiting room is to be lit with four 600 mm × 600 mm prismatic recessed fluorescent luminaires each housing 4–18 W lamps each emitting 1400 lumens (Figure A3.1).

Calculation of illuminance and illuminance ratios using manufacturer's data

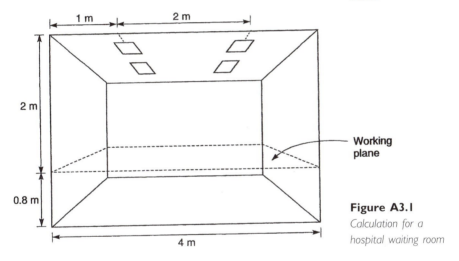

1 m   2 m

2 m

Working plane

0.8 m

4 m

Figure A3.1
Calculation for a hospital waiting room

$$E_{av} = \frac{n \times F_L \times UF \times MF}{A_{WP}}$$

$$= \frac{16 \times 1400 \times UF \times MF}{16}$$

$$= 1400 \times UF \times MF$$

The utilization factor is obtained from the manufacturer's data in terms of room index and room reflectances (Figure A3.2).

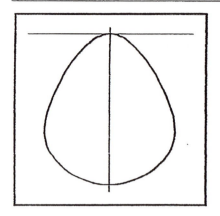
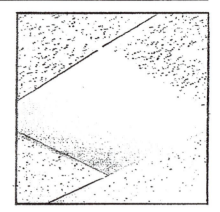

Light Output Ratio   Up 0.00   Down 0.47   Total 0.47
Max. Spacing to Height Ratio   SHR MAX 1.33

Utilization Factors UFCF]										SHR NOM = 1.25	
Reflectances			Room Index								
C	W	F	0.75	1.00	1.25	1.50	2.00	2.50	3.00	4.00	5.00
0.70	0.50	0.20	0.31	0.35	0.38	0.40	0.45	0.45	0.47	0.48	0.50
	0.30		0.28	0.32	0.35	0.38	0.41	0.43	0.45	0.47	0.48
	0.10		0.25	0.30	0.33	0.35	0.39	0.41	0.43	0.45	0.47
0.50	0.50	0.20	0.30	0.34	0.37	0.39	0.42	0.44	0.45	0.47	0.48
	0.30		0.27	0.32	0.35	0.37	0.40	0.42	0.43	0.45	0.46
	0.10		0.25	0.30	0.33	0.35	0.38	0.40	0.42	0.44	0.45
0.30	0.50	0.20	0.29	0.34	0.36	0.38	0.41	0.42	0.43	0.45	0.46
	0.30		0.27	0.31	0.34	0.36	0.39	0.41	0.42	0.44	0.45
	0.10		0.25	0.29	0.32	0.34	0.37	0.39	0.41	0.43	0.44
0.00	0.00	0.00	0.24	0.28	0.31	0.33	0.36	0.38	0.39	0.41	0.42

Angle (deg)	Mean luminaire intensity in vertical plane (cd/1000 lumens)
0	218
5	218
10	215
15	211
20	205
25	197
30	186
35	167
40	189
45	107
50	82
55	70
60	44
65	31
70	23
75	17
80	13
85	8
90	0

Figure A3.2

Manufacturer's data sheet for the luminaire

$$RI = \frac{W}{2H} = \frac{4}{4} = 1.0$$

The decorations are planned to be light in colour and so the table is entered at ceiling reflectance 0.7, wall reflectance 0.5 and floor reflectance 0.2.

$UF = 0.35$

The initial illuminance will therefore be

$E = 1400 \times 0.35$
$= 490$ lux

The maintained value will be

$490 \times MF$
$MF = LLMF \times LMF \times RSMF \times LSF$ (see Chapter 10)

Typical data are obtained from Tables A2.1, A2.2 and A2.3.

LLMF = 0.85   (10 000 hour figure)
LMF = 0.82   normal 1 year cleaning
RSMF = 0.94   normal 1 year cleaning
LSF = 1.0   lamps replaced on failure

$MF = 0.85 \times 0.82 \times 0.94 \times 1.0$
$= 0.66$

Maintained value $= 490 \times 0.66$
$= 324$ lux

In this case the manufacturer does not provide the utilization factors for the walls and ceiling which are needed to calculate the ratios of ceiling to working plane and walls to working plane illuminances. However, the manufacturer does provide the ULOR, DLOR and LOR as well as the UF for zero reflectances $UF_{0.00}$. These, together with transfer factor tables, enable these UF values to be obtained.

Transfer factor tables for ceiling, walls and floor (WP) are given in Tables A3.1, A3.2 and A3.3 (see below).

$$UF(W) = DF(F).TF(F,W) + DF(W).TF(W,W) + DF(C).TF(C,W)$$

For reflectances 0.7, 0.5 and 0.2, RI = 1.0

$$UF(W) = DF(F) \times 0.22 + DF(W) \times 1.422 + DF(C) \times 0.646$$

To complete the calculation we need DF(F), DF(W) and DF(C).

DF terms are the proportion of light from the lamps that reaches the surface in question directly.

DF(C) relates to the ceiling and is equal to the ULOR. In our example *no* light reaches the ceiling directly and so DF(C) = 0.

DF(F) is equal to the UF value for zero reflectances – $UF_{0.00}$ in this case.

$$DF(F) = UF_{0.00} = 0.28$$

DF(W) is the proportion of the downward flux that does not fall directly on the working plane.

DLOR is the downward proportion of the lamp flux and so $DLOR - UF_{0.00}$ is the value required. The DLOR = 0.47, giving DF(W) = 0.47 – 0.28 = 0.19.

$$
\begin{aligned}
UF(W) &= 0.28 \times 0.220 + 0.19 \times 1.422 + 0 \times 0.646 \\
&= 0.062 + 0.270 \\
&= 0.33
\end{aligned}
$$

$$E(W) = \frac{n \times F_L \times UF(W) \times MF}{A(W)}$$

Aw is the area of the walls above the working plane

$$= \frac{16 \times 1400 \times 0.33 \times 0.66}{32}$$

$$= 152 \text{ lux}$$

The illuminance ratio $\dfrac{E(W)}{E_{av}} = \dfrac{152}{324} = 0.47$.

E(C) is obtained in a similar way:

$$
\begin{aligned}
UF(C) &= DF(F).TF(F,C) + DF(W).TF(W,C) + DF(C).TF(C,C) \\
UF(C) &= 0.28 \times 0.121 + 0.19 \times 0.231 + 0 \times 1.130 \\
&= 0.034 + 0.044 + 0 \\
&= 0.078
\end{aligned}
$$

$$E(C) = \frac{n \times F_L \times UF(C) \times MF}{A_C}$$

$$= 16 \times \frac{1400 \times 0.078 \times 0.66}{16}$$

$$= 72 \text{ lux}$$

The illuminance ratio $\dfrac{E(C)}{E_{av}} = \dfrac{72}{324} = 0.222$.

For clarity, the calculations has been shown in full, but in fact since the lamp flux $n \times F_L$ and the maintenance factor MF are the same in each case they cancel and could have been omitted, if only the *ratios* were required.

So,

$$\frac{E(W)}{E_{av}} = \frac{A_{WP}}{Aw} \times \frac{UF(W)}{UF}$$

and

$$\frac{E(C)}{E_{av}} = \frac{UF(C)}{UF}$$

The example is repeated below to illustrate the calculation of UF when only the polar curve scaled in cd/1000 lamp lumens is provided (Figure A3.2). If there is upward intensity then the flux this produces is assumed to fall on the ceiling or ceiling cavity. The value of this flux would be calculated by using the 90–180° zone factors from Table 9.1.

Example 2 Calculation of the utilization factor when only the polar curve is available

In our example there is no upward flux component and DF(C) = 0.

To calculate D(F) we must calculate the direct flux to the working plane. This is done by point source calculations. There are four luminaires symmetrically placed and so the calculations are only required for one luminaire. Again, because of symmetry even though the working plane is divided into 16 1 m squares only six point source calculations are required (Figure A3.3a).

Consider square 3

$$Q = \sqrt{1.5^2 + 1.5^2}$$

$$= 2.12$$

$$\mathrm{Tan}\,\theta = \frac{Q}{H} = \frac{2.12}{2}$$

$$\theta = 46.7°$$

From Figure A3.2 by interpolation

$$I_\theta = 98.5 \text{ cd}$$
$$\cos^3\theta = 0.3228$$

$$E_3 = \frac{I_\theta \cos^3\theta}{H^2} = \frac{98.5 \times 0.3228}{2^2}$$

$$= 7.95 \text{ lux per 1000 lamp lumens}$$

By similar calculations values for each of the other squares can be assigned (Figure A3.3b).

Figure A3.3

(a) Only six point source calculations are required because of symmetry; (b) results of the point source calculations

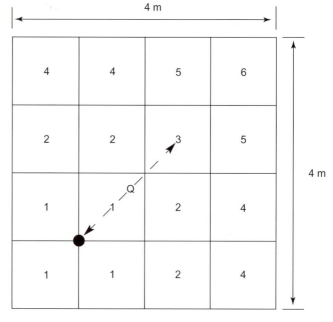

(a)

4.58	4.56	2.72	1.28
18.97	18.97	7.95	2.72
43.14	43.14	18.97	4.56
43.14	43.14	18.97	4.56

$\Sigma E_h/klm = 109.83 + 109.81 + 48.61 + 13.12 = 281.4$

(b)

For I luminaire $\quad E_{av} = \dfrac{\Sigma E}{16}$

For 4 luminaires $\quad E_{av} = \dfrac{\Sigma E}{16} \times 4$

Flux received by working plane

$$= \frac{\Sigma E}{16} \times 4 \times \text{area of WP}$$

$$= \frac{\Sigma E}{16} \times 4 \times 16$$

$$DF(F) = \frac{\text{Total flux to working plane}}{\text{Total lamp flux}}$$

$$= \frac{\Sigma E \times 4 \times 16}{16 \times 4000}$$

(Since the polar curve for each luminaire is scaled for a 1000 lumen lamp output)

$$= \frac{\Sigma E}{1000}$$

$\Sigma E = 281$ from Figure A3.3(b)

giving $DF(F) = 0.281$ which is the value given by the manufacturer in Figure A3.2.

The proportion of lamp flux received by the walls is

$$DF(W) = DLOR - DF(F)$$

where the downward light output ratio (DLOR) is the proportion of lamp flux emitted into the lower hemisphere.

For the purpose of this example only the intensity distribution in cd/1000 lamp lumens is available and so the DLOR must be calculated. This is done using the zone factors for 0–90° from Table 9.1.

Zone limits (degrees)	Zone factor	Mid zone intensity (cd/1000 lm)	Zonal flux (lm)
0-10	0.095	218	20.71
10-20	0.283	211	59.71
20-30	0.463	197	91.21
30-40	0.628	167	104.88
40-50	0.774	107	82.82
50-60	0.894	70	62.58
60-70	0.993	31	30.78
70-80	1.058	17	17.99
80-90	1.091	8	8.73
			479.41 Total downward flux

$$DLOR = \frac{479}{1000}$$

$$= 0.48$$

So,

$$DF(W) = 0.479 - 0.281$$

$$= 0.198$$

Transfer factors for the working plane UF are given in Table A3.3.

$$UF(F) = DF(F).TF(F,F) + DF(W). TF(W,F) + DF(C), TF(C,F)$$
$$= 0.281 \times 1.067 + 0.198 \times 0.275 + 0 \times 0.423$$
$$= 0.3 + 0.054$$
$$= 0.35 \text{ which agrees with the manufacturer's value.}$$

Full details of how to calculate the transfer factors will be found in *Lighting Engineering: Applied Calculations* (Simons and Bean, 2001).

Approximate cavity reflectance formula

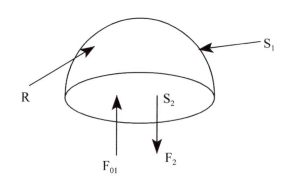

Figure A3.4
Calculation of the equivalent reflectance of a cavity

Consider Figure A3.4. Reflectance (R) of cavity surface is the weighted average of the reflectances within the cavity. The equivalent reflectance of the cavity is R_E:

$$R_E = \frac{F_2}{F_{01}}$$

where F_{01} is the flux entering the cavity
          F_2 is the flux leaving the cavity
          F_1 is the total flux received by the cavity including interreflection within the cavity

$$F_2 = RF_1 f_{12}$$

where f_{12} is the fraction of the flux leaving surface 1 that passes through aperture 2
          F_1 = the initial flux on surface 1 + the reflected flux received by surface 1
          $= F_{01} + RF_1 f_{11}$

So,

$$F_1 = \frac{F_{01}}{1 - Rf_{11}}$$

Where f_{11} is the function of flux leaving surface 1 which falls on surface 1 (being curved it 'sees' itself), giving

$$F_2 = \frac{RF_{01}f_{12}}{1 - Rf_{11}}$$

$$\frac{F_2}{F_{01}} = R_E = \frac{Rf_{12}}{1 - Rf_{11}}$$

$$f_{12} =$$

$$\frac{\text{the area of aperture } 2 \times \text{received flux density from } 1}{\text{area of cavity surface } 1 \times \text{reflected flux density from } 1}$$

But the received flux *density* is the same as the reflected flux *density* and they cancel

$$f_{12} = \frac{S_2}{S_1}$$

Subtracting this fraction from unity gives the fraction transferred within the cavity. So,

$$f_{11} = 1 - f_{12}$$

$$R_E = \frac{R \dfrac{S_2}{S_1}}{1 - R\left(1 - \dfrac{S_2}{S_1}\right)}$$

which can be rearranged as

$$R_E = \frac{RS_2}{RS_2 + S_1(1 - R)}$$

An uplighter produces a luminous patch on the ceiling, which then acts as a light source for the working plane below.

In Chapter 9, the point source formula was re-written as:

$$E_p = L\omega\cos\theta$$

From Figure A3.5 we can see that the illuminating power of any element of that luminous patch can be reproduced by an element of the spherical cap filling the same solid angle and having the same luminance as the patch element and the same angle θ at the illuminated point.

Each element of the patch will have a corresponding element on the spherical cap, which can be paired in this way, so that the illuminating effect of the patch on the ceiling can be reproduced by part of this assumed spherical cap.

In addition, also in Chapter 9 it was shown that any uniformly diffusing luminous element δa of a sphere will

Illuminance at a point from an uplighter: the approximate direct component method

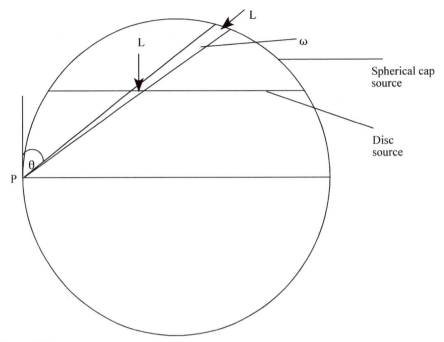

Figure A3.5

Each uniformly diffusing patch reflecting light from the ceiling can be paired with its equivalent on the sphere

produce an illuminance on all other elements of the inside of the sphere, given by

$$E = \frac{I_m}{4r^2} = \frac{L\delta a}{4r^2}$$

where I_m is the intensity normal to the element δa and r is the radius of the sphere.

Since *no angle* appears in the formula both the luminous element and the illuminated element can be anywhere on the inside of the sphere. We can, for *calculational* purposes, replace the individual projected elements by a single point source element, which has all the illuminating power of all the elements of not only the projected patch on the spherical cap, but also of the luminous patch on the ceiling itself. It is obviously convenient to centre this point source element directly above the uplighter (Figure A3.6).

A single point source can be assumed to create an illuminance vector in the direction of the illuminated point equal to the maximum illuminance that it could produce at that point because of the cosine law. The horizontal illuminance and the sphere wall illuminance would each be components of this vector. In the simple case shown in Figure A3.6 it is obvious that each of these components is at the same angle to the

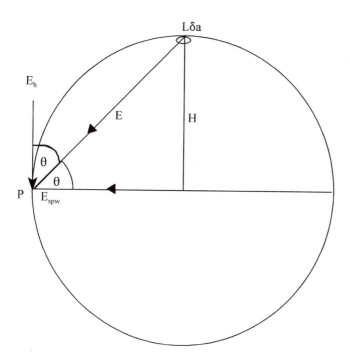

Figure A3.6

A single equivalent source would have an illuminance vector that always bisects the horizontal illuminance and spherical wall illuminance components

illuminance vector. Therefore, they must be equal. This is because the illuminance vector *always* bisects the angle between the horizontal illuminance and the spherical wall illuminance components when the source is located at the top of the sphere, that is, at the end of the diameter that is normal to the horizontal plane.

If the point source formula is now applied in the form

$$E_p = I\cos^3\theta/H^2$$

it is easy to see that when the ceiling height is changed the illuminance values must be adjusted for the new H^2 values and that the horizontal distance to which this applies must also be adjusted to keep $\cos^3\theta$ the same. Doing this ensures that the intensity related to the original illuminance value will still apply.

Since the ceiling reflectance used to produce the original illuminance curve is usually 0.8, if the installation has a different value of ceiling reflectance the final illuminance values must be adjusted in proportion.

Table A3.1　Transfer factors (ceiling)

Transfer factor ($TF_{c,c}$)								
R_C	R_W	R_F	0.75	1.00	2.00	3.00	4.00	5.00
80	50	20	1.140	1.151	1.167	1.176	1.179	1.181
80	30	20	1.079	1.090	1.123	1.140	1.149	1.155
70	50	20	1.120	1.130	1.145	1.150	1.153	1.155
70	30	20	1.068	1.079	1.106	1.120	1.128	1.134
50	50	20	1.083	1.089	1.099	1.103	1.105	1.106
50	30	20	1.047	1.055	1.073	1.083	1.088	1.092

Transfer factor ($TF_{F,c}$)								
R_C	R_W	R_F	0.75	1.00	2.00	3.00	4.00	5.00
80	50	20	0.101	0.123	0.169	0.189	0.200	0.207
80	30	20	0.083	0.104	0.153	0.176	0.189	0.196
70	50	20	0.100	0.121	0.165	0.184	0.195	0.202
70	30	20	0.082	0.103	0.151	0.174	0.186	0.194
50	50	20	0.096	0.116	0.159	0.177	0.187	0.193
50	30	20	0.081	0.101	0.146	0.167	0.179	0.187

Transfer factor ($TF_{w,c}$)								
R_C	R_W	R_F	0.75	1.00	2.00	3.00	4.00	5.00
80	50	20	0.210	0.235	0.283	0.303	0.315	0.321
80	30	20	0.105	0.120	0.152	0.168	0.177	0.183
70	50	20	0.206	0.231	0.278	0.297	0.308	0.315
70	30	20	0.103	0.118	0.151	0.165	0.174	0.180
50	50	20	0.199	0.222	0.267	0.285	0.295	0.301
50	30	20	0.101	0.116	0.146	0.161	0.168	0.173

Table A3.2 Transfer factors (walls)

Transfer factor (TF$_{w,w}$)

R$_C$	R$_W$	R$_F$	0.75	1.00	2.00	3.00	4.00	5.00
80	50	20	1.520	1.445	1.279	1.207	1.164	1.138
80	30	20	1.259	1.226	1.152	1.114	1.092	1.078
70	50	20	1.497	1.422	1.265	1.195	1.155	1.129
70	30	20	1.249	1.217	1.144	1.108	1.088	1.074
50	50	20	1.453	1.381	1.235	1.172	1.137	1.114
50	30	20	1.230	1.198	1.129	1.097	1.078	1.065

Transfer factor (TF$_{F,w}$)

R$_C$	R$_W$	R$_F$	0.75	1.00	2.00	3.00	4.00	5.00
80	50	20	0.264	0.232	0.151	0.112	0.089	0.074
80	30	20	0.219	0.196	0.137	0.103	0.083	0.070
70	50	20	0.253	0.220	0.142	0.105	0.083	0.068
70	30	20	0.211	0.188	0.129	0.097	0.078	0.065
50	50	20	0.232	0.198	0.125	0.091	0.071	0.058
50	30	20	0.196	0.101	0.114	0.085	0.067	0.056

Transfer factor (TF$_{c,w}$)

R$_C$	R$_W$	R$_F$	0.75	1.00	2.00	3.00	4.00	5.00
80	50	20	0.895	0.753	0.453	0.324	0.252	0.206
80	30	20	0.741	0.639	0.408	0.299	0.236	0.195
70	50	20	0.769	0.646	0.389	0.277	0.215	0.176
70	30	20	0.642	0.553	0.351	0.257	0.203	0.168
50	50	20	0.531	0.445	0.267	0.190	0.147	0.121
50	30	20	0.450	0.386	0.244	0.178	0.140	0.115

Table A3.3   Transfer factors (floors)

Transfer factor (TF$_{F,F}$)

R$_C$	R$_W$	R$_F$	0.75	1.00	2.00	3.00	4.00	5.00
80	50	20	1.060	1.075	1.112	1.134	1.144	1.152
80	30	20	1.039	1.051	1.093	1.116	1.130	1.139
70	50	20	1.055	1.067	1.099	1.116	1.125	1.132
70	30	20	1.035	1.047	1.081	1.100	1.112	1.121
50	50	20	1.045	1.053	1.073	1.083	1.089	1.093
50	30	20	1.028	1.036	1.059	1.071	1.079	1.084

Transfer factor (TF$_{W,F}$)

R$_C$	R$_W$	R$_F$	0.75	1.00	2.00	3.00	4.00	5.00
80	50	20	0.248	0.289	0.378	0.419	0.443	0.458
80	30	20	0.124	0.148	0.204	0.232	0.249	0.262
70	50	20	0.237	0.275	0.355	0.392	0.413	0.426
70	30	20	0.119	0.141	0.193	0.218	0.233	0.243
50	50	20	0.217	0.248	0.311	0.339	0.355	0.365
50	30	20	0.119	0.129	0.171	0.191	0.202	0.210

Transfer factor (TF$_{C,F}$)

R$_C$	R$_W$	R$_F$	0.75	1.00	2.00	3.00	4.00	5.00
80	50	20	0.406	0.492	0.674	0.754	0.798	0.826
80	30	20	0.333	0.418	0.613	0.704	0.756	0.790
70	50	20	0.349	0.423	0.578	0.645	0.683	0.707
70	30	20	0.288	0.362	0.528	0.605	0.649	0.678
50	50	20	0.241	0.291	0.396	0.442	0.467	0.483
50	30	20	0.202	0.224	0.304	0.397	0.430	0.451

Glossary

The adjustment of the visual system to changes in brightness of the visual field.

Adaptation

The arithmetic mean of the specified illuminance over a plane or a surface (e.g. horizontal illuminance, cylindrical illuminance, scalar illuminance.

Average illuminance

Subjective response to luminance in the visual field.

Brightness

SI unit of luminous intensity.

Candela (cd)

    The fundamental definition of the candela is inconvenient for general use. Conceptually, it is easier to define it as 'a solid angular flux density of one lumen per steradian'.

    One lumen is the result of converting 1/683 watts into visible radiation at the 555 nm wavelength (notionally, at the peak of the human eye response curve where $V_\lambda = 1.0$). (At any other wavelength 1/683 watts converts to V_λ lumens.) The constant 683 arises from the need to relate lighting quantities to power quantities when both systems originally developed separately.

    The fundamental definition of a candela is: 'The luminous intensity in a given direction of a source emitting monochromatic radiation of frequency 540×10^{12} Hz and whose radiant intensity in this direction is 1/683 watts. (540×10^{12} Hz corresponds to a wavelength of 555 nm in air.)

A Munsell system term which represents numerically the increasing intensity or vividness of a colour on a scale starting from zero.

Chroma

Colour quality of a stimulus which can be given numerical definition in the CIE system.

Chromaticity

The capacity of a light source to provide the wavelengths necessary to reveal the true colour reflective qualities of an object.

Colour rendering

Correlated colour temperature	The temperature of a theoretical 'full radiator' which would emit radiation having the closest match to the chromaticity of the light source to which it is applied.
Contrast	A term used to describe the difference in luminance or colour of two elements of a visual field. Also used to numerically define the luminance difference between a task luminance (L_T) and its background (L_B)

$$\text{Contrast} = |\frac{L_T - L_B}{L_B}|$$

(The difference in sign is ignored)

Cylindrical illuminance	A term used to denote the mean vertical illuminance at a point. (The term average cylindrical illuminance usually refers to its value over a horizontal plane, e.g. the working plane.)
Daylight factor (df)	The illuminance at a point in an interior expressed as a percentage of the exterior daylight illuminance from an unobstructed hemisphere of sky responsible for both illuminances.
Disability glare	Glare from a source of light that impairs vision either directly or through reflection.
Discomfort glare	Glare from a source of light that causes discomfort.
Distribution Factor (DF)	Proportion of light from the lamps that reaches the surface in question directly, e.g. DF(C), DF(W), DF(F).
Downward light output ratio (DLOR)	The ratio of the light output of a luminaire below the horizontal to the light output of the lamp. (This is based on the light output of the lamp outside the luminaire. Placing the lamp inside the luminaire can create temperature changes that alter its light output. The DLOR includes this effect.)
Full radiator	A theoretical thermal radiator, described by Planck's radiation formula, which is the basis of the concept of colour temperature.
Full radiator locus	The line on a chromaticity diagram indicating the colour of a full radiator as a function of its temperature.
Hue	An attribute of colours that allows them to be classed as red, blue, green, etc. A term used to indicate numerically values associated with these properties in the Munsell system.
Ingress protection number (IP number)	A two digit code indicating the degree of protection that is associated with a particular luminaire. The first digit relates to protection from the ingress of solid objects and the second from the ingress of moisture.
Illuminance (lux)	The luminous flux density on or at a plane or surface, e.g. lumens per square metre.

Illuminance, point or average, for a new lighting installation (at 100 hours) before deterioration due to age or environmental conditions.	**Initial illuminance**
The ratio of light output of a luminaire to the light output of the lamp. (Based on the light output of the lamp outside the luminaire. Placing the lamp inside the luminaire can create temperature changes that alter its light output. The LOR includes this effect.)	**Light output ratio (LOR)**
The luminous flux emitted within unit solid angle (one steradian) by a point source of uniform luminous intensity of one candela.	**Lumen (lm)**
A device for suitably housing a lamp or lamps, connecting it to the electrical supply, controlling the light distribution and fixing it in position.	**Luminaire**
A physical stimulus related to the sensation of brightness, but not directly equivalent to it. (Measured in terms of intensity per unit apparent or projected area.)	**Luminance (L) (cd/m^2)**
The ratio of the luminous flux emitted by a lamp to the power consumed. It may be just for the lamp or as a circuit. Circuit luminous efficacy includes control gear losses. Overall luminaire efficacy would also include the LOR of the luminaire.	**Luminous efficacy (lm/W)**
Ratio of the luminous flux leaving a surface to the area of the surface.	**Luminous exitance (M) (lm/m^2)**
A space filled with electromagnetic radiation capable of stimulating the eye to vision.	**Luminous field**
Light emitted by a light source or received, reflected or transmitted by a surface. Related to the radiant power emitted in watts by the relative spectral sensitivity curve (V_λ) and the agreed constant 683.	**Luminous flux (Φ,F) (lm)**
A measure of the illuminating power of a source of light in a specified direction. Equal to the ratio of the luminous flux to the solid angle of the cone through which the flux travels.	**Luminous intensity (I) (cd)**
The SI unit of illuminance, equal to one lumen per square metre.	**Lux (lx)**
The illuminance at which the maintenance procedure should be carried out to avoid the illuminance falling below the design value.	**Maintained illuminance**
The factor by which the initial illuminance is multiplied to obtain the value of maintained illuminance. It is calculated from the lamp lumen maintenance factor (LMF), the lamp survival factor (LSF), the luminaire maintenance factor (LLMF) and the room surface maintenance factor (RSMF).	**Maintenance factor (MF)**

Mounting height (H or hm)	Generally the distance between the plane of the luminaire and the working plane. The working plane is sometimes taken as being the floor.
Munsell system	A long-standing system of colour classification based on colour scales of hue, value and chroma.
No-sky line	This denotes a position within a room from which no direct view of the sky can be obtained. It indicates the limit of direct daylight within the room.
Reflectance (R or ρ)	Ratio of the luminous flux reflected from a surface to the incident luminous flux.
Refractive index (μ)	Ratio of the sine of the angle of incidence to the sine of the angle of refraction. In practice the index assumes the ray is incident on the denser medium from air (($\mu = \frac{\sin i}{\sin r}$) Snell's Law).
Relative spectral sensitivity (V_λ) (or relative spectral luminous efficiency)	A numerical function that indicates the variation of the standard eye response to the wavelengths of the visible spectrum on a scale from 0 to 1.0.
Room index (K or RI)	A means of classifying rooms in terms of the ratio of horizontal to vertical surface area used in tabulating lighting data. $$RI = \frac{\text{length} \times \text{width}}{\text{mounting height (length + width)}}$$
Scalar illuminance (lux)	The ratio of the luminous flux falling on the surface of a small sphere to the surface area of the sphere.
Solid angle (sr)	A multidirectional angle subtended at a point by an area, measured in terms of the area that the same solid angle would project onto an enclosing sphere centred on the same point divided by the square of the radius of the sphere.
Spacing to height ratio (S/hm)	The ratio of the spacing between the centres of adjacent luminaires to the mounting height of the luminaires.
Steradians (sr)	The unit of solid angle, equal to $1/4\pi$ of the solid angle subtended by the surface of a whole sphere at its centre.
Transmittance (T, τ)	The ratio of the luminous flux transmitted through a material to the incident luminous flux.
Unified glare rating (UGR) system	A system whereby limiting values of glare rating may be specified for discomfort glare. Proposed lighting installations can be evaluated by using the UGR formula to check that they comply with the appropriate limiting value.

A perfectly matt surface obeying the cosine law of reflected intensity or a transmitting medium having a cosine distribution of the emitted intensity. **Uniform diffuser**

The ratio of minimum illuminance to average illuminance over a specified surface or area. **Uniformity**

The ratio of the light output of a luminaire above the horizontal to the light output of the lamp. (This is based on the light output of the lamp outside the luminaire. Placing the lamp inside the luminaire can create temperature changes that alter its light output. The ULOR includes this effect.) **Upward light output ratio (ULOR)**

The proportion of the lamp flux that reaches the working plane including interreflection. **Utilization factor (UF)**

(see **Relative spectral sensitivity**) V_λ

A similar function to V_λ but related to scotopic vision. V'_λ

A term used in the Munsell system to numerically indicate the increasing lightness of a surface on a scale of 0 to 10. **Value**

The capacity of the eye/brain combination to distinguish between the illuminance and the reflectance components of the surface luminances seen under normal well-lit conditions. Also to distinguish between the illuminance effects and the intrinsic colour of a surface under normal well-lit conditions. **Visual constancy**

The whole space viewed when looking in a particular direction. **Visual field**

The visual aspects of the work being carried out. **Visual task**

The plane on which the visual task lies, often the horizontal plane. **Working plane**

Bibliography

British Standards Institution, 389 Chiswick Road, London W4 4AL (tel: 020 8996 9000)

Standards and lighting guides

British Standards

British Standards are being harmonized with CEN Standards (European) Committee for Standardisation) and where this has been done BS etc. becomes BS EN etc. Where they are harmonized with ISO (International Organization for Standards) they become BS ISO.

BS ISO 8995	Lighting of indoor workplaces (2002)
BS ISO 15469	Spacial distribution of daylight (1997)
BS EN 1838	Emergency lighting (1999)
BS EN 60598	Luminaires: Pt 1 (2000) general requirements; Pt 2 particular requirements
BS EN 12193	Sports lighting (1999)
BS 5225	Photometric data for luminaires: Pt 1 Photometric measurements (1975); Pt 3 Photometric measurement of battery operated emergency lighting (1982)
BS 5489	Road lighting (Pts 1–10) (1992) under revision
BS 8206	Lighting for buildings: Pt 2 Code of practice for daylighting (1992)

CIBSE, 222 Balham High Road, London SW12 9BS

Society of Light and Lighting publications

Code for Lighting (CDRom) (2002)

Lighting guides
LG2	Hospitals and healthcare (1989)
LG3	The visual environment for display screen use (1990)
LG4	Sports
LG5	The visual environment in lecture, teaching and conference rooms (1991)

LG6   The outdoor environment (1992)
LG7   Lighting for offices (1993)
LG8   Lighting for museums and art galleries (1994)
LG9   Lighting for communal residential buildings (1997)
LG10   Daylighting and window design (1999)
LGHHE Hostile and hazardous environments (1983)
LG11   Surface reflectance and colour (2001)

RIBA   66 Portland Place, London WIN 4AD

RIBA01 Electric lighting for buildings (1996)

Department of   HMSO   Building Bulletin 90: Lighting design for schools (1999)
Education and
Employment
(DfEE)

Books   Coaton, J.R. and Marsden, A.M. (1977) *Lamps and Lighting*, 4th edn, Arnold.
Cuttle, C.C. (2003) *Lighting by Design*, Architectural Press.
Jay, P. and Crawforth, B. (2001) *Church Lighting*, Church House Publishing.
Simons, R.H. and Bean, A.R. (2001), *Lighting Engineering: Applied Calculations*, Architectural Press.

Index

Accuracy in calculations and measurements, 25, 66, 90–3
Adaptation, 8, 21, 32, 41, 246, 301
Age and vision, 224–5, 261
Apparent brightness, 104
Appearance of people, 63, 103
Area source, 110
Atrium, 208
Average illuminance, 301
    measurement, 92
    sports, 255
    values for floodlighting of buildings, 233

Baffle, 146
Bathrooms, 224
Bedrooms, 224
Brightness, 29, 32, 40, 65, 301
Building
    floodlighting, 229–41
    regulations, 125

Candela, 30, 301
Cavity equivalent reflectance, 175, 294–5
Chartered Institution of Building Service Engineers (CIBSE), 18, 21, 27, 32
Checking a lighting installation, 92
Chroma Munsell, 52, 301
Chromaticity coordinates, 47, 301
Churches, 210–15
CIE (Commission Internationale de l'Eclairage)
    chromaticity diagram, 47
    general colour rendering index, 50, 51
    overcast sky formula, 117
    Unified Glare Rating (UGR), 32
Colour
    after images, 8, 45

appearance, specification of, 47
constancy effects, 5
in lighting, 45–54
mixture additive, 50
    subtractive, 50
rendering, 47, 50, 203, 301
sample systems, 51
vision, 8, 45
Compact fluorescent lamp, 139–40
Computer programs, 90
    checking accuracy, 91
Cone diagram of illuminances, 242
Cones, 8
Contrast, 27, 40, 302
Control
    factor, 125
    gear, 134
Control of Lighting, 123–5
Cosine cubed illuminance formula, 74
Cosine law, 72, 296
Coordinate system
    Bβ, 71
    Cγ, 69
    VH, 71
Correlated colour temperature, 51, 301
Critical angle, 153
Cylindrical illuminance, 77–9, 103, 302

D cubed illuminance formula, 74–6
Daylight
    calculations, 115–21
    coefficients, 119–20
    factor, 13, 115–17, 302
    importance of, 13
Design, first stage, 6
DF (Distribution Factor), 289–93, 302
Diffuse transmission, 150–1

Diffusion in light control, 150–1
Direct lighting, 59
  scalloped effects, 61, 62
Disability glare, 33, 58, 166–71, 302
Domestic lighting, 221–5
Downward light output ratio (DLOR), 289,
  302
Discomfort glare, 29
Disc source, 296
Display lighting, 203–5
Displaying a building after dark, 229–42

Efficacy, 20, 303
Electric lighting, 130–62
Emergency lighting, 157–60
Energy management, 123–7
Exitance, 110, 303
Eye, 7–9
  sensitivity, 19

Faceted reflector, 150
Fibre optics, 154–5, 219
Flicker, 33
Floodlight distributions, 232–3, 236
Floodlighting, 230–55
Fluorescent lamp, 134–40
Full radiator, 48, 49, 302
  locus, 49

General lighting, 169
Glare
  disability, 33, 58, 302
  discomfort, 29, 302

High pressure sodium lamp, 142–3
Highlights, 38
Hospitals, 215–18
Hostile and hazardous environments, 157
Hue, 52, 302

I table, 69, 259–60
Illuminance, 302
  curve, 180–2
  cylindrical, 77
  initial, 93, 237–40, 302
  ratios, 63, 103
  received by a surface, 21
  scalar, 79
  schedule of recommended levels, 25–7
  specification method, 105, 211–14

variation, 37, 38
Incandescent filament lamp, 129–32
Indirect lighting, 60
Induction lamp, 140
Industrial lighting, 185–91
Ingress Protection (IP) rating, 156, 302
Integrating sphere, 86–8
Interreflection, 59, 82, 182
  factors, 182
Intensity distribution photometry, 67–9
  photometric distance of measurement,
    67, 70
Inverse-square law, 66

Kitchens, 221, 224

Lamp output calculation, 20
Lecture theatre, 196
Libraries, 216–17
Lighting
  as a language, 9
  Code, 26, 27
  controls, 123–5
  general, 168–9
  levels, 17, 25
  local, 169
  localized, 169
  measurements, 67–71, 81, 88–90, 92–3
  quantity, 18
  schedule of recommended levels, 25–7
Lightmeter, 92
Light output ratio (LOR), 83, 88, 303
Light source
  compact fluorescent lamp, 139–40
  fluorescent lamp, 134–9
  high pressure sodium lamp, 142–3
  incandescent lamp, 129–32
  induction lamp, 140
  LED, 145
  low pressure sodium lamp, 140–2
  mercury vapour lamp, 143–4
  metal halide lamp, 144–5
  tungsten halogen lamp, 132–4
Line source, 109
Louvre specular, 149
Lumen, 19, 303
  method, 97–103
Luminaire, 129, 145–57, 303
  construction, 155–6
Luminance, 30, 31, 303

measurement, 80, 81
Luminous efficacy, 20, 235, 303
Luminous exitance, 110, 303
Luminous field, 5, 303
Luminous flux (light flux) 21, 30, 88, 302
Luminous intensity, 30, 65–70, 88, 303
Lux, 17, 21, 303
Lynes, J.A., 9

Maintained illuminance, 99, 237–40, 302
Maintenance Factor
    exterior, 235
    interior, 99, 175
Measurement
    of illuminance, 92
    of luminance, 80, 81
    of luminous intensity, 67–71
Mercury vapour lamp, 143–4
Mesopic vision, 21
Metal halide lamp, 144–5
Modelling, 63
Munsell system, 51, 52, 53, 304

No-sky line, 117, 304

Office lighting, 165–83
Obstruction in light control, 146–7

Photometric data, 174, 180, 288
Photometry, 67–71, 81, 88–90, 92–3
Photopic vision, 21
Places of worship, 210–15
Planck's (Full radiator) formula, 49
Point source
    concept, 65
    illuminance formula, 71
Polar
    curve, 69
    solid, 69
Preferential reflection, 147
Prismatic
    control, 153
    diffusers, 152
Public buildings, 207–19

Quality of the lit environment, 165

r table, 259–60
Ratio of cylindrical to horizontal
    illuminance, 78–9, 103–4

Reflectance, 29, 82, 85, 233, 304
Reflection types, 146
Reflector profiles, 147–50
Refraction in light control, 151–5
Refractive index, 152, 304
Relative spectral sensitivity (or relative
    spectral luminous efficiency) 19, 21
Retina, 7, 8
Road lighting, 257–71
Rods, 8
Room Index (RI), 92, 100, 175, 289, 304

Scalar illuminance, 63, 79, 304
Schools, 193–6
Scotopic vision, 21
Shadows, 41
Sheen, 41
Shops, 201–5
Sky zones, 120
Snell's Law, 152, 304
Society of Light and Lighting (SLL), 18
Solid angle, 30, 31
Spacing to height ratio, 100–2, 304
Spectral luminous efficiency functions, 21
Specular reflection, 146
Sports
    hall, 197
    outdoor, 245–55
Staircases, 41
Statues, 230, 241–2
Steradian, 30, 32, 304
Street lighting, 275–80
Stroboscopic effect, 33

Threshold Increment, 33, 261
Transfer factor, 179
Transmittance, 30, 119, 304
Tungsten
    filament lamp, 129–32
    halogen lamp, 132–4
Tunnel lighting, 269–73

Unified Glare Rating, 32, 178–9, 304
Uniform diffuser, 84–7, 304
    flux emitted, 84, 85
Uniformly diffuse reflection, 84, 147, 304
Uniformity of illuminance, 93, 304
Uplighter, 179
Upward Light Output Ratio (ULOR), 179,
    289–90, 305

Utilization Factor, 98, 100, 175, 235, 252, 287–94, 305

Value, Munsell, 52
Vector scalar ratio, 63
Visual
  comfort, 29, 166
  constancy, 37, 38, 305
  field, 57
  perception, 7
  performance, 17–18, 168
  satisfaction, 166
  scene, 33, 40, 166
  task, 57, 168, 185

Visualization, 91
Vλ relative spectral sensitivity (photopic vision), 19–21, 140, 305
V'λ relative spectral sensitivity (scotopic vision), 21

Waldram, J.M., 257
Windows
  area, 116
  importance of, 13
  performance of, 13
Working plane, 98, 100, 109, 116, 179, 305

Zone factors, 88